TWO'S COMPANY

TWO'S COMPANY

*A Fifty-Year Romance with Lessons Learned
in Love, Life & Business*

SUZANNE
SOMERS

HARMONY
BOOKS • NEW YORK

Photograph credits appear on page 283.

Library of Congress Cataloging-in-Publication Data
Names: Somers, Suzanne, 1946– author.
Title: Two's company / Suzanne Somers.
Description: First edition. | New York : Harmony Books, 2017.
Identifiers: LCCN 2017021476 | ISBN 9780451498267 (hardcover : alk. paper) |
    ISBN 9780451498274 (ebook)
Subjects: LCSH: Somers, Suzanne, 1946– | Somers, Suzanne, 1946—Marriage. |
    Actors—United States—Biography. | Hamel, Alan. | Hamel, Alan—Marriage. |
    Entertainers—Canada—Biography.
Classification: LCC PN2287.S63 A3 2917 | DDC 791.4502/8092 [B] —dc23
    LC record available at https://lccn.loc.gov/2017021476

ISBN 978-0-451-49826-7
Ebook ISBN 978-0-451-49827-4

Printed in the United States of America

Jacket design: Caroline Somers and Danielle Shapero-Rudolph
Jacket photographs: (front) Cindy Gold; (back) Hank Saroyan

10 9 8 7 6 5 4 3 2 1

First Edition

To my husband, my family, and my therapists.
You all know who you are, how much you mean to me,
and how deeply all of you have enriched my life.

To live is the rarest thing in the world. Most people exist, that is all.

—OSCAR WILDE

This life is what you make it. No matter what, you're going to mess up sometimes, it's a universal truth. But the good part is you get to decide how you're going to mess it up. As for lovers, well, they'll come and go too. And baby, I hate to say it, most of them—actually pretty much all of them are going to break your heart, but you can't give up because if you give up, you'll never find your soulmate. You'll never find that half who makes you whole and that goes for everything. Just because you fail once, doesn't mean you're gonna fail at everything. Keep trying, hold on, and always, always, always believe in yourself, because if you don't, then who will, sweetie? So keep your head high, keep your chin up, and most importantly, keep smiling, because life's a beautiful thing and there's so much to smile about.

—MARILYN MONROE

ACKNOWLEDGMENTS

A t the top of the list is Heather Jackson, my editor extraordinaire. You remind me when I'm redundant, repetitive, or too wordy. You force me to cut to the meat. You are ruthless in your comments. You make me mad, and then I see it. Your eye is impeccable, and my trust in your instincts gives great comfort. This is our eighth book together. I look forward to the next and the next. Thank you for being a great friend, and thank you for your enormous talent.

Alan Hamel, my cool, sexy, hot, smart (supersmart), honest, kind, and savvy husband. My chairman/CEO, the guy at the top of the company, is a true executive who oversees but allows his executives to do their thing. Unlike most people in these roles, Alan is extremely creative. For this book, I asked him to tell it his way: without polish, without any political correctness. To be truthful, shocking, and compelling. You are consistently true to yourself. You don't care what anyone thinks; you see it as you see it, and you tell it as it is. I like that, and so will the readers. You are the real deal, a straight talker, and a real man. I love you more than anything.

Bruce, you are part of all my stories. You *are* my story. You came through me to teach us both about the life we live. Just seeing you walk through the door makes me smile and my heart soar. I am a proud and happy mother, and I love you with all my heart. (Alan wanted me to remind you, "I taught you to walk!")

My daughter, Leslie Hamel, thank you for your unbelievable talent. Thank you for all the costumes you've designed for me that I've written about extensively in this book, and no small thing, for the Doodle Shirt you designed from your father's doodles that became the shirt on the cover of this book. Here's to a great new business! Thank you for accepting me as your other mother. It means so much to me. I love you.

Thanks once again to Sandi Mendelson, my lucky charm, my one and only publicist. This is our nineteenth book together. It doesn't matter how great the book; if the public doesn't know about it, the work gets lost. Sandi makes sure all the right outlets—the most prestigious TV shows, social media, print, Facebook, every source available—give coverage. The result has been a string of bestsellers. You are the best and such fun to work with.

Marc Chamlin, my literary lawyer—we turn it over to you, tell you what we need and want, and then you go get it, and no one ever feels screwed over. That's true talent and diplomacy. Thanks.

Caroline Somers is now president of our company, after a long run as creative director and executive vice president of branding and product development. There is no one better or smarter to be at the helm. You wear so many hats, you keep all the plates spinning, and nothing suffers. It all gets done, and it gets done great. You are my right hand. Johnny had Ed, Oprah has Gayle—and I have you, Caroline. You anticipate my every need, you help me execute my vision, and you represent us at the highest level of professionalism. I loved our collaboration on the photo shoot and design for this jacket. Most important, we are in sync. You are my son Bruce's wife and mother to my darling granddaughters, Camelia and Violet. You are one of those women who does it all. I love you dearly—and I love being your "earth mother."

Thank you to Danielle Shapero-Rudolph for the fantastic jacket design. I love the fun, the energy, and the style. I love your enormous talent and what you've brought to the company and the brand.

Thanks to Cindy Gold for the fantastic jacket photo. I love working with you and your talented team.

Roger Ball, our senior vice president in charge of production. In other words, "our everything guy." You are the best; a dear friend, a master of lighting, and a lot of fun. It's been thirty years.

Julie Turkel, our dear sweet assistant, who lies awake at night thinking of nice things to do for us and the company.

Thanks to Mooney, as always, for giving me my trademark Suzanne Hair. And it's just cool to be with you.

Thanks also to Jill Schugardt, vice president of procurement. She handles all interfacing for ordering, delivering, and distribution of our products. Your work is incredibly detailed, and you're really good at spreadsheets and things I know nothing about!

Sam Harwit, director of social media, manages all my social media platforms and helps me stay current with emerging apps. You're smart, savvy, and adorable.

Jason Latshaw, vice president for e-commerce and sales, you're the heart of my sales team, running the website and ensuring that my customers have a smooth experience in finding my products and that they are delivered promptly to their homes.

Dave Henson, my computer guy—how I've written so many books with such limited computer skills speaks highly of your input. When I call you in tears saying, "Helllllp!" you are there and put it all back together again. Thanks so much.

Herb Schmidt, who handles the money, our CFO for many years. Thank you.

My partners at Crown are Diana Baroni, vice president and editorial director; Tammy Blake, publicity director; Christina Foxley, assistant marketing director; and Aaron Wehner, senior vice president and publisher at Clarkson Potter, Ten Speed Press, and Harmony Books.

On the production side, thank you to Christine Tanigawa, production editorial director; Heather Williamson, production manager; Maria Spano, managing editor; and Elizabeth Rendfleisch, vice president and director of interior design.

Thanks to John Gray (*Men Are from Mars, Women Are from Venus*) for writing his praises for this book.

And finally, thanks to our wonderful late president of Somers Companies, Jim England. You were one of the great gentlemen; your loss is felt every day. Both Alan and I miss you, love you, and send all our love to your dear wife, Debbie, and your beautiful family. RIP, you dear, sweet soul.

CONTENTS

TWO'S COMPANY

PROLOGUE

My therapist, wisely, once told me, "There is no such thing as perfect." My thinking at that time was that I *had* to be perfect. Like so many women, I have spent a lot of my life being controlled by self-imposed perfectionist issues. This thinking is most likely a carryover from my growing up a child of an alcoholic. (Not understanding the disease, I believed [wrongly] that if I could just be perfect he—my father—would love me enough not to have to drink.) Over the years, I've learned you can drive yourself crazy trying to be perfect. The goal instead is to do and be your best, learn from your mistakes, and move forward. With the advent of wisdom—the greatest gift of aging—I am more relaxed. I live my life the best I can, succeeding and failing, learning to forgive myself and others, being "present," and feeling incredibly grateful and thankful for my life's good fortune.

We must learn from our mistakes otherwise they hold no value.

My life is our life: my life with him—my husband, Alan Hamel—and his with me. No kidding. He is what makes the day begin. He makes me smile before I fall asleep and wake up happy in the morning. I don't like to be away from him. Others criticize this togetherness, tell us we are crazy and that if something were to happen to one of us, we would be so lost. I figure, I'll take my chances. We have the dream. We have what everyone wants; what poets write about, why love songs are written, why movies get made. We have achieved it.

1

As with all love stories, though, we had a rocky beginning, a bumpy middle, and a lot of problems and imperfection along the way. Yet with the perspective I now have, we clearly are living the greatest life together two people could imagine. You see, it's never perfect. As M. Scott Peck says in *The Road Less Traveled,* "It is the wise man that welcomes problems and mistakes, for through them we learn to grow spiritually and emotionally." Growth is agitating, but it is what allows us to move forward as people.

When you are living a relationship you never want to end, then good health is a responsibility. It is respectful to want to stay healthy for each other.

None of us knows what tomorrow will bring, but Alan and I live together each day wanting another day together tomorrow, and the next day and the next. I want to be with him forever. We have a true love aligned in deep commitment to each other, to our mutual desire for optimal health, and to the business we created from scratch. We have fun together doing all of it. We are two like-minded people who respect and encourage each other, we are each other's best friend and most trusted confidant. We love our children and grandchildren; family is where we connect and enjoy the "stuff" of life—food, meals together, holidays. My husband is the man I have loved with all my heart for fifty years.

I have not always been a perfect wife. When I look back at hurtful, stupid things I have done or said, I feel a pain in my gut so palpable, I can hardly live with it. When it overwhelms, I run to my therapist to remind me (again) that we all screw up and we all have the capacity to forgive and be forgiven. Then I use those actions like judo; using forward energy to win.

We must learn from our mistakes otherwise they hold no value. What we have is an almost-perfect relationship (there I go again). I never get tired of him, am always amused by him, am completely turned on by him, and rarely feel annoyed with him. I admire him and his thinking. We are in sync. Our sex life has been part of our cultural lore ever since an offhand comment on *The Talk* that we often have sex twice a day. That information follows us everywhere, when the bigger question is why two people, after fifty years together, still feel so drawn to each other sexually.

The questions I am asked most often are *Why does it work?* and *How can two people spend 24/7 together 365 days a year and get along so great?* Everyone seems to want the combination for this love lock. I call it

Allow yourself to be humbled by each other.

a figure eight: never beginning, never ending. Lovers, best friends, companions, business partners, each holding our individual strengths and rarely getting in the other's way. This story is an attempt to share our unexpected life as a couple. Perhaps you might recognize yourself and find inspiration when times are hard, knowing that dreams can come true but that growing up takes time and is hard work.

The health component of our relationship, and anyone's, truly is not to be downplayed. We are two people who take it seriously; when you are living a relationship you never want to end, then good health is a responsibility. It is respectful to want to stay healthy for each other, so you can enjoy quality of life, vitality, longevity, mental clarity, and all-around superb health. As you know, if you've ever read any of my other work, I believe this wholeheartedly: without health, you've got nothing.

We all are capable of the worst behavior; can you still love each other even then?

So what is the magic? How do you get it? Is there a formula, or are we just a once-in-a-lifetime almost-perfect match, two chemistries that mesh and meld together? I'll tell you what it isn't. It isn't about luck. A great relationship takes work and tremendous respect. You must hear each other, and that takes time. Sometimes you'll have to wait for the other person to grow up enough to be ready to hear you; sometimes it's the reverse. You also need to allow yourself to be humbled by each other. It requires seeing each other, not only in the best light but also in the worst, and still knowing that it's okay. We all are capable of the worst behavior; can you still love each other even then?

This is our love story.

Let's start at the beginning.

3

CHAPTER 1

IN THE BEGINNING

Nothing's impossible I have found, for when my chin is on the ground,
I pick myself up, dust myself off and start all over again.
—JEROME KERN AND DOROTHY FIELDS, "PICK YOURSELF UP"

Alan Hamel is an interesting guy, and I would say that even if he weren't my husband.

That we even met is the stuff of dreams; he was the son of Polish immigrants who luckily escaped from the jaws of Hitler. His father lived in a settlement called Little Pietrokov on the Polish-German border with dirt floors and thirteen children. Somehow in 1905, at thirteen years old, he managed to get the equivalent of eight dollars (an enormous sum of money at that time) to ride steerage on a ship to America. With that many children, it probably wasn't noticed much when he took off on foot to Bremen to a new life. He wanted to get himself to Texas and become a cowboy. Speaking no English, amazingly he did just that. And then eventually at sixteen, he wound up in Chicago, where he was clubbed over the head and blinded in his right eye by police on horseback who were rounding up union troublemakers. (He was not one of them, just a casualty.) That incident led him to seek out relatives who had immigrated to Canada, and that is where he stayed.

Alan's mother's mother also emigrated to Canada, but she became lonely and returned to Poland. Sadly, once back home again, she was rounded up by Hitler in the worst of ways along with boxcars of her family and met with an unthinkable death.

Alan's mother wanted to expose him to all cultures, so as a young boy he was sent to Knox Presbyterian Church for his first year in nursery school. That year he was chosen to perform in the Christmas play and dressed up as one of the three wise men. He carried one of the gifts to put under the manger for Baby Jesus but was so intrigued by the glitter of the gifts that after the ceremony he grabbed the present and ran all the way home and up the stairs to the bedroom. He ripped open the beautifully wrapped gift to find it . . . empty. It was his first life lesson. He cried when his mother was angry with him for stealing. He hadn't thought of it that way.

Alan was your typical Canadian kid, loved playing ice hockey in the winter. He was typical, that is, until he was eight, when a gang of monsters, teenage bullies, hung him by a rope and left him to die. An angel in the form of an old man heard the whimpering of this small boy inside an abandoned building and cut him down in the nick of time. He repressed this horrible memory until much later in life, when his mother told me about it, but surely this incident shaped him in ways that took a lifetime to understand.

At home his life was idyllic. He grew up in a boardinghouse run by his mother; sixteen people all lived together; his parents and sister, a black Nigerian prince, eight Chinese brothers, a Presbyterian minister, a stripper whose name was Rita (who took him to his first girlie show), a British engineer, and a blind alcoholic trumpet player who smoked in bed and almost set the house on fire on a regular basis.

His mother worked morning till night, cooking dinner for the group, cleaning, and doing laundry (whatever it took), and in her spare time she ran a candy store. Every morning Alan—or Sonny, as he was called—came down the stairs to find his mother holding his still-warm, fresh-pressed shirt and a spoonful of castor oil; mothers at that time ruled the roost, and refusing the spoonful of "dreck" (his word) was not an option.

So that was his life. Who knew this son of immigrants would grow up to be one of the most popular and beloved TV personalities in Canada? In Canada today, he is referred to as a television pioneer. His picture is positioned front and center and prominently displayed in the Ryerson Hall of Fame. Lucky for me, being Mr. Canada just wasn't enough for him. Though still to this day, whenever he hears "O Canada," he tears up.

I was raised in San Bruno, California, a lovely, small, middle-class town about twenty miles from San Francisco. Ducky Mahoney was my father, and his father emigrated from Ireland. His people were hardworking, staunch Catholics, with more than a bit of an alcohol problem. And in and from that, I was shaped and formed. The Irish are fun-loving, and my father was no exception. He told great stories and was a true entertainer, although he didn't realize it; he was able to hold the attention of a crowd, whether at a dinner table or at a school assembly. He would make people laugh, and his stories had an element of great physical humor, which he acted out using his body to make a joke work. On the dance floor, he could wow a crowd.

In his twenties, he was an all-star baseball player and won a scholarship to the University of San Francisco, at a time when very few went to college. It was quite a special honor, and for sure everyone thought he was destined to play professional baseball. He was in line to be chosen for the farm team for the San Francisco Seals, a pro ball club. Their star player then was Lefty O'Doul, and my father most likely would have ended up in the same league as Lefty—everybody was sure.

With the onset of World War II and like so many men of that time, his dreams were cut short to serve his country. He became a Merchant Marine stationed on a ship outside Nagasaki, during the time the atom bomb was dropped on Hiroshima. He describes his job as the worst on the ship, loading bombs into the bottom of the hull, knowing that if the ship were hit, there would be no way out for him. His stories of that time were horrific and must have shaped him in some deep way. The demons were surely in his dreams. After he came home in 1945 (I was born in 1946), he put aside his aspirations of pro ball out of necessity and he took a job at a brewery—a terrible choice for a budding alcoholic. And with that choice, and in that moment, all he could and would have been slipped away.

Everyone loved being around Ducky, the fun-loving, funny, life-of-the-party guy. But by the time I was growing up, his disease had progressed, and that person was rarely the reality anymore.

That great guy faded, and the person who emerged was the drunken one: mean, frightening, abusive. Laughter was replaced by long scary nights hiding from him in a locked closet (rigged on the inside by my brother Danny), where my brother, sister, mother, and I trembled in fear, praying he wouldn't find us and hoping he would just pass out. In an alcoholic family, everything revolves around the needs and feelings of the alcoholic, so the rest of the family is left to figure it out on their own. I feared him, loved him, hated him, *loved him,* an unhealthy vicious cycle, which never ended until a teenage pregnancy shamed me from living in the only environment I knew and condemned me as bad.

In these horrifying nights of my childhood my self-esteem took a hit; in his drunkenness, my father decided each night who would be the object of his rage and ridicule. The booze made him act viciously and say terrible things: "You're stupid, hopeless, worthless, you're nothin', you're a big zero!" He also repeatedly told me, "You're gonna get knocked up." I didn't even know what knocked up meant; I had never even had sex at this point. Sadly, his rants became my reality. I believed I *was* what he said, and the only time I did have sex (if you can call it that) I got knocked up. My mother, confined by her Catholicism, stated sadly, "You made your bed, Suzanne, now you must lie in it." Abortion was out of the question. On the night before the wedding, my father once again drunkenly ranted, "I always knew you'd get knocked up," which had me sobbing on the floor of my closet wishing I could die. I was convinced he was right about my worthlessness and felt I deserved my punishment.

In this chaos, I found myself not only pregnant, but a teenager with neither the means nor the skills to be a mother. This time was, in retrospect, the hardest period of my life.

My new husband was a nice guy, a good guy, but we were both kids. The responsibilities of being parents and of being married and starting a real life just didn't and couldn't work out for us. We parted amicably and I got custody of our son, which was the custom of the time. The whispers in my small town for being their first divorcée were too much to bear, so I moved away to try my best to make a good life for us.

Life has a way of sending you what you need when you need it, even if you don't feel ready. And "it" was my child, my beautiful little baby son, Bruce, who would give me my reason for living. As they pulled him from my body, while still on the delivery table, we locked eyes. His stare was so intense, and he looked so worried that I said out loud, "I promise I will make a good life for you." I meant it. I would keep that promise. When I think back on it, I believe Bruce was sent to save me. My childhood had so damaged my self-worth that I was a walking ball of shame. But with Bruce there was no shame, only love and acceptance, and somehow together we would survive and thrive.

My low self-worth was soothed only by my mother, a woman of divine sweetness whose example was such that it didn't feel right to feel sorry for myself. Her life was terrible; if she could do it, I could do it.

Even though we had very little money for luxuries, my mother, Marion Mahoney, was an elegant woman with exquisite taste who always dressed beautifully. She had few pieces, but all were of great quality, an ethic she taught me. "Buy good," she would always say.

"Better to have one great cashmere sweater than a bunch of junk."
She was right. It didn't take me long to figure out that the cashmere
felt better, looked better, and lasted longer. She had attended Lux
School of Design, a prestigious San Francisco design and art school.
But once she was married, like so many women of her time, she put
her dreams aside. Who knows what she dreamed of being? She was
a wonderful seamstress with a great eye, and lucky for me she made
most of my clothes as a girl, allowing me to create my own styles
with great fabric we would buy together in the theater district.

*How many great
love affairs never
come to fruition
because it is too
easy to walk away?*

I imagine my mother thought that by
marrying the most popular guy in town—
the sports hero, the life of the party—she
was going to have the life she dreamed of,
that he'd bring her out of her shell and
release her shyness. Instead, his drunken
behavior horrified her and made her feel
even more shy and withdrawn in public. Everyone in our community liked her a lot because she was so sweet. She never said a bad
thing about anyone and was always happy for any good thing that
happened to people. There was a real purity about her.

After the divorce, my ex and I had no qualms over visitation,
the more the better. I was at least responsible enough to want the
best for my little boy whom I loved fiercely. The mother instinct, I
believe, is wired into the birth process. From the moment of delivery, a protective feeling takes over and regardless of your age and
what you think before becoming a mother, afterward, you instinc-
tively know that you'd throw yourself in front of a bus to protect
your child.

And so I began a new life, one that revolved around me and my
darling baby child. Two of us against the world. My little pal. So
close and so bonded; a teenage mother with a baby.

And then life sent me something and someone else unexpected:
Alan Hamel.

In the beginning, passion, for sure, was the initial draw. The "I gotta have you now, and then again, and then it's still not enough" kind of passion. Flying to each other's cities, even if just for a few hours, knowing that any time together was worth any difficulty of pulling it off. That went on for years, and it's what got us through the bad times. And yes, there were years of bad times.

When I think back, it would have been so easy to cut and run. I did think about it—a lot—in the early years. How many great love affairs never come to fruition because it is too easy to walk away? But I am getting ahead of myself.

It was 1967, and I was broker than broke, a teenage mom, and a divorcée, at a time when no one I knew had gotten a divorce, and I was too ashamed to go home and ask for help. Even if I had gone home, the dysfunction of alcoholism that had my family in its grip would not have allowed me to improve my situation. Besides, since I was the one who had screwed up, I had to figure this out on my own.

I did what I could to keep my little boy, Bruce, and me with shelter and enough food. I worked odd jobs, played extras in movies, and sewed children's dresses. I was an Avon Lady going door to door and a convention model—my big job was dressing like a squirrel for the American Walnut Association and passing out nuts. I made chocolate desserts for local restaurants, and I did odd modeling jobs for different companies, like for the ad that liquor stores put on their doors that showed me as the girl smoking extra-long cigarettes. (I've never smoked a cigarette in my life.) I was also the girl standing next to the Chevy on a bluff in Monterey, and I was the budding bride modeling wedding veils. Once in a while, I'd get a commercial, but nothing national, and that was where the money was.

I tried to get a job at the telephone company, but they said I wasn't qualified. I tried to get a job as a waitress, but I couldn't "stack." My mother had stressed the importance of being a good typist and being able to take dictation. She was a medical secretary, so it made sense to her that I would want the same. I learned to type in high school and was a pretty fast typist, and I learned shorthand. I applied for a job working for a goofy-looking lawyer. The moment he saw me, he hired me. The first day, he called me into his office to take a letter. My heart was pounding—I had never done this before. He spoke very quickly, and I didn't want to ask him to slow down, so I wrote my shorthand as fast as I could. Trouble was, I couldn't read it back. When I returned to my desk, I knew he would fire me when he realized I had wasted his time. I felt stupid. Rather than go through the humiliation of hearing him do it, I fired myself. To this day, I doodle (and think) in shorthand, and to this day I'm unable to read it back. Go figure.

My skill set was limited, but I was willing and able to work. I was smart and knew how to connect with people. It was just that work was hard to come by, and my schooling had been cut short because of my pregnancy. I really disliked typing and never really saw myself in an office. Deep down, showbiz was my lure. I wanted it but hadn't yet gained the confidence that someone like me could pull it off.

At twenty-one, I tried out for weather girl on the KPIX Westinghouse station in San Francisco. It was the late 1960s, and girls weren't wearing bras, so I wore a thin jersey mini-shirt dress (my best dress) and thought I looked pretty nice. They handed me a thingy, and I was pointing it at all the wrong cities, and I couldn't ad-lib, so I'd say, "It's going to be very cold here and not so cold there." They laughed me out of the studio.

Then one day I got a job as a prize model on a TV game show. It was a trial run, one day of work for sure, and then depending on how I did, it could become a regular gig. I walked into the local ABC station in San Francisco, and there *he* was, the center of attention, everyone standing around him while he held court, handsome, sexy, with intense blue eyes, laughing with a throaty laugh. A guy who knows he's attractive. Men were charmed by him and women were drawn to him. He was wearing a red alpaca sweater and bell-bottom jeans. It was a very hip, cool look for the times. I had never seen that. No one I knew had clothes like that.

I stood off to the side. I didn't have the confidence to walk into that energy field. I looked around for someone to direct me to wherever, but suddenly I was aware he was staring at me. I looked away because it scared me. I wanted to disappear. And then he walked toward me and my heart started pounding while his eyes took me in. Blue. Deep light pools of blue. I guess he asked my name, I guess he asked me other questions, but I was too involved with his stare and his intensity.

Shortly after arriving in Los Angeles from Toronto, I sold a ninety-minute comedy special to ABC called You Can't Do That on Television *and was offered a hosting job on a game show called* The Anniversary Game. *It would shoot in San Francisco because studios in Los Angeles weren't available. I always heard that San Francisco was the New York of the West, very sophisticated and very into the arts, so I jumped at the opportunity. I moved into a Japanese suite at the Miyako Hotel with tatami mats on the floor for beds, translucent sliding shoji screens everywhere, great lighting, and it was quiet.*

First day on set, I was talking to my production team, on the way to my dressing room to change for the first show, and I looked up and saw this angel standing alone in the corner of the studio. She was the most beautiful girl-woman I had ever seen. At that moment, everything the group was saying sounded like blah blah blah blah. I didn't hear the chatter from the crew setting up. I didn't hear anything. I didn't see anything except her. I had to say something. What do I say? I was always lousy at come-on lines because they always sounded like come-on lines. My eyes were riveted on her as I made my way across the studio, with my heart pounding. And finally we were face to face. Now what?

"Uh," I blubbered, "would you mind getting me a cup of coffee?"

Nice, huh? How stupid was that? Thankfully, she said yes, and that was our beginning.

Suzanne says it was love at first sight. For me, the animal, it was lust at first sight, but it was a lot more.

I was still married at the time, but my wife and I had started conversations about a divorce.

I had known my wife for only two weeks when we married; we should have only been good friends. But I was twentyish, and at that age you think you can handle anything that comes your way. This union was simply another challenge. I'd make it work! Right.

On our honeymoon, I felt trapped, but didn't know how to broach the subject. She had moved out of her parents' home into mine. We were kids. During the ten years we were married, I was away most of the time with work in TV, radio, and commercials. I created a show that allowed me to choose subjects and locations, so I was in and out of foreign countries constantly.

Back to day one: Suzanne was hired to be the prize model on the show but was fired the first day because when she opened the refrigerator door, she looked toward the wrong camera. No one told her it was the one with the red light. With her gone from the set, I had to figure out how to get in touch with her. The booker had her phone number but refused to give it to me. But I finally got it after much taunting from him.

I called Suzanne, and a child answered. It was her four-year-old, Brucie.

"Is your mommy home?"

"Yes," he said, and then put down the phone.

For the next ten or fifteen minutes, I listened to Brucie playing and Suzanne singing. Brucie had answered my question and then moved on. Yes, his mommy was home. Suzanne finally saw the phone off the hook, picked it up, and said hello, and we were joined at the hip from that moment.

Years later Suzanne told me she called her mother that day to announce she had met the man she wanted to marry. I had no one to call, but I knew even then this was not a fling; this was serious, very serious.

What are the odds of a guy from Canada getting a gig in San Francisco and meeting his one and only who came from a little blue-collar town in Northern California?

"*C*an you get me a cup of coffee?" Is that what he said? I thought to myself. Get him a cup of coffee?!

"Ummm . . . sure," I answered.

I asked someone, "Where do I get coffee?" I was told it was upstairs in the third-floor cafeteria. I took the elevator and found a vending machine. Fifty cents! Shoot, did I have fifty cents? I rummaged through the bottom of my purse, found it, and took the coffee downstairs to Blue Eyes.

"Thanks," he said, as I saw that someone had already gotten a cup for him.

We stood awkwardly for a moment looking at each other, and then he was called to the set. *Geez. What was that?* It was just a nanosecond, but there was something powerful about it.

I was awful as a prize model. I kept looking at the wrong camera. At the end of the day, the producer told me not to come back. I rushed out of the studio, mortified.

I went back home that evening to my life with my little son. I cooked our dinner and put him to bed, then lay down with my stomach grinding, trying to understand why my heart felt like it was tied in a knot. It was no use even thinking about Blue Eyes; he was as out of reach as Siberia.

The next day the phone rang. Bruce, who was four, answered it. When he was asked if his mommy was home, he said yes and then walked away. Kids are literal. I just happened to walk by and picked it up. How long had it been off the hook? I wondered. "Hello?" I asked, about to hang up, and then I heard someone saying, "Wait, wait, wait . . ." I recognized that voice. *Oh my god, it was* him!

"I want to take you to dinner." His voice was even deeper on the telephone, strong and sexy. Demanding.

I was barely able to get the word *okay* out.

"Meet me tonight at the Miyako Hotel, seven o'clock, my room." We were on.

The Miyako is an upscale hotel in the Japanese section of San Francisco. There was no parking anywhere, so I reluctantly parked in the hotel's subterranean parking lot. *I'm already in trouble,* I thought. *I don't have enough money to get my car out of here.* But as was my usual reality back then, I decided, like Scarlett, that I'd think about that tomorrow. I'd face that problem later.

I had very few nice things to wear—the bulk of my clothes were the inexpensive (cheap) hippie Indian type of the 1970s; flowy shirts, jeans, and boots. I was a San Francisco girl, and the city look was considered sophisticated. In retrospect, he most likely would have preferred my easy-to-get-under, no-bra, flowy shirt that was the style of the time. But I wanted to impress and didn't know what kind of guy he was, so I wore my best outfit. I had read in the society pages that the "right" women wore hostess skirts in the evening, and I wanted to be with it, so I wore my new one. I didn't know that women wore hostess skirts only at home when they were hostessing. My Yves Saint Laurent white silk blouse was opened to just above my bra, to reveal what I knew were spectacular breasts. We Irish women are known to have lovely bosoms, and I inherited a good pair. Underneath my hostess skirt were platform shoes that made me look very tall. My hair was freshly washed, long and blond, and I didn't wear much makeup—some mascara was about all.

I knocked nervously on his hotel room door, and as it opened, I felt my body turn to Jell-O. *Him.* Inches away from me.

"Hello there," he said in his deep, sexy way while gently taking my hands. "It's a Japanese suite, so you have to take off your shoes."

I hesitated momentarily, then blurted out, "What else do I have to take off?"

He laughed his throaty laugh and pulled me inside. I really didn't mean to be funny; it was just the first thing that came out of my mouth.

My skirt was too long without shoes, and I tripped on something because it was dark. It smelled like chocolate. *Oh my god,* he had lit chocolate-scented candles, and they were glowing everywhere. The only actual light came from the TV set, and it was all screwed up to appear like a psychedelic light show.

I think I'm going to be dinner.

There was no bed that I could see, just a tatami mat on the floor, but cracked crab was laid out on top of it with lemon slices and sake, which he was able to warm up in his bathroom sink with hot water. He had done this before, I was sure.

We sat down on the tatami mat, and he handed me a brownie. I thought it strange to have dessert before dinner, but nothing about this evening was like anything I had ever experienced. So I figured I'd go for it.

I took a bite and said, "Yuck, it tastes like dirt."

"That's because it's a pot brownie," he stated matter-of-factly.

Oh my, another first. I had never tasted sake, had never been to a man's hotel room, and had never had a pot brownie. I had never tried pot. I had hardly gone out with anyone since my divorce.

I had a moment of guilt while setting the stage for what I hoped would happen, but the moment Suzanne knocked on the door, all guilt disappeared. I stood there staring at this incredible woman, someone who was trusting enough to spend our first date in my suite. We had barely finished the crab and shared some gentle kissing and touching, when clothes were flying everywhere, and we were at that place poets write about.

After the pot brownie, we nibbled delicious sweet Dungeness crab, and took sips of warm sake. The effects took hold, and soon I was laughing hysterically over the dumbest things. The TV set made me laugh, the nervousness of sitting on his "bed" on the floor made me laugh. Suddenly my silk blouse was unbuttoned and then slipped off. He expertly unfastened my bra, and in an instant my breasts were in his hands. I was spinning. I had never felt anything like this. His chest was beautiful, smooth and muscular, with just enough hair to be perfectly manly. I couldn't believe I was touching *him*. He pushed me gently onto the floor, although it was a little uncomfortable trying to remove the cracked crab shells poking into my back without breaking the moment.

Then it was a beautiful blur, crazy excitement, mouths every-where. I was lost in the greatest feeling of my life. And I was in love. Then . . . right then. I never wanted to leave.

Our love affair had begun.

Oh, and he paid for my parking.

That was fifty years ago, and I remember it like it was last night.

And then we lived happily ever after. Right?

Not so fast. This was about to be some journey.

CHAPTER 2

GETTING TO KNOW YOU

An invisible thread connects those who are destined to
meet, regardless of time, place, and circumstance. The
thread may stretch or tangle. But it will never break.
—ANCIENT CHINESE PROVERB

We met again the next night. He didn't ask me, he *told* me to
meet him at his hotel and that we'd drive to the restaurant
for dinner at an upscale San Francisco place. The tables had white
tablecloths, and the lighting was dim. It was quiet, with the tinkling
of crystal glasses in the background and soft-speaking waiters in
black tuxedos.

*Our second date was at Fleur de Lys. Frankly, I ordered champagne
and dessert so we could get out of there. All I could think of was getting
naked again.*

"We'll have two chocolate soufflés," he said to the waiter.
I guess we're not going to have dinner. But I really didn't
care. I knew what this night was going to be. My insides were already heating up. I felt excited and had a hard time believing this

was real. It all felt crazy. I mean, who goes out to a fancy restaurant and just orders two chocolate soufflés and a bottle of Dom Pérignon?

The waiter popped the cork on the champagne bottle and poured us each a perfectly chilled glass: my first expensive champagne. I had had champagne before at weddings, but compared to this, I realized that what I had thought was champagne was rotgut. This was different: colder, the bubbles were smaller, it tasted . . . expensive. It went to my head quickly. I hadn't eaten all day. My appetite was gone. We sat in a leather-padded booth like a cocoon, shielded from the rest of the room. His hand rubbed my thigh, and each sip of champagne intensified the feel of him. He leaned in and kissed my lips. I wanted them to stay there forever, but it felt awkward being this romantic in public.

"You know," I said, slightly tipsy, "I saw you on television a few years ago. You were hosting a show called *Wedding Party*. I used to watch you every afternoon while I was giving my baby his afternoon bottle."

"Really?" he asked.

"Yes," I continued. "I thought you were an ass." *Oh my god, did I just say that?* I laughed nervously. "Sorry!"

Thankfully, he laughed too. "Why did you think I was an ass?"

"I don't know," I said. "You kind of made fun of your guests, and it made me uncomfortable."

"Well," he said, "that's probably why that show was a flop."

Geez, why do things just blurt out of me? I thought. *I always say the stupidest things.* "I really didn't mean to hurt your feelings."

"Oh, come on," he said. "You'd have to do a lot worse than that to hurt my feelings."

As I sipped another glass of Dom, he went on to explain. "I really enjoyed doing *Wedding Party*. It was one of my first jobs in America. I had gone as far as I could go in Canada. At one point I was hosting thirteen shows a week on the Canadian network, including *Nightcap*. When I asked for a raise, they said, 'If we pay you what you are asking, you'll be making more than the president of the network.'

That was when I realized I needed to move on and come to the States."

"How can anyone do thirteen series at a time?" I asked incredulously.

"Canada is different. I was in the right place, right time, and I had had some lucky breaks. I had gone to Ryerson University, which was the MIT of Canada; I was in the radio and television arts department. I loved it. When I was taking my midterms in my second year, my professor came up to me and whispered in my ear, 'They're holding an audition for a classical radio show, and I think you could get it.' I said, 'Okay, great.' He said, 'No, put down your pen and go right now.' So I did and got the job. I can thank my mother for that too. She'd forced me to go to the Royal Conservatory of Music in Toronto, so I knew how to pronounce all the classical names, like Dvořák.

"It was a great morning gig. From that point on, I started living my life. I was eighteen years old and had a small apartment on the Detroit River. I got myself an outboard motorboat and went out on the river every day. Soon I started getting called for auditions for jobs in Toronto. In Canada, Toronto is New York and L.A., as in 'the place to be.' I landed a job as a CBC announcer, which is the plum job of jobs, kind of like Walter Cronkite, the most prestigious of all positions. And I was just a kid with a deep voice. I was on air in the studio every night but out in the field during the day.

"Because of my youth and ratings, soon I was at the top of that field. More jobs started coming, and I found I could handle them all. I had an afternoon kids' show called *Razzle Dazzle,* it was one of those shows with a peanut gallery of screaming kids, and I would come out, and instead of saying hi to the kids, I yelled at them: 'Aw, shut up.' They screamed with laughter. Howard the Turtle was my foil.

"But the plum gig was *Nightcap.* We were the most popular late-night show in Canada—everyone watched. The show was satire and very irreverent. We made fun of everybody. One night I interviewed a topless dancer—topless on national TV—and we got away with it! Canada at that time was much looser than the States, and they understood satire."

I listened with rapt attention while sipping the cold champagne. He was wearing a black leather sports jacket and jeans. Around his neck was a necklace made of rope with a small silver deep sea diver dangling from it. I wondered at its significance. It looked amazing against his tanned, strong, gorgeous chest. I couldn't wait to touch him again.

"I was gone all the time, which I'm sure is another reason my marriage didn't work out. I was never home. I hosted the Tokyo Olympics for the CBC, the World Rowing Championships in Bled, Yugoslavia, skydiving in British Columbia, ballooning over the Alps, Thailand boxing, a deep-sea-fishing tournament in the Bahamas, the Highland Games, Denmark, Sweden, Germany, France, Spain. I loved being on the road, and I created several tournaments around the world so I could get away.

"But then one day I realized I couldn't go any further in Canada. I loved the sun, but Canadian winters can get you down, and I was curious about the big-time aspect of L.A. and Hollywood. If I made it there, it would be a whole different thing. So I got on a plane and flew to L.A. The door of the plane opened, the sun was shining, the air was fresh, and I thought to myself, 'I'm home.'"

I was hanging on his every word. I felt so special to be having this intimate conversation with him. I had never known anyone famous before, and here I was the complete object of his attention.

"I moved my wife and kids out a few months later, but by that time we had grown too far apart."

I was glad to hear that his marriage was over. I had been so overwhelmed by him, I hadn't thought about the possibility that there could be someone else. I still couldn't believe I was sitting so close to him. I could feel his breath. I loved the sound of his voice.

"We had two children together," he said. "And when I think of my failure in that marriage, I am so grateful that out of this never-should-have-happened marriage, I had two really great kids.

"I started a new life, moved to L.A. to tape my first TV special. I brought in a lot of my regulars from *Nightcap,* people I used to work with, including writers. I hired R. J. Wagner as my special guest star and put it on the air. That's when I 'got' that Americans did not understand satire. In Canada we did outrageous satire. The people were used to it. But Americans were clearly uptight with this form of humor. The switchboard at ABC was bombarded with outraged viewers, so I knew we'd struck a nerve. We were the highest-rated show for that time slot. But what I had hoped would be a series was brought down by the right, the left, the Christians, the evangelicals, the Girl Scouts, the Catholics, and pretty much everyone else.

"Moving to L.A. was the best choice I ever made, though. I met Dick Clark shortly after arriving, and we hit it off. We think alike, so we formed a partnership. We are very similar, get along great, understand business, and now we produce several shows together and have many in development."

"Oh, so you live in Los Angeles and not in San Francisco?" I asked.

"Yes, three days a week there, and four days a week here."

Good, I thought. *Maybe I can see him four nights a week.* I took another sip of champagne. Glass number three.

The soufflés arrived on a silver tray: perfect and high, puffing with air, the waiter expertly opened little mouths in the top of the soufflés and poured hot chocolate sauce into them, and then topped them with a spoonful of fresh, cold whipped cream. Now I knew what the word *mouthwatering* meant. Drooling in anticipation, I took my first bite. *Wow.* Chocolate, hot soft puffs of chocolate, rich and luscious mixed with cold whipped cream; it was a dreamy combination, an incredible explosion in my mouth. I took a second bite and then another—I couldn't stop, it was so good. Another sip of champagne followed, cold, sparkly, bubbly. My senses were exploding.

"This is so good," I said, then noticed him watching me. "What?"

"I like to watch you eat. You eat with gusto. I like women who like to eat."

I thought about the night before . . . his hand was now caressing slightly higher up my thigh. I felt chills. I took another bite and then another. Now I was scraping the bottom of the soufflé dish. Gone.

He leaned in and moved my hair away to kiss my neck, and I heard him whisper, "Let's get out of here."

The drive back to the Miyako seemed to take forever. The champagne had me feeling very loose, and he was able to drive while touching every part of my body he could reach. We opened the door to his room and walked in, and in an instant, we were kissing furiously. It was dark and warm as we made our way to the floor onto the tatami mat, and within minutes we were connected, intertwined, one.

For night number three, I took Suzanne to her first concert at Fillmore West, Bill Graham's rock 'n' roll establishment. I gave her a brownie, and an hour later we were laughing our asses off and walking in to see Janis Joplin & The Kozmic Blues Band. Suzanne wore a powder-blue coat dress, with matching purse and shoes. Everyone in the Fillmore was loaded and, in Haight-Ashbury, wearing really funky 1960s street clothes.

There was a layer of dope smoke hovering above the crowd, but the cops disregarded it and let everyone enjoy the music. They were there in the event of a disturbance. But stoned people don't fight—they love.

After that I wanted to spend every night with her, and when I was away, we talked on the phone for hours. We were falling into that glorious place where love and sex and food intersect, and we wanted a lot more of all of it. We didn't know where this was going, but I was prepared to handle it. I had to. This was very real, important, and urgent. No way was I going to allow anything to get in the way.

That's how it started. We made love every night he was in town, everywhere, in every room, every place we could find ourselves alone. I had read about love affairs like this but never thought they really happened.

A few months later Alan leased a hip, small, but sexy apartment on Telegraph Hill. It was very private, located in an interesting neighborhood overlooking the San Francisco Harbor. It was a sublease, so it was furnished in someone else's style.

"Come over tonight—I want to make you dinner," he said. There it was again, that demanding tone in his voice, yet I liked it. I found his strength a turn-on. I had had a controlling father, and something about Alan was controlling in a way I understood. (We'd work that out later, in therapy.) Tonight I knew up front that I was going to be dinner, and I was a willing participant. I couldn't wait.

Whenever I went to see Alan, I first did my nightly ritual with Bruce. I gave him a yummy dinner and his bath, and then I would rub his back until I heard his even deep breathing, the sleep only a child enjoys. I stared for a while at my darling child, such a good boy, sent to me to teach me true love. I was doing my best to keep my promise to take care of him. He knew he was loved, and that gave him a sense of safety. Only when his regular babysitter arrived did I dress for my date with Alan.

That night Alan and I were staying in at his new apartment, so I wore the clothes he seemed to prefer on me: soft and casual, easy to get into and out of. I spent twenty dollars, part of my rent money, to buy new bell-bottom jeans (I wanted to be with it, and when I saw his bell bottoms, I had to have a pair), my hippie T-shirt, no bra, and a Peruvian poncho. It was the look of the times, and it was good for me because it cost nothing. I was young enough that I didn't need a lot of embellishing; besides, I didn't have the luxury of an extensive wardrobe, so this look fit our evenings together perfectly.

The door opened, and I took an inward breath. Would I ever get over this feeling? There he was in front of me, so gorgeous it made me feel faint. I gazed into his soft but strong blue eyes. *Geez!* I could hear my heart pounding. He was wearing jeans and no shoes, with his shirt open. I loved his chest. I buried my face in his beauty, and then he lifted my mouth to his. He had made sure, as always, to set the mood with music.

Alan had an extensive musical background from attending the

Royal Conservatory of Music and from hosting a three-hour daily classical show on CBC Radio. But there were also his years of *Nightcap,* with big-band live music and rehearsals. Music was everywhere. I could only imagine the thrill of being enveloped daily with great live music. It's what I love now about performing in Vegas and other venues. The rehearsal is as fun as the show. He often spoke of standing right in the middle of the band when they were rehearsing just to have the experience. Toronto is and was a big jazz town, and on any given night, downtown clubs blaze with incredible live music. Alan's show band was much like Doc Severinsen's on *The Tonight Show.* Alan's bandleader was Guido Basso, a world-class trumpet player who remains to this day a dear, dear friend to both of us.

But back to that moment . . . music was blaring, Fred Neil was singing "Everybody's Talkin'" as we fell into each other's arms, an embrace so close and passionate, it didn't have the patience to get further inside. It had to be now, kissing as though it were the last time. Later would come dinner, more crazy kissing, and then passion out of control. The experience was heavenly.

Having an apartment was more fun for us. He could play music as loud as he wanted. He could cook. There were no hotel hallways with passing strangers. It was just us, all alone. The sound of this music was moody, bluesy, and melodic. I had never heard Fred Neil's voice before, but it was deep and rich like Alan's: sexy and effective. No one could have talked me out of falling in love with Alan Hamel, no matter how improbable it seemed.

Everybody's talkin' at me
I don't hear a word they're sayin'
Only the echoes of my mind.

I knew the feeling. I felt deaf when I was with Alan. I'd never felt anything like this in my entire life. Every moment, every touch, every look sent chills down my spine. The rest of the world was filtered out.

. . .

Alan served dinner on the floor, large bowls of fresh oyster stew with big oversize napkins—oyster stew is messy. He had gone to Fisherman's Wharf in the afternoon and brought home a pile of fresh oysters for a romantic dinner with me, which was sweet of him. Only problem was, I loathed oysters. The idea of eating slimy muscles made me want to dry-heave. So I drank cold white wine and did what children do when their mothers aren't looking: I spat each bite into my napkin. I would have to find a place to bury the evidence later. I was too young and insecure to let him know that oysters, and frankly most fish, were not my cup of tea.

After dinner and a *lot* of wine, he pulled out a large roll of plastic bubble wrap that he had taken from the studio and covered the entire floor of his apartment. *Are you kidding me?* There was a big kid inside Alan Hamel, a guy who liked to have fun. He started jumping on the plastic bubbles, popping them. I stared incredulously, and then he grabbed my hand. He and I were jumping up and down on the plastic bubbles, popping them, laughing, falling on the ground; pop, pop, pop! Soon we were making wild and crazy love on the plastic floor, our passion accented with the sound of plastic bubble gunshots going off. It was a wild crazy night, incredibly funny and incredibly sexy.

I was madly in love.

But every week he had to go back to Los Angeles. Each week his leaving became more painful for me. I longed for him, waited for his phone calls; he was all I could think about.

Our dating was serial, and it was nightly. Every night when he was in town, I would leave my apartment to be with him. I always came home long before Bruce was awake, like an alley cat.

Our affair was crazy, wild, and sexy, and when we were out in public, it felt like we were the only two people in the room. I saw nothing else. "I can't get enough of you," he whispered to me again and again. I felt the same way.

I had never met a man like Alan Hamel. I grew up with super-nice Irish guys. Really nice. They were fun and laughed a lot. I understood their psyches. We were alike. I could have happily married any number of them, but I was attracted to Alan because he was so different from me. He laughed a lot, but even that was different. There was an intensity about him, all man and animal in one. He wanted me, all the time. He was used to getting what he wanted, and I wanted to give it to him; I wanted to feel possessed by him. I liked it.

You don't have to create crises—they come without invitation.

I had a small but nice apartment in a good district in San Francisco, but I was going to have to move out very soon because the rent was more than I could afford. I had never invited him to my apartment, but now I wanted to show off my cooking. "Come to my house tomorrow night and I'll make you dinner," I said nervously. I was a very good cook. I had very little money, but I'd use some of my rent money to buy groceries. I did stupid things like that all the time back then. Like I had to create a crisis to feel good. This was going to get me in trouble down the road. I learned later that you don't have to create crises—they come without invitation.

This would be the first time I introduced Alan to my son, Bruce. I told Bruce that Alan was my friend; that was okay with him. I invited Alan to come at Bruce's bedtime, which was seven-thirty. They were fine with each other. Alan joked with him a bit, and then I put Bruce to bed. At that age, children go to sleep almost instantly, so I rubbed his back for a bit while Alan was in the other room opening a bottle of Margaux he had brought over (whatever Margaux was).

I decided to serve dinner on the floor in front of my fireplace; it seemed like we were doing a lot of things on the floor lately, and besides, I didn't have a dining table. I had chocolate-brown shag carpets, the style of the time, so lying side by side on the floor, we sipped his delicious red wine by firelight in between passionate kisses.

I went into the kitchen and took my incredible (if I don't say so myself) roast honey-vanilla duck from the oven, hot and steaming, with crackling skin, the kind you pull apart, eat with your hands, and lick your fingers after for the sweetness. Another dish had fresh-steamed green beans, unseasoned, crisp and hot. I could tell he loved them.

"This is delicious," he said between bites.

"Just wait, save some room," I said. "I have a surprise."

I waited until he finished his duck, then went into the kitchen and proudly brought out a perfect hot chocolate soufflé, along with a big bowl of fresh cold whipped cream. I knew he liked soufflés from our date at Fleur de Lys, and I wanted to impress him.

We sat on the floor while I placed spoonful after spoonful of hot chocolate and cold whipped cream into his mouth. The wine was now gone. My head was spinning, a delicious combination of wine, chocolate, lust, and love. He pushed all the dishes to the side and pulled me close to him. He felt warm, safe, and delicious, then hot and crazy.

Listen to your gut. Sometimes in life you have to leap, take the chance, not "be safe."

"Let's go to my room," I whispered. I loved being in front of the fire, but in case Bruce woke up, I wanted to be behind a locked door. As soon as we were inside, he expertly had all my clothes off. He grabbed me by the torso, turned me around, and thrust himself inside. I buried my head in the mattress to muffle my screams.

He left at four a.m., after hours of sex. My hair was dripping wet from sweat; I was exhausted and overwhelmed with our passion. I appreciated his sensitivity in leaving then. Even though I never wanted him to go, I would not want Bruce to wake up and find him in my bed. I lay in the dark wondering where this was going, knowing I had never felt like this before in my life.

WHAT I KNOW NOW

Go for life. When it presents itself, give in and fill your heart. Listen to your gut. Sometimes in life you have to leap, take the chance, not "be safe." Those that can jump without the safety net are the risk takers; you might lose, but you might win. I took a deep breath and followed my heart. I didn't want to live a life filled with I-wish-I-hads.

But let's get back to the story.

CHAPTER 3

SAUSALITO

The only real security is not in owning or possessing, not in demanding
or expecting, not in hoping, even. Security in a relationship lies
neither in looking back to what it was, nor forward to what it
might be, but living in the present and accepting it as it is now.

—ANNE MORROW LINDBERGH

Being with Alan, my hot, sexy boyfriend, was like a fantasy. For four days a week, most weeks, I got to be with him. I didn't introduce him to anyone. I kept "us" to ourselves, our private affair. He came over to my place more and more often, after Bruce was asleep, and I would make him one amazing meal after another, always followed by crazy, incredible sex. Each time with him was better than the last, if that was possible.

I could tell he more than liked me, but there was no commitment, and I took each time as maybe the last time. Not in my wildest dreams did it enter my thoughts that it could be permanent. One night he slipped into the conversation, "I'm never getting married again," and I didn't comment. The fact that I was getting this much of him, for as long as it could last, was all I cared about. I was living for this moment and for the next. I was in love for sure, but I planned on never, ever letting him know. Things were fine just the way they were.

It had been impressed upon me growing up that you never asked for anything; my father had ingrained in me the blue-collar ethic of "owe nobody, nothin'." So I wasn't looking for anyone to take care of me. With Alan, I wanted love and love only. Money was my problem to fix. I got a commercial here, a commercial there that paid the rent and food and not much else, A successful month was making $300 to $400. My rent was $250, and the other $100 was for food and expenses. Pretty tight, but at least I was taking care of myself and my child.

In San Francisco, acting jobs that came available were mostly the ones film companies planned on picking up locally. I signed with a modeling/commercial agency hoping for a chance at a national commercial. They paid *really* well, sometimes as much as $50,000 if you landed a good one. At least, that's what I'd heard. When you sit in interview waiting rooms, everyone brags about how well they're doing and how much money they're making. It's all BS. If anyone was really doing so well, they wouldn't be sitting in an interview room. That's not how it works. But insecurities run rampant in acting; you're not anyone till you're someone. That's why in most interview waiting rooms, everyone talks as though they are the next Tom Cruise.

I wasn't really an actress—the extent of my training was having the lead in my high school musical, *Guys and Dolls,* playing Adelaide. But at the time, it had been quite the big deal for me. I won a college scholarship for it. My performance was brought to the attention of Walter Winchell, a very famous New York columnist on whom Damon Runyon had based one of his characters in *Guys and Dolls.* Walter Winchell actually came to see the show, which was extraordinary for a high school production. After the finale, he came onstage and walked directly over to me and said in his heavy New York accent, "You're goin' someplace, sister." I was stunned. My picture was with him in the newspaper the next day, and for a minute

I was quite the celebrity. No one as famous as Walter Winchell had ever come to our little small town of San Bruno, California.

Upon graduation that year, I was thrilled to receive a scholarship to college from the fine arts department. You didn't automatically go to college in those days. There was no money for it. My mother had been adamant that I learn to type so I could get a good job as a secretary. As a blue-collar family, the general thinking was that having a college education was not necessary; you graduated high school, got a job, found a nice husband, and started making a family. Getting a scholarship opened up my thinking. It gave me a glimpse of the possibilities for a life I had not entertained. Few people I knew went to college, except my father, who had received a baseball scholarship to the University of San Francisco and would have played major league ball (he was that good) except, as I mentioned, for World War II and a major drinking problem once he returned home.

So for me, going to college was an event. I did it. I was proud. Unfortunately, I screwed up by getting pregnant, so I got to spend only a couple of months at Lone Mountain, the San Francisco College for Women, a place totally inappropriate for my skill sets, who I was, and what I dreamed about. I had the show-business bug and this school was not the place to be for that dream, but I had felt that by applying to this impressive school I could be seen as more than the daughter of the town drunk. My pregnancy required that I put aside any dreams/plans to do the right thing. I was devastated, and my family was embarrassed (small towns are very gossipy, plus it was the thinking of the times), as though getting pregnant was the worst thing one could do. I kept out of sight for most of the nine months and, for the sake of appearances, I made up some bullshit story about my baby, Bruce, being born premature to try to make the numbers work out between my wedding date and Bruce's birth.

Making things up was how we survived during my childhood and adolescence. When you live with a major alcoholic who is running crazy at night, every night, you make up stories to save face. I needed reasons to explain why I was so tired all the time, why my mother had a black eye (again), and why I didn't do my homework. And I needed something to say for why the fence had been knocked down (again) in front of the house—my dad was so drunk, he kept missing it when he pulled into the driveway. We had to keep the secret all the time, so you make up shit to cover for it all. In the process, there is humiliation that further degrades self-esteem, and you learn to be on all the time; so it makes sense that acting felt second nature to me.

At night when Dad was especially violent, we would all get hurt. These were not direct assaults but he was so strong and booze made him violent so his arms would swing out at everything, often connecting with one of us, then my brother Dan would go crazy on him and on more than one occasion my dad ended up getting his ribs broken. It was awful. When he was down, we took advantage. It was the buildup from being emotionally traumatized night after night. When the situation presented itself, we would all go after him. The experience was frightening and shameful.

I always felt so sorry for my mother, who was a quiet, sweet Irish woman. The character I'd later play of Chrissy Snow on *Three's Company* was greatly inspired by her. Clearly this was not the life she had envisioned for herself and her children. She had married the life of the party, the star athlete, the guy on scholarship, the baseball hero, but then the war came, and when he returned, it all went dark. It happened for so many men at that time. They lost their window of opportunity. Dreams had to be abandoned and were replaced by the mundane reality of needing to put food on the table.

> *Seeing our success is how we manifest what we want.*

I grew up in what some now refer to as the idyllic 1950s, a baby boomer as we are called. The people on TV at the time were Betty Furness and Kate Smith, who opened her daily afternoon television show singing "When the Moon Comes Over the Mountain." She was a rotund woman with a big voice. I loved her. The movie stars were Marilyn Monroe and Betty Grable; I idolized both and loved their glamour. In my dreams, I wanted to be an entertainer, performing in front of big crowds on any stage anywhere, especially for soldiers as they did. My high school production of *Guys and Dolls* gave me an inkling of what it felt like. Performing wasn't hard for me. I loved singing; I loved the music, and I wasn't afraid to do it. Strangely, I felt more confident on stage than I had ever felt in my personal life.

I was a bundle of insecurities most likely due to the dark secret we had to protect all the time. I knew my dreams were just fantasies I had tucked away; I never told anyone what I fantasized about so as not to sound stupid. I had low expectations. I thought people like us weren't the kind to do anything extraordinary. One night when my father was raging drunk and telling me how worthless I was, I blurted out in anger, "You wait and see, one day I'm going to be a big star." And he said, "Oh shut up—you sound like an asshole." It knocked me down. I retreated, embarrassed. Who *did* I think I was? How was I to know that years later, I would walk into a TV studio, meet the man of my dreams, and eventually become a big star!

WHAT I KNOW NOW

I now realize that *seeing* our success is how we manifest what we want. My saying it out loud was a moment, a nanosecond, where I *saw* it but I just wasn't ready (yet) to believe in it or that I had a chance.

I had moved to Sausalito to find a place with more reasonable rent. Sausalito at that time was a picturesque, small village, directly across from the famed Golden Gate Bridge. I had been seeing Alan for over a year at this point. My new place was close to the city, so I could have fairly easy access to Alan, plus the small-town-ness of Sausalito spoke to me. I found a great place on the hill overlooking San Francisco, the beautiful San Francisco Bay, and Tiburon Island, directly across the bay. It was a perfect apartment (duplex) for Bruce and me: inexpensive, quiet, and safe. Across the street was a public school and playground, and on our first day there Bruce met Thomas, who would become his best friend. Thomas lived down the street. They were the same age, and it was a perfect friendship for both.

I moved to Sausalito around the same time as Suzanne did so I could be nearer to her. I loved knowing she was up the hill, while I lived on a houseboat below her. I loved the life. Although I had never sailed, I had a sailboat. It almost got me killed when I got trapped under the Golden Gate Bridge with a naval tanker headed for me. Stupid of me.

Every night, after Suzanne gave Bruce a bath and dinner, read him a story, and rubbed his back till he was asleep, she would join me on my houseboat. Suzanne was a good mother. I admired that.

Most nights I poured her cold white wine while I cooked dinner for us. After eating our meal while watching the moonlight, we would settle into the carpeted "fire pit" of the living room of the houseboat. It was like a sex pit—we couldn't keep our hands off each other. As the moon rose over the Golden Gate, we made love by the roaring fire and talked nonstop about ourselves and our lives and our families and our passions and our needs. Our relationship was the only thing we never discussed.

> Sometimes what we want is buried in our subconscious.

We explored and made love all over Marin County. One sunny afternoon on top of Mount Tamalpais, we were naked and "engaged" when an entire Boy Scout group marched by carrying flags. I was grateful for the long grasses.

Bruce and I settled into life in Sausalito, still interrupted regularly with nasty little details like not having enough money for the rent. Ugh. Money, money, money—it was always such an issue. A low-paying commercial here and there and low-paying day work as a movie extra filled in the gaps. I probably would have been a good waitress because I'm so friendly, but it was not in the cards for me. I was inexperienced, I was told, and unqualified. I decided to use my wits and do what I knew how to do, so I made desserts for local restaurants. But with my costs, the restaurant would have had to sell each slice of my incredible chocolate mousse cake for $3.35, an enormous sum at the time.

I also tried making children's dresses, but with the cost of materials and the time it took me to put these dresses together, I needed to sell them for $120 to $150—way too expensive for almost everyone. They hung in the windows, these beautiful handmade confections. I lost money on them. (Today they'd be worth a fortune, wouldn't they? How funny is that?) So local modeling jobs, a rare commercial here and there, and extra work on movies was how I paid my bills. When I think back, what was I going after? Why not go after something steadier—as a shopgirl, an office worker, a flight attendant—anything that would bring in money regularly so I could depend on keeping the lights turned on? Why didn't I do that?

Negatives that happen to us as children will follow us into adulthood unless we find a way to correct them.

Sometimes what we want is buried in our subconscious; deep down I wanted to be somebody. I didn't want to be the daughter of the town drunk—I wanted more. And subconsciously, I wanted to finish the dream my dad started.

I never let on to Alan how broke I was. I didn't want him to see me as pathetic. No wonder my first autobiography was called *Keeping Secrets*. It was how I grew up. We had to keep the secret at all times, at all costs. As they say in Alcoholics Anonymous, "We are as sick as our secrets." Negatives that happen to us as children will follow us into adulthood unless we find a way to correct them.

During this time, the women's lib movement was beginning. Women were burning their bras and fighting for corner offices, but that wasn't my reality. I just needed to put food on the table for us. I wasn't looking to change the world. (Ironically, years later I would be the first woman on TV to demand to be paid commensurate with the men—but that story comes later.) I had pride. I didn't want help from anyone. Somehow, I hoped, I would figure this out on my own. I learned to put on a happy face.

WHAT I KNOW NOW

My lack of confidence was a habit ingrained from a childhood where I learned to hold in my anger. For survival, I hid the hurt inside to protect myself. It was my sickness. When you have low self-esteem, you know inside that *you* are the problem. I knew *I* was the problem. I always felt everything was my fault: *If I could just be a better daughter, my father wouldn't have to drink so much.* I blamed myself for everything, including problems I didn't create. I looked right, but I was damaged, and it was playing itself out over and over in my adult life. Everyone would point to my sister and my brothers as the ones with the problems because they were all now clearly alcoholic, but in reality, they were more honest than me. They hurt, so they drank. It took the pain away. I hid my hurt by pretending. I became expert at putting on a happy face. Today it's easy to say "You've got to fix yourself," but back then I had no perspective or clarity. Thankfully, I would do that work to heal in the future.

Sometimes we need to escape from our realities; how we choose to do this can be healthy or unhealthy.

Those dreamy hours and nights with Alan allowed me to escape from my daily struggle and the sense of isolation I felt raising a child by myself with very little support or knowhow. Sometimes we need to escape from our realities; how we choose to do this can be healthy or unhealthy. It's the coping mechanism of being human, and it's a necessary part of evolution. I loved and needed Alan. In fact, besides my son, Alan was the best thing that had ever happened to me. While I had him, I was going to get everything I could from "us": drink him in, get lost in him, escape with him.

Life has a way of opening doors if you're willing to walk through to the unknown. One fateful day in San Francisco a phone call from my low-end agent had changed my life. It certainly wasn't the job as a prize model that was life-changing; it was the opportunity to meet Alan Hamel. Through him, I got a peek into a world I didn't know existed.

I was ecstatic when Alan moved to Sausalito to live on a houseboat. Was it to be closer to me? I think so. All I knew was, I loved having him so close with such easy access. Without discussing it, it was understood that we wouldn't spend much time together anymore at my place. I had no idea if he and I would ever be more than we were at present, and I didn't want Bruce to look at Alan as someone who was going to hold a place in his life.

Life has a way of opening doors if you're willing to walk through to the unknown.

Divorce at that time was such a new phenomenon that I was the only single parent I knew. No one from my hometown had gotten a divorce at that time, to my knowledge. Things have changed drastically, but in the early 1970s, Bruce's cousins and friends thought that not having his father living with us made him different. I didn't want anyone to feel sorry for Bruce, and I tried my best to make his world great with just the two of us. He was good and darling, and I loved being with him. He was my little friend, and we did everything together.

Alan's son was the same age as Bruce, and his daughter was a little older, but we kept them separate. Maybe it was selfish that we wanted to be alone with each other, but most likely it was because introducing the kids to one another would provoke questions, fear, and insecurities. It wasn't the right time to create this complication.

My daytime life with Bruce was about the two of us, and for four nights a week my night life (after Bruce was asleep) was with Alan. I'd meet him on his houseboat, he'd make dinner, and we'd share a bottle of wine. We'd look at the moon, talk, hold each other, and make incredible love. It was dreamy. Sexy.

I had dated very little in high school because it was always difficult. Back then the boy came to your house to pick you up, and meeting the parents was part of the uncomfortable ritual. I never knew what shape my dad was going to be in, and I didn't want to be embarrassed, so I just didn't date. So with (and through) Alan, I was working out a part of life that I had never explored. I wasn't analyzing us; I was thrilled to realize what falling in love was about. It was all better than I had ever imagined.

But now I had this cool, sexy boyfriend who lived in the moment, and I took each time for what it was, not knowing if it would ever be anything else. Deep down I fought—was it resentment?—and covered it with my easy smile. I still hadn't gotten up the nerve to tell Alan I loved him. I didn't want to rock the boat. Two years together, and I was still afraid to ask for what I wanted. I was too afraid to share my most vulnerable feelings! Too afraid to say, "I love you."

> *I was working out a part of life that I had never explored. I wasn't analyzing us; I was thrilled to realize what falling in love was about.*

One evening I could feel something was wrong. Alan was quiet and very tender with me. Suddenly in the silence of the moment, he blurted out one word: "Canceled!" We had been luxuriating in the fire pit of his houseboat when he suddenly dropped the word. It hung over us like a dark cloud. I was shocked into reality.

"My show was canceled today," he repeated quietly.

I was speechless; I had not seen this coming. Of course, all shows have their run, but I had been living in a dreamworld and hadn't let the thought enter my mind.

His show was canceled. The word *canceled* in all its finality just hung in the air. I was startled. It felt like the lights had gone out. What would it mean for *us*?

My four days a week with him were coming to an abrupt halt. Two years into our love affair, it was about to become more complicated. With easy access gone, how would we see each other? Our love affair was about to become . . . what? *Would* we see each other?

Alan would need to stay in Los Angeles for his work and to see his children. He never brought up the subject of my moving to Los Angeles to be near him. He knew I couldn't—I was a mother with responsibilities. Bruce was enrolled at a school he loved, plus he had friends and an important family support system. "Can't you come stay with me in Vancouver?" Alan kept pleading. "I can't," I would tell him, torn between my two great loves. "I don't want to leave Bruce with a babysitter."

I was sad (*traumatized* would be a better word) that Alan's time in San Francisco was now over. He understood and told me not to worry. He would stop in San Fran-

You get used to dysfunction when it's all you know.

cisco every week on his way back. But it would be only for a night.

Our time together was unbelievably passionate, but now with even less time, it became almost frantic. I felt if I exerted any kind of pressure on him, if I asked for what I wanted from him, it would send him packing, drive him away. Today, when I look back at who I was, what we were, and what we had, I find it amazing that I was afraid he would leave "us" behind, but self-esteem was something I still lacked.

Up to this point, I never allowed myself to get angry with anyone, including my father, even when he treated us kids and my mother so badly. I always just wanted to love my father. This is classic child-of-an-alcoholic thinking, and it doesn't dissipate until you do the work to fix yourself. I had no comprehension of this phenomenon back then. Looking back, I can see that the nighttime scenes of violent alcoholism were emotional brutality, but we accepted it then as kind of normal. You get used to dysfunction when it's all you know. With today's perspective, I see clearly that our life was *not* normal.

I dealt with my feelings by writing about them. All my life I had been writing down my feelings; I would write when hiding in the closet as a kid, and I would write when I was scared at the responsibility of raising a son when I was still a kid myself. I was always questioning: Was I doing my job correctly? Did Bruce feel safe? I didn't want to screw it up.

Frankly, unknowingly, poetry was my first form of therapy and a perfect outlet for me. I wrote about my feelings and all that I didn't understand about everything. There was my little bit of wisdom (as much as one could have in their early twenties). Poetry is pure thought. I didn't and couldn't understand the impact my life's journey had had on me so far, I didn't have a clue about all the layers of complexities. That understanding would come later.

I had a friend who was a published poet, James Kavanaugh, a former Catholic priest. We had become friends over the years through mutual acquaintances. He taught me poetic form and was so encouraging and helpful in my putting together a nice collection.

A lan is never idle. He immediately went to work creating a new show called *Mantrap*. He would produce and host it in Canada, but it would be syndicated in the States. The premise was three articulate and interesting women taking on one male celebrity guest. The women's lib movement was front and center, so the idea was timely. It was another of his co-productions with Dick Clark.

> As a parent, sometimes the best you can do still leaves you feeling like you've not done enough, or it pulls and tears at you no matter which direction you turn. Whatever choice you make tugs at the other part of your heart.

Once he got his show up and running, he offered me a semiregular job on it. Golden handcuffs. It was a great offer and a great opportunity for me, I needed the money, and I wanted to be with him. But it would not be the best situation for Bruce, and it would be emotionally difficult to commute. My sister, Maureen, and my mother said they would help me out with taking care of Bruce. I would be able to drop him off on my way to the airport.

But I didn't want to leave him at my mother's because my father's alcoholism was so frightening, and I didn't want to impose too much on my sister. She and her husband had four children of their own. Yet how could I turn this down? I told Alan I could come up to Vancouver to tape his show once a month for a few days. That was the best I could do. As a parent, sometimes the best you can do still leaves you feeling like you've not done enough, or it pulls and tears at you no matter which direction you turn. Whatever choice you make tugs at the other part of your heart. Thankfully, Bruce enjoyed staying with his cousins, so it was a good compromise for now.

From a career perspective, as I said, it was a great opportunity. Up till then I didn't really have any credits, just several local and regional commercials. Now, because of ACTRA (Canadian TV) unions, I would be able to make a good fee for appearing on his show.

I was the young one on the show, the one without much to say except for things I blurted out that turned out to be funny. I didn't try to be funny—it just came out that way. I didn't have the wardrobe of the other women, so I wore the look of the day and my age: hot pants and my tight-fitting Superman T-shirt with knee-high boots. Alan loved having me with him, so I turned up regularly.

On one of these shows, Alan had booked an author named Jacqueline Susann (the Jackie Collins of her day), a lovely and very sincere woman, and she took a liking to me. I told her over dinner one evening that I had a secret hobby of writing poetry as an outlet for my pent-up feelings.

Jacqueline Susann asked me to show her a couple of my poems. I didn't know if she meant it, but later I dropped my poems off at her room anyway.

The next morning she said, "These are wonderful and moving and deep and well-written."

"Really?" I asked, disbelieving.

I told Alan. He said, "That's great—you should get them published."

He said things like that: *Get them published.* Like I had a magic wand.

Jim Kavanaugh, my good friend, set up an appointment with his publisher, Nash Publishing. To my surprise, they decided that I was a poet who didn't look like a poet, and that that could be a good gimmick. (Not much was said about my content, or the feelings and emotions that my poems evoked. It was my first experience with business. These men weren't interested in anything other than the bottom line. But in retrospect, they made a good choice.) I was thrilled when they said yes. I had sold my first book! I couldn't believe it. What an incredible accomplishment! My deepest thoughts and feelings were now going public, and hopefully would resonate with others.

CHAPTER 4

WHAT DOESN'T KILL YOU…

In the depth of winter, I finally learned that within
me there lay an invincible summer.

—ALBERT CAMUS

It was a chilly Sausalito day, and the sky was gray. Bruce, who was five years old, asked if he could go outside to play with his new Christmas gift, a scooter board. "Okay," I said, "but just in the driveway."

As parents, we relive every mistake we make over and over in our minds, endlessly chastising ourselves. This one stays with me to this day. I was just about to take a bath when I heard the most terrible screech outside, and then a hard, frantic pounding on my wooden front door, and a neighbor screaming, "It's your little boy." I looked out the window, and there was Bruce lying in the middle of the road, with blood running down the hill. In front of him was a car with the door open. He was alone. He had lost control of his scooter board and it had shot out into the street just as a car was coming over the crest; it ran over him.

> As parents, we
> relive every mistake
> we make over
> and over in our
> minds, endlessly
> chastising ourselves.

I grabbed my robe and ran outside. I lifted his bloody little head into my lap. He looked up at me and said, "Mommy," then passed out, or at least I prayed he had passed out. An ambulance arrived, and suddenly we were in the ER, and everyone had snapped into action.

"He's going to need surgery," the doctor said. "It looks like his spleen has been crushed, and we have to operate to see what other damage might have happened. His head has been badly injured. We have to go immediately."

"Is he going to live?" I asked, terrified.

"He's got a fifty-fifty chance," and then the doctor took off.

They wheeled his motionless little body past me, and I sobbed as I've never sobbed before in my life. I prayed and begged God to save him, to please save him. I sat outside the operating room for what seemed like hours, like years really.

Then the doctor finally came out. "He's got some very bad injuries, but we were able to save his spleen. He has a concussion, and we stitched up his head. From what I see, he's a very lucky little boy. We need to keep a watch over him, so he'll have to stay in the hospital for quite some time. And then you'll have to keep him quiet and inside for a while. Watch for dizziness, watch for anything out of the ordinary."

I would have done anything for him. I would have traded my life for his at that moment.

After surgery, Bruce was wheeled into intensive care. Twenty-four hours later he was taken out of ICU and put in a hospital room, but he was sedated and in a deep sleep. I sat next to his bed, touching him, reassuring him and myself through that touch, hoping he could hear.

The nurse said to me, "Mrs. Somers, I think you should go home and get some rest and change your clothes."

I looked down. I hadn't noticed until then that my robe was covered in Bruce's blood. I had no shoes on. I also realized I had no car. So I called a friend to come and get me, and I called my parents to come to the hospital and keep watch until I could return after cleaning up.

All the way home I was lost in my thoughts: I kept asking my-self, *Why, why, did I do something so stupid?* It brought me back to my childhood, when my father told me over and over during his drunken rages that I was "stupid, hopeless, worthless, nothing, a big zero." I knew in that moment, I was all those things. My life would fall apart without Bruce. It was us against the world. From the day he was born, at every moment of every day, I had been pre-occupied with him and what he needed.

Bruce survived, but it was a long recovery. He needed constant attention, and I was more than willing to give it to him. I loved taking care of him, and I was deeply grateful to see him gradually getting well. I would make him delicious dinners and bring them to him on a tray, and I would sit with him while he ate. I prepared all his favorites, anything to make him happy. I made his room perfectly tidy and organized, because that was how he liked it. I wanted to do anything that would provide him with healing calm and peace.

His cousins visited often, friends came by, and I warned every-one to keep him quiet and not get him too excited. I gave him a bath every evening before dinner, but in shallow water, always careful not to get his wounds wet. Then I'd rub his arms and shoulders to help him go to sleep. He couldn't sleep on his back because of his head wound, and he had a scar on his stomach that went from his chest to below his navel. Finding a comfortable position for him was challenging. I changed the dressings several times a day. I did everything I could to get him well and recuperated.

After weeks of recuperation, Bruce finally went back to school. He was getting back to normal except for the continuing night-mares. Every night he would wake up screaming and shaking reliv-ing his accident over and over in his dreams.

Kids need to feel secure, but for Bruce, the accident had taken away that security. It created a deep emotional trauma for him. He learned early on that life is fragile and that what seems solid can be split in two. That's a lot for someone so young. Even though his little body was healing, his dreams were terrifying. He would wake up every night shaking with terror, reliving the horror over and over again.

I didn't know what to do. I would rock him and hold him and stay with him through the darkness of the night. I would take him to my bed to soothe him back to sleep. But the weight of all of it was getting to me. I was strong, but I felt overwhelmed with so much responsibility. I realized he needed help I was not able to provide.

His father mentioned to me that the community mental health center might be the place to find help—they charge you according to your ability to pay. I called the clinic, and they encouraged me to bring Bruce over the next day.

At our first meeting the therapist, Mrs. Kilgore, said she felt she could help him but in order to work with him she would also need to work with me. It would require that I also come in once a week. "Of course," I told her, "I'd do anything for Bruce." It never entered my mind to go to therapy for me. I'm sure I didn't feel I was worth it.

Little did I realize the life-changing effects these visits were going to have on both of us. Bruce's weekly visits with the therapist would help Bruce come to terms with the accident and the night traumas and allow him to start believing again that his life was safe. She was truly our angel—she worked so lovingly and intelligently with him.

She charged me only a dollar a visit. This was good, as I was swamped in debt. Bruce's doctor bills amounted to twenty thousand dollars. I had no insurance, the woman who ran over him had no insurance, and his father had no insurance. So the bills came to me, and along with the bills came bill collectors. The phone was constantly ringing with collectors harassing me for money that I didn't have.

I had to get some work.

Back then money was always my issue: I never had enough. I was always late on the rent. I never received child support, and most months I just wasn't making enough money to get by, so my checks bounced regularly. It was a dangerous survival mechanism that was going to get me into trouble. I'd go to the grocery store and pay by check, crossing my fingers that a modeling check I was expecting would come in time. Most times it worked out, but when it didn't, I made up lame excuses (lies) and hoped I would be believed. It was a terrible cycle that further eroded my self-esteem.

To keep the police away, I had to regularly go to the Sausalito bank and make nice with the manager, a married guy with a big crush on me. I didn't mean to manipulate him, but I was a survivor, and survivors do what they need to do. I smiled and talked to him and asked him about himself. I never let it get to the point I could tell was coming; dinner, drinks, anything? I always left before he could get up the nerve. I needed him to be understanding about my checking account and that I always got the money into it somehow but was often a little late.

My agent called one day, again showing no particular enthusiasm for me. I was used to it. Her tone was dry, matter-of-fact, bored: "I have a modeling trip for you. You'll fly to Baja Mexico to shoot a brochure for Mexican Airlines. It's three days. It doesn't require any talent. They chose you from your picture; all you need to bring are your bikinis. It pays fifteen hundred dollars." She gave me the time and place to show up, then hung up.

Wow! Fifteen hundred was a lot of money. Three days later I boarded a rickety-looking twin-engine Cessna with a crew of three (plus the pilot), the photographer, and his two male assistants. The plane was jammed with equipment.

As we flew over Baja, I looked down at a vast wasteland of dry, hot desert. I noticed a car being pushed by two men. Obviously, they had car trouble, but I could see what they couldn't, that ahead of them was . . . nothing. As far as my eyes could see, there was nothing. I hoped they had water and food with them, otherwise I didn't see how they would make it. *How terrible to be stranded in that wasteland,* I thought to myself.

We arrived at Puerto Vallarta, which was beautiful. I had never really traveled, so I was thrilled. A rickety taxi drove us to wherever it was that we were staying. It was then that I realized my agent probably hadn't vetted anything about this trip. Here I was in Mexico with four men I didn't know, flying in a run-down plane, and now riding in a run-down taxi. I had very little money with me, and a checking account that was barren. I had a credit card, but it was maxed out; when I tried to use it, red lights and beeps came on at the register alerting to all that I was a poor risk. I thought of Bruce. I was desperate for money, and because of that, I had allowed myself to be put in a potentially dangerous position, with no power.

One advantage of being a child of an alcoholic is that you learn to be adaptive; another is that we possess a "radar" that allows us to constantly assess a situation to see if it's dangerous.

I had no choice but to take this job. My enormous medical debt, coupled with the bill collectors who were constantly hounding me, had me seriously stressed all the time. Bruce needed his medicine, and now the hospital had turned me over to credit agencies. It was terrible and stressful with strangers constantly calling my number, and then they started showing up at my house, humiliating me for being a deadbeat. I was too proud to take welfare, and I didn't qualify for unemployment. My family had no money, and we grew up being told that after eighteen we were on our own, so I never even bothered asking.

We pulled up to a gorgeous Mexican villa on the sea, and I thought, *Well, maybe this is going to be okay after all.* I was shown to a beautiful room that had two twin beds with mosquito netting around them. The doors were wide open to the sea; it was just stunning. I started unpacking my things.

Then the photographer walked in. "We're bunking together," he said cheerily.

"Aren't there other rooms for you to stay in?" I asked, alarmed.

"No, there are only three bedrooms. So this one is for you and me. Don't worry, I'm not going to bother you."

It didn't feel right, but I didn't know what to say. I was very bothered to be sharing a room with this photographer, a huge hulk of a guy.

"Okay," I said half-heartedly. I talked myself into feeling safe. *He's not going to do anything. I'm sure this is a reputable advertising agency who has hired him.*

I wished I could go home.

That night dinner was served in a picturesque dining room by live-in local servants. The food was great and authentic Mexican. One of the servants kept looking at me creepily. One advantage of being a child of an alcoholic is that you learn to be adaptive; another is that we possess a "radar" that allows us to constantly assess a situation to see if it's dangerous. As a girl, I could determine the level of my dad's intoxication just by looking at the back of his head. Now, my radar was on high alert about this guy. Something about him bothered me.

I delicately questioned everyone about where they were from, trying to garner as much information as I could. There were no cell phones at the time, but my agency in San Francisco must have known who the ad agency was. *Right?*

I had my first margarita. *Geez, these drinks go straight to your head.* All the men were drinking heavily. Everyone was laughing except me. I was in a strange house with four drunken men, plus a creepy servant. I was overcome by alarm.

"I'm going to turn in," I announced. "I know we start shooting early, and I need my beauty sleep, so good night everybody." No one seemed to notice my departure.

It was boiling hot and sticky in my—our (gulp)—room. I liked to sleep nude, but no way was I going to do that here. *I'll be fine,* I reassured myself. That margarita made me so sleepy, I soon drifted off, wrapped in a cocoon of mosquito netting.

I awoke at dawn to the sound of clicking. The photographer guy was taking pictures of me sleeping. The blanket was pulled down, and my breasts were exposed.

"Wow, you have beautiful tits," he said.

I was horrified.

"Just sit up for a bit. I see nude women all the time. Sometimes I photograph for *Playboy* magazine. I shoot nudes for them. With your body, I bet I could get you a centerfold. They pay fifteen thousand dollars, plus all the side benefits. Some girls walk away with tens of thousands of dollars."

I grabbed the sheet to cover what had been my exposed breasts. Had my nightgown and the covers slipped off naturally? Or had he uncovered me? How creepy. I was a jumble of nervous feelings. Fifteen thousand dollars—that would get me out of debt and free me from my noose of always being broke. But nude—*oh my god.*

"Just look away and let the blanket drop to your waist. Make it look like you don't know the camera is shooting," the photographer encouraged me.

I slowly dropped the blanket as the *click, click* of the camera took picture after picture.

"These are great. You should see the light—it's blue and beautiful. These are fantastic. Your tits look great from the side. They are so firm and young—beautiful. I bet they're going to love these at *Playboy.* We'll take more later, at the end of the day. Maybe find a waterfall, and you can sit nude in the water."

Without consenting, I had consented. My insides were torn up. The small-town good girl in me was pulling against the reality of the money that could set me free. What would Alan think? He wouldn't like it.

We shot all day for the airline brochure: predictably, the pictures featured the blond girl in the bikini. She was sipping an exotic drink with a little umbrella, smiling and happy, sitting in a chair in the water, running on the beach, lying next to a local male model. These pictures would make anyone stuck in a Connecticut blizzard want to pack up and take a vacation.

At the end of the day, the ad guys left, and the photographer and I continued to do what was hoped to be the *Playboy* test photos. He did find a waterfall. At first I couldn't bring myself to be completely nude, so I wore a flowy top over my naked body and let the water fall, cling, and reveal. The look on my face was nervous and shy, not the come-hither come-get-me photos we are so used to today.

After a while, he convinced me to remove the top and then the bottom and let the water flow over my naked body. To do this, I had to go somewhere else in my mind, and I felt myself leave my body. It was another survival mechanism: escape to that place in the brain that allows terrible situations to occur without it seeming out of the ordinary. These pictures would be my ticket out of my terrible debt. I just sucked it up; I didn't know what else to do.

At dinner that evening, I felt more than a little depressed. I didn't feel like drinking with these strange men, so I quietly left the table and walked down to the pool area. I was lying on a chaise longue looking at the starry night, wanting to go home, missing Bruce, worried about him. He wasn't healed yet, and leaving him for this trip had been traumatic for both of us. I had explained to him that if I hadn't needed this money so badly, I would never leave him. I explained that his favorite babysitter was going to stay with him day and night. If there were any problems, she would call my mother, his grandmother. Also, his father promised to visit him as often as he could. I knew he would keep his word.

I also missed Alan, as I lay under the stars in the warm balmy air, thinking of what it would be like if he were lying here with me.

Suddenly, my thoughts were shattered by the creepy guy from the villa, who came from . . . where? Had he been watching me? Had he followed me down here and been hiding somewhere?

He sat down next to me—too close—and asked if I wanted a drink.

"No, thanks," I said nervously. I wanted him to leave.

"You want some weed?"

"No thanks," I said, uncomfortable.

He then moved farther in on my chaise longue and sat down right next to me. He reached for me and tried to push me down. I could smell alcohol on his breath. He started kissing my neck and reaching for my breasts. "You are very beautiful and very sexy. I like to look at you."

I furiously tried to push him off me, but he was strong and insistent. He had come for what he wanted. Luckily for me, he had had so much alcohol that his balance was off, and I was able to throw him to the side.

I ran upstairs screaming, but no one was around when I got to the dining room. They had all gone to a nightclub in town. So now I was alone in this villa with a guy who was clearly intent on raping me. I went to a dark corner of the vast living room and hid behind a large stone sculpture. Trembling, I heard him walk intently toward my room. *Where can I go? Where can I go?* I hid in the shadows for what seemed an eternity, listening to him go from room to room calling, "Susan, come here, Susan."

I prayed he wouldn't find me. I prayed I wasn't going to end up getting raped or, worse, killed by this crazy man. If I went down on the beach and he found me, I feared I'd never be seen again, and my family would never know what had happened to me. He could kill me and throw me into the water.

Finally, I heard sounds signaling that the group had come back. Not that they were going to be much help. What did they care about me? I heard them call for creepy guy to open the bar and serve them yet more drinks and bring food to them.

What had I gotten myself into? I was terrified that I would get raped by any of them. No one here cared about me or would protect me. I felt anger welling up that my agency had sent me on this trip with no regard for my safety. They, at least, owed me that.

I slept fully dressed that night, with one eye open, and by the time dawn came, I was packed and ready to leave. I just wanted to go home.

I was still unnerved as we piled into the rickety plane, and I noticed that the pilot was high. He smelled like liquor. I told the rest of the group, but they said, "Oh, he's fine." It was laughed off. I was terrified. As we flew up the Baja coast, I looked down at the spot where I had seen the two men pushing the car on the way in. I didn't see their car anywhere. Someone must have rescued them.

I looked over at our pilot. He was *asleep*! I shook him violently and yelled, "Are you crazy? You can't sleep! None of us knows how to fly a plane." For the rest of the flight, I watched him like a hawk and shook him if his eyes started rolling back into his head. Imagine!

The idiots I was traveling with were sleeping off their hangovers, oblivious that the pilot was drunk and the plane was old and probably not well maintained, and that at any moment we all could die. When the plane landed, I wanted to cheer. I certainly never wanted to see any of these people again. The photographer waved goodbye and said, "I'm sure we'll see each other at the shoot." I smiled a half smile, not sure how I felt about any of it.

As I drove across the Golden Gate Bridge toward Sausalito and home, I could feel the stress leaving my tense body. I walked through my front door, and there was Bruce, his happy little face and smile, with his arms outstretched for a big hug. For the moment, everything was okay again.

CHAPTER 5

THREE LITTLE WORDS

No matter how many mistakes you make or how slow you
progress, you're still way ahead of everyone who isn't trying.
—TONY ROBBINS

Every week Bruce and I had our separate therapy session. It
didn't take long before both of us looked forward to seeing this
incredible woman, Mrs. Kilgore.

The therapy brought up that Bruce felt unsafe about his family.
Divorce hadn't been common when he was born, so he was one of
the first kids in his world to experience it, the only one of his cousins and friends—as the rest all had intact families. I hadn't realized
it, but divorce did make him feel different, and he didn't know how
to express those feelings.

Mrs. Kilgore did doll therapy with Bruce: there was a Mommy
doll, a Daddy doll, an Alan doll, and a Bruce doll. She would put
Mommy and Alan in the same bed, and Bruce would move the Alan
doll out and replace it with the Daddy doll. An interesting way to
express what he couldn't explain. Children don't know how to say
I wish you and Daddy were still together. It made me sad but also relieved that if anything positive resulted from his terrible accident,

it was the therapy where he was able to express himself in a safe arena. He wouldn't have to spend a lifetime with unresolved feelings and end up on a psychiatrist's couch as an adult. Slowly but surely his debilitating nightmares were subsiding.

Bruce began sleeping through the night again, and his therapy sessions were having a remarkable effect on his self-confidence. Instead of feeling "different," his accident made him feel special. He was the talk of his class, and he showed his scars like a war hero. He was a hero. He was such a cheerful and sweet little boy. He didn't complain, and to my relief the wounds, both outside and inside, were healing very well. I was so deeply grateful.

One year into it Mrs. Kilgore announced that Bruce was fine and didn't need to come anymore. "He's going to be okay," she told me. "You've been a good mother." I felt humbled. I had always worried that being so young, with no skills in how to raise a child, I would mess up terribly. But clearly there is a mothering instinct, and I just followed that feeling. Besides, I had had a wonderful, sweet, and loving mother who provided a sense of sanity for all of us while we were growing up. What I knew I did right was to love Bruce dearly and deeply. That had to count, and I know now it counted for a lot.

I couldn't ask for what I wanted—I didn't feel worthy.

But Mrs. Kilgore then surprised me: "I want *you* to keep coming to therapy."

"Me?" I asked, startled. "Why?"

Her next statement stopped me in my tracks. "You have the lowest self-esteem of anyone I have ever met." I just looked at her, uncomprehending. She continued, "You apologize for who you are, what you are, what you look like, where you come from, what you do. You are a walking apology."

I sat quietly, lost in thought. I didn't know how to process this information, but I knew it was resonating.

I began my own intense therapy with Mrs. Kilgore to focus on issues I didn't realize I had, namely low self-worth. I continued to see her once a week.

Mrs. Kilgore talked about my low self-esteem and tried to figure out why I felt so negatively about myself. "Where did you get the feeling you were worth so little?" she kept asking, session after session.

At first I really didn't know what she was talking about. "I'm fine!" I kept protesting. I thought I was okay. I talked about my money problems, my overwhelming bills, and the horrible modeling trip.

I couldn't see that my low self-esteem had been keeping Alan from *having* to commit to us. Since I wouldn't force the issue, he could easily avoid making a decision. In retrospect, an ultimatum would have changed the entire paradigm. But I couldn't ask for what I wanted—I didn't feel worthy.

Every week Mrs. Kilgore had me write down what I liked about myself and what I didn't like. The list of "What I don't like" was filled up, but the other list was virtually empty. "I like my hair," I wrote. "What else?" she would ask. "Umm . . . I have nice breasts . . . kind of." That was about it. Pathetic. Clearly, we had a lot of work to do.

With each visit to her, I felt something . . . unraveling. She took me back, way back, into the closet at night, filled with fear, hiding with my mother and brother and sister in the dark, all of us so afraid. We could hear him downstairs ranting and raving, throwing food from the refrigerator all over the kitchen. The sounds were frightening, dishes breaking, him swearing. I could see my mother cry. I had always felt so badly for her. During therapy sessions, I remembered him coming up the stairs booming in his drunken voice, *"Where are you?"* (Reminds me now of creepy guy.) Thank god my brother Danny had installed a lock on the inside of the closet. If Dad suspected we were in there, he would at least have difficulty

Gifts are always hidden in the negative.

opening it—unless he kicked the door down, which was not out of the range of possibility.

I told her about the nude pictures I had let someone take because I was desperate for money.

"How will you feel if you are chosen as a Playmate?"

"It scares me," I told her. "I feel like my family will be embarrassed. I haven't told Alan about them yet."

"Have you asked yourself why you would put yourself in this position?"

"What would you do?" I asked her somewhat angrily. "How am I supposed to pay these bills?"

"I just want you to think about your choices and find peace with your actions," she said compassionately.

WHAT I KNOW NOW

Gifts are always hidden in the negative. As horrible as the accident was for Bruce, it was the bridge to repairing him from the effects of divorce and his fear of being unsafe, and it pushed me to look at my negative image of myself. The sessions returned Bruce to feeling safe and happy, and they saved me from the debilitating belief that I wasn't enough. I never would have gone to therapy for myself. I went because of Bruce. Little did I know that through Mrs. Kilgore, I was going to be "re-parented," but this time correctly.

Our childhoods have a major impact and effect on who we are. Problems that don't get fixed just compound, and life gradually deteriorates.

In retrospect, how could I have been anything other than emotionally crippled? My sister and brother used alcohol as a way of coping. (They have been in recovery for decades. The exception is our brother Michael who sadly died early, at forty-six.) I might easily have done the same thing, tried to ease my pain and low self-esteem with booze, but giving birth to my darling child so young took away any such inclinations. Frankly, at that time I couldn't even afford food, let alone alcohol.

Looking back, Mrs. Kilgore was an angel sent to help me unravel a lifetime of unresolved feelings. I had no idea that I was the problem holding me back from my own development as a person. As a form of self-protection, I hadn't been telling myself the truth about anything, and in doing so I had been holding myself back from true happiness. Anger and hurt were just below the surface, but I covered them up with my easy smile. Feeling everything was my fault was a big part of my sickness. Children of alcoholics blame themselves and get through each day by putting on a happy face. Our childhoods have a major impact and effect on who we are. Problems that don't get fixed just compound, and life gradually deteriorates. Anger and resentment build up and can make you sick. (I got cancer later in life. When did it begin? Just a thought . . .)

The phone rang—it was my uninspired agent. "*Playboy* likes your test photos. They want to shoot you for a centerfold. The pay is fifteen thousand dollars upon publication. You need to fly to Los Angeles this week, and they'll shoot at the *Playboy* studio. They'll provide hair, makeup, and wardrobe, whatever that is." She laughed.

Geez, she was almost nice to me, I thought. *I guess congeniality improves as the money goes up.*

I told Alan about Mexico and the test shots. I didn't mention the creepy guy. Somehow I felt it was my fault it had happened. The child of an alcoholic always feels they are the cause of the problems. It's not the alcoholic's fault or the would-be rapist's—it's yours. I wasn't *well* yet, but I was getting there. I was beginning to see the light.

Alan was quiet about the nude shots. He really didn't have any right to tell me what I could or couldn't do. I wasn't his wife. Besides, I needed the money.

"Okay, I'll pick you up next Wednesday," he said.

The following week I arrived at LAX. Alan was waiting for me out front in his big dark green 1965 Cadillac convertible. I loved his car and the way he looked in it. He kissed me so hard and long and intensely that we both forgot where we were until a cop came up and rapped on the car window. "Keep moving," he said briskly. I sat as close to Alan as I could in his big front seat.

We didn't discuss what I was about to do, which was odd; he was strangely quiet, and so was I. I was a jumble of nerves at the thought of being naked in front of so many people. And then to think that these pictures would be seen everywhere by everyone. My appointment for the big shoot was at two p.m., with an undetermined end time. It was going to take hours. We drove silently up Sunset Boulevard toward the *Playboy* building, and then there we were, right in front. *Playboy* was written everywhere.

I sat in the car for a minute, then smiled at Alan and moved to get out. He gently took my hand and quietly but firmly said, "Just remember, for the rest of your life, you are going to be thought of first as a *Playboy* Playmate." He looked at me with a wisdom that penetrated right through me. His words played over and over in my head. *Is that what I want? Is this the kind of success I am seeking? Is this all I can be?* I just sat in his front seat, feeling paralyzed. I didn't know what I wanted, but I knew I wanted to be more than this. I had not thought of this as defining me, a *Playboy* Playmate! Is that what Walter Winchell meant when he singled me out as a teenager and said, *"You're goin' someplace, sister"*? Is this where I was *goin'* with my life?

An entire crew, a costly crew, was waiting for me upstairs in the photo studio. I sat and stared at nothing, deep in thought. Alan didn't say anything else. We both just sat in silence.

Finally, I looked over at him and said, "This is not who I want to be."

He took my hand and pulled me to him. We drove off. I never took the pictures.

Now back in my reality, I was still deep in debt, but I knew I had made the right choice. Somewhere, somehow, I'd figure out how to earn the twenty thousand dollars to pay Bruce's doctor and hospital bills. I should have sued the person who ran over him, but I didn't, for all the reasons I now know had to do with my low self-esteem. It still amazes me how broken I was at that time. But I was starting to heal, and this choice was a big step toward the light.

I was glad Alan said what he said. Without judgment or pressure, he helped me make the best choice for myself. It was a better choice for Bruce, too. I wanted to be more for him. I would be more for me, too.

It was 1973, and Alan and I had been together for five years. I had moved to a new duplex down the hill and around the corner. I wanted to be in a place without the horrible memories of Bruce's accident. My brother Dan helped me move the chocolate-brown shag carpet (again) from my last apartment to this one. This place was one large room lined with glass and a full view of San Francisco and Tiburon. It was amazingly inexpensive ($250 a month), with two small bedrooms, a deck with a swing (which Bruce loved), and a wood-burning fireplace. At that time you got a lot more for your money. The only problem with the apartment was that the guy who lived downstairs was always coming on to me in a way that made me uncomfortable. So that needed managing. I couldn't make him mad, but I also couldn't lead him on.

I didn't know it yet, but 1973 would be a big year for me. My first book of poetry was published, thanks to Jacqueline Susann and her earlier encouragement. It was called *Touch Me,* about a young woman's feelings and emotions culled from my

Life is about the journey and love and passion and food and doing the right thing.

life as a broken bird. (I'm going to go out on a limb and say the book and these poems hold up even today.)

The book had heart. It had sincerity. It was my young truth. I wrote about my lack of power, about pining for love and feeling crippled by lack of money. I wrote of having no skills (amazing that

I couldn't see them). I realized early on that without money or skills or a way to make a living, you feel powerless.

Yet I also saw the bright side, the glass half full, that it would and could work out, that life is about the journey and love and passion and food and doing the right thing. *Touch Me* was who I was at that time in my life. A young woman, naïve and wounded yet optimistic. It was all learning-from-the-journey stuff.

The poems were who I was, sadness about the pain of our unbelievably dysfunctional home and its effects, yet also moments of pride when the best parts of us shone through. My alcoholic father had a light within him. Everybody liked him, especially now that after fifty years of drinking, he was sober. He had started out as the life of the party and ended up as a greatly compassionate man who was very sympathetic toward seniors his age and older. He helped those who needed his help, no matter how vulnerable they were.

> *Forgiveness is a gift you give yourself.*

He wrote me an apology, which says everything. It took a big man to do so, and it was a big part of my healing.

Because of it and because of the work that I would do on myself, I was able to truly forgive him. Later on, in a book of mine, I would write, "Forgiveness is a gift you give yourself." I still feel that way today.

The next thing that happened to me in 1973 was that my sort-of agent in San Francisco called about an interview. As always, she was very unemotional. Since I had walked away from the *Playboy* shoot, she probably felt I was a total loser. You may wonder why I continued with this agent, but anyone who lived in the San Francisco Bay Area at that time knows there were only two agents. Period. No other choices. I needed whatever money could come my way, so I put up with all of it.

She said, "They are looking for a blonde for a part in a movie."

"Oh. My. God!" I screamed. "Are you kidding me? Can you get me a script?"

"You don't need one," she said. "It's a very small part, three words. You say, 'I love you.'" Then she hung up on me. Again.

I didn't care. The day of the audition, I needed to go to San Francisco, but I literally did not have fifty cents to pay the bridge toll. I rummaged through every purse and couldn't find it, so I decided to figure it out when I got there. When I told the bridge toll-taker, "I forgot my wallet!" he said I had to leave collateral. I left him a tube of lipstick and went on my way.

The waiting room was filled with beautiful blondes. I was worried it would take so long to get into see George Lucas (whoever that was) that my car would get towed. I had parked in a no-parking tow-away zone. When I told the casting agency that I couldn't afford to stay, he said, "Mr. Lucas was very interested in your picture."

"Really?" I asked, dumbfounded.

They let me go in next.

George Lucas didn't stand up, just sort of slumped behind his desk. "Can you drive?" he asked me.

"Umm, yes," I said nervously. He stared at me for a bit. It was uncomfortable. And then he said, "Thank you."

Some audition. I drove home disappointed. I walked in the door, and the phone was ringing. "You got the part," said my agent drily. "It pays $136.72 and shoots tomorrow night. They'll pick you up at your house at seven p.m. And think fifties." She hung up.

That was it.

I called Alan and said, "I got a part in a movie! It's really small, one night's work."

"That's great," he said. "What's it called?"

"*American Graffiti,* by some guy named George Lucas. I'm going to be the mysterious Blonde in the Thunderbird." Of course, I had no idea that *American Graffiti* would go on to become iconic, the biggest-grossing film of the year, and that finally I was going to have a real screen credit.

The set of *American Graffiti* was in Petaluma, California, best known as the egg capital of the country; it is also where they hold the World Armwrestling Championships every year. I knew nothing about the movie, the director, or any of the actors. There was one very quiet guy who I later learned was Harrison Ford.

George Lucas, the director, called us all into the makeup trailer to tell us that this movie was going to be a blockbuster and that we should be excited to be in something this special. I looked around at Cindy Williams, Candy Clark, Paul Le Mat, George Lucas, Ron Howard, and Harrison Ford and thought, *No way!* That's how good my judgment was! All of them went on to become giants in the industry, but at the time I didn't know who any of them were, and neither did anyone else.

Three words: *I love you.* That was it. But they changed my life. Years later, when I was the star of the number one show in America, ABC announced that it would be airing *American Graffiti* for the very first time on TV starring . . . Suzanne Somers. I wasn't even credited in the movie! But that's showbiz.

The next thing that happened was a fluke. Sausalito, where I lived, was way out of the Los Angeles loop, so I read the trades a lot, researching what parts were up for audition. One issue mentioned a show (a sitcom) called *Lotsa Luck,* starring Dom DeLuise. They were looking for a girl who in their description sounded like me; small town, not aware of what she looks like, naïve and bosomy.

I decided it was worth a try, and besides, it would give me a reason to stay overnight with Alan. I would have done anything to find a reason to spend the night with him. I always wished he would tell me to stay permanently, but then suddenly we would be into unspoken complications. He would be living with my son and not with his own; they were the same age. We weren't committed (at least he wasn't). I left it alone and was grateful to take what I could get. My weekly therapy sessions were flushing out my feelings, and in this welcome healing, I was allowing myself to feel a little resentful, as in *Soon we were going to have to get this out in the open.*

The trades said the audition was the following Monday at two p.m. I didn't know the protocol. I didn't know there *was* a protocol, like that your agent calls and sets up a specific time for you. Back then things were much looser than they are today, and what happened for me probably would never happen now. In retrospect, it was a really ballsy thing to do, but I didn't realize it then. I told Alan I had an audition and asked if he would drive me to NBC's studio in Burbank. Ignorance is bliss, so when the NBC guard asked me why I was there, I said proudly, "I'm here to audition for the Dom DeLuise show," and I was pointed in the right direction.

Good things happen in life when we are ready to receive them. But if your nose is squashed against the mirror, you have no perspective.

I signed in and grabbed a script like the other girls, was called in, and read for what I guessed were the producers and writers. It wasn't hard for me; the girl in the script *was* me. I didn't even have to act.

After I finished the audition, the producer, Sam Denoff said, "Veeeery nice!" and "We are going to give you a callback."

"Thanks," I responded nervously.

When I went back to the reception area, I said to the assistant, "I have a callback."

She said, "How great."

"What is that?" I asked.

She looked at me strangely. "It means they're going to call you back."

"When?" I asked.

Now I was becoming her problem. "I don't know. Today for sure," she said, annoyed.

"Well, where do I go?"

To get rid of me, I'm sure, she said, irritated, "I don't know. Why don't you go wait in the commissary?"

Little did I know that that one direction from her was about to change the course of my life!

. . .

As I was sitting in the commissary all by myself (here comes the life-changing part), Johnny Carson walked in. He was the biggest star on television at that time. He looked at me and walked over and said, "Hey little lady—what are you doing here?" I lost my voice, I literally couldn't speak. Nervously, I handed him my book of poetry. I was using it as my résumé, because I didn't have a real one. I couldn't believe Johnny Carson was *talking* to me.

I told him proudly, stuttering a bit, "I—I—have a callback for the Dom DeLuise show."

"Well, good for you. I hope you get it." He walked away with my book of poetry in his hands.

> *Follow your heart.*
> *It's smarter than we*
> *give it credit for.*

That was Wednesday. Two things happened that day. I got the part on the sitcom, and that Friday I was booked on *The Tonight Show* with Johnny Carson, my first live national TV appearance. That Friday night in 1973, as I walked out in front of that famous curtain with Johnny Carson and Ed McMahon standing and clapping, my life changed.

WHAT I KNOW NOW

We never realize the pivotal nature of things while they are happening. I believe this is because good things happen in life when we are ready to receive them. But if your nose is squashed against the mirror, you have no perspective. I was in the right place with the right motivation, with the right talent at the right time, all inadvertently because of meeting Alan Hamel.

It never occurred to me then that connecting with Alan was no accident. I now know that we were supposed to meet and have this life we share today. My instant love for him was my motivator for everything. I wanted to do his show in Canada not so much to be on television as to be with him. Alan's show was how I met Jacqueline Susann. Showing her my poetry and then getting her encouragement gave me the confidence to find a publisher. That book led to getting an audition for *American Graffiti*, where I had three words to say. That movie and my book led to my—unknowingly— being able to bluff my way into the audition, then sitting by myself in the NBC commissary I had the great good fortune of having Johnny Carson walk in. This just doesn't happen to people, does it? But it did, and none of it would have happened if I had not fallen in love with Alan. Follow your heart. It's smarter than we give it credit for.

Johnny Carson liked me, really liked me, so much that he started having me on once a month. Over the next three years, I became a regular on his show. I would read to him about feelings and emotions while he would mug to the camera. Sometimes he would pretend he was crying as I sincerely read my poems. Imagine! He made me be funny. The audience loved the bit. I'd blurt out things that I didn't even realize I'd said, and we'd both get big laughs.

Relationships are about steps, a gradual moving forward toward an unknown end point.

My book became the best-selling book of poetry that year, alongside one by the well-known poet Rod McKuen. Now I had access to other TV shows because I was "that girl" from *The Tonight Show*, and the "mysterious Blonde in the Thunderbird" from *American Graffiti,* and a poet who didn't look like a poet.

My unexpected small success gave me some confidence for the first time. I wasn't a loser after all. I was starting to believe that I deserved to take up the little space I occupied on the planet.

One evening at my Sausalito apartment, after lavishing Alan with one of my seductive dinners—buttery chicken pieces cooked in coconut curry sauce over jasmine rice, with a bottle of perfectly chilled white wine, a lovely fire, moonlight over the San Francisco Bay, soft candlelight, and Carole King singing "You're So Far Away," from her hit album *Tapestry,* I took the chance . . .

Lying in front of the fire, wrapped in his arms and fortified by the wine, the mood, and the romance, I whispered to him, "I love you." I had wanted to say it for so long, and now I couldn't hold it in any longer. Regardless of the consequences, I had to say it. I had fallen in love with him the first night. I always knew he was the one for me, but I'd never felt we had a chance of forever until now.

He was silent. I felt as though the air had been sucked out of the room, waiting, waiting for *some* response, anything. He stroked my hair, touched my face, and finally lifted mine to his.

"I love you, too." My body felt weak. He had said it.

"You do? Really?" I asked, not wanting him to change his mind.

"Yes. I've loved you for a long time. Do you think I'd turn my life upside down to be with you if I didn't?"

I didn't need any more words than those. *Later down the road,* I thought, *we'll both know what this means.* It was a real step. Relationships are about steps, a gradual moving forward toward an unknown end point. We had taken a big step. It had been worth the wait, and I felt happier than I'd felt in a long time. He loved me. He loved *me.*

Bruce was with his father for the weekend, so soon Alan and I were undressed and making passionate love on the floor in front of the fireplace. It was thrilling, and now it had another layer. I buried my face in his beautiful chest. He loved me.

CHAPTER 6

FEELIN' GROOVY

Slow down, you move too fast
You got to make the morning last.
—SIMON AND GARFUNKEL

L ife had taken a remarkable turn.

The Tonight Show was a godsend. Appearances on the show didn't pay much, a few hundred dollars apiece, but they sold books, and that was bringing in some decent money. Finally we got the all clear on Bruce's health. It was a huge relief, and I felt I could resume my part-time job with Alan. I'd be gone every two or three weeks for two days. When I was away, I arranged for Bruce's father to stop in on Bruce when he could. I began flying regularly to Vancouver to appear on Alan's show, and now I was both the "resident poet" and the "girl from *The Tonight Show*."

All I could think about during the taping was being alone with Alan that night—sex was such a huge part of us. I had never had this with anyone else. I never went through the normal sexual escapades, as I'd married so young. After my divorce, I had dated some men but was "with" very few, so essentially Alan was my one and only. But what a one and only! Whenever there was any kind of imposed abstinence, all I wanted or needed was to be alone with him.

I wrapped my naked body around his under the covers, and we lay together holding each other like we never wanted to let go. "I missed being with you so much," he said. I couldn't even speak. There were no words. I loved him. I wanted and needed to be with him. He was everything I wanted for my life.

I would return home to Sausalito, momentarily satisfied by our brief time together but restless. I wanted to move to Los Angeles—after his show was canceled, Alan had let go of his houseboat and moved back to L.A. I was tired of this routine—I wanted to be with Alan full time and I really felt I might be able to make a career there. San Francisco felt like a dead end for me. I had bills to pay, and I needed to be where there was more action or possibilities, where things could have a chance of opening up for me. But more than anything, I wanted to be with him.

"Even though Alan is divorced, he's not going to be ready to get married again for a long time," Mrs. Kilgore said to me repeatedly. "Don't set yourself up for disappointment. Know that you deserve to ask for what you want. I just want you to be prepared for his answer. Think it through. What are you willing to accept? Is it all, something, or nothing?"

She kept at me, pushing my emotional buttons. "Don't you feel you're good enough for him?" she would ask.

Yes, no, I don't know, I thought.

"Make a list again."

I had been doing this with her since our first visit, the same exercise over and over. Then one day I heard myself answer her differently; it was a moment of clarity.

There it was, the aha moment they talk about with therapy. She finally pulled it out of me. I had buried it so deep inside, I had had no idea it was driving me. Deep down I felt I had ruined the family by being born. After the terrible violent nights, my brother Danny, trying to make me feel better, would often say, "You know, it wasn't always like this. Before you were born, we had good times, parties."

There it was. I had always thought it was my fault, I had bought into it, I had grown up believing I was (as my father relentlessly told me in his drunken tirades) "stupid, hopeless, worthless." I had unconsciously thought I ruined everything. After seeing Mrs. Kilgore that day, I drove home feeling that something big had changed.

I decided to ask for what I wanted. But when I pushed the issue of living together or just living in the same city, he felt like I was putting him up against a wall. Declaring our love for each other was a big step. By living in Sausalito, I was still allowing the relationship to be safe without real commitment to a life together, but moving to Los Angeles would mean a much deeper commitment.

I didn't enjoy forcing the issue of living together, and it made him feel trapped. He was so intent on never getting married again that this was threatening. We got angry. We broke up. We got back together because we couldn't stand to be apart. We argued more, had more sex, and finally we gave in.

"Let's just try it," I said tearfully one night. "If we can't live in the same house, I'll get my own apartment. I just want to be nearer to you all the time. I want to be part of your life for real."

There—I had asked for what I wanted. Big leap forward.

The topic of the three children and how we would handle sharing this news with them now moved to the top of the list of things I needed to work on with Mrs. Kilgore. It was uncomfortable. Alan and I had kept our children separate from our relationship for the most part. We were an after-hours love affair, and we liked it that way. He wasn't opposed to raising my son, but his involvement was with me; Bruce was just part of the package. When he said this, my feelings were hurt because I wanted and needed him to know how special Bruce was. I was hoping that since he loved me, he would love what was a part of me.

Blending families is complex, and logic is not part of the equation. It often requires professionals who can set all the parties straight. Alan's children couldn't make the leap to liking me because they had loyalty to their mother. That was completely understandable. In blended families, there is often unresolved anger at the original relationship not working out. If the mother is angry, then the children must rise to her defense. Again, it's completely understandable. The new mother- or father-substitute is not welcomed with open arms. Everyone involved has an emotional stake, and the result is a lot of pain all around.

At one point, we all must learn to fly on our own.

All Alan wanted was to have me to himself, but we knew that wasn't realistic. I wasn't much more of a grown-up, and to be honest, I wasn't very interested in sharing him with his kids, so it was difficult all around. I might have been more receptive if they'd liked me, but the more I tried, the more it seemed to be resented. Again, can you blame them? There were no rules for blending families then, no books, and besides, I was just his girlfriend. It wasn't like I was his wife.

I had been seeing Mrs. Kilgore for a few years at this point. One day she said to me, "I don't want you to come anymore."

"Why?" I asked, shocked. I had come to lean on these sessions. They were that important. "I come, I do the work, I pay you the dollar. I need to keep coming."

I felt distraught at the idea. It was like Mommy sending me out of the nest. At one point, we all must learn to fly on our own. But I didn't feel ready. Clearly, she was pushing me out of the nest.

"I want you to go live your life. You *are* ready—you'll see. I'll always be here. You're ready to face the world." She was dead set. I couldn't dissuade her. Finally, I got up from my chair and slowly walked to her office door. I felt shocked, sad, lost, and adrift.

As I opened the door, I heard her say sternly, "Suzanne," and I turned to face her. "Remember this," she said deliberately. "The worst is over!"

The worst *was* over. I had been trapped in low self-esteem, something I never realized I had or was, and that fog had kept me from realizing that I was enough. That my personal life and what was happening to my career were phenomenal. I had never considered that what I was doing was a career, yet here I was a regular on the biggest TV show in history, *The Tonight Show*. I was one of Johnny's girls! I had a best-selling book of poetry, and I was a regular on *Mantrap,* so I was becoming well known in Canada, too. I had the most beautiful little boy, and I was in love with the most incredible man in the world, and he loved me.

By the time I got home, I was smiling broadly. I felt ready to tackle life in a way I had never felt before. Up until that point, I had been looking at all jobs as simply a means to cover the basics: food, shelter, and clothing (and not much new clothing). I hadn't seen any of it as major breaks and stepping stones to accomplish whatever I wanted. How had I missed the significance? How had I not realized that I was experiencing something akin to Eliza Doolittle, that this unlikely girl from nowhere, the daughter of the town drunk, had broken through and succeeded? Was it all luck? Being at the right place at the right time? Maybe a little of both. Either way, I was ready. It was my time. And as they say in comedy, timing is everything.

Bruce and I moved from Sausalito to Los Angeles. It was 1974. Bruce cried as we drove across the Golden Gate Bridge. Ironically, as we crossed the bridge, Karen Carpenter was singing on the radio, "We've Only Just Begun." I felt bittersweet and teary-eyed. I was leaving behind my mother, father, sister, and brothers, all my relatives, Bruce's friends, Bruce's school, and my own friends. I had no guarantee of a job or a career, no guarantee of the life I hoped for with Alan. He was happy I was coming, but he hadn't fully committed. "We'll see how it goes" was all he gave me. I know now that he was just protecting himself, because he was in deep with me.

I figured I had no choice. I had to move one way or another. Either it worked out with him or it didn't. I loved him madly, but if it didn't work, I would figure out a way for me and Bruce. At least in Los Angeles there would be work and the possibility of turning my recent opportunities into something big.

I looked into the rearview mirror: behind us, the Golden Gate Bridge was getting smaller. San Francisco and the long five-hour drive to L.A. were ahead of us. We would stay at Alan's place until I figured out what to do. I felt heavy-hearted and frightened. Finally, we were going to be together every day and—I hoped—every night. It had been a long and difficult journey getting to this point, requiring a lot of growing up on both our parts. His children were living with their mother, and if it worked out and we lived together as a real couple, my son would be living with us.

Bruce and I moved in with him—and we never left. He never asked us to. Instead, it was his idea one day to go and get all my things out of storage and move in for real.

I was ecstatic. It was everything I wanted it to be, except for the dynamics with the kids.

WHAT I KNOW NOW

Man, we women are hard on ourselves. I look back at all the time I spent beating myself up. I often wonder what would have happened or where I'd be today had I not been in intense therapy, which essentially undid all the damage from my early life family's dysfunction. Would I ever have come to believe in myself? Would I ever have gone for the dream? Would I ever have had the courage to ask for what I wanted in my relationship with Alan?

Most people find therapy too vulnerable, too revealing, too introspective, too painful. To get well, you must look at yourself for who and what you really are, but mainly you must see the part you played in your life drama. It's uncomfortable. It's much easier to blame someone else for your problems. I learned that I owned this, that it was up to me to learn and grow and move on. I wasn't the child hiding in the closet anymore.

What I *saw* through therapy was someone I didn't respect, someone who was weak, someone who didn't feel like she deserved the little spot she occupied on the planet. No more. Now I was ready to move forward and go for this incredible journey ahead of me. Those four words, *The worst is over,* freed me. It is a mantra I still use to this day. I've been through the worst times, so today with whatever happens, I look back and say, *It's not as bad as that. I'm free.* What a great feeling. I was freed to soar.

The biggest song of this era was "Feelin' Groovy," Simon and Garfunkel's sweet, melodic, promising voices telling us all to chill out and enjoy the lives we had. It played on the radio all the time. Bruce and I did everything together from morning till night. He was my little pal, my best friend. I loved being with him and he with me.

But unfortunately, at first, we weren't always feelin' groovy. Divorce is traumatic for all involved. If you're lucky and it works itself out, a new relationship emerges, but it rarely happens smoothly. Blending families is hard. It causes tension. A new life partner is a part of a new journey that kids don't like, and neither Bruce nor Alan's kids liked it.

Children of divorce get used to the new dynamic of having each parent all to themselves, and they don't want new ones. Alan's daughter liked having Daddy to herself, as did his son, and I don't blame them. How wonderful to be the sole focus! I never had a relationship like that with my father, so I listened with awe when Alan would run down his weekends of fun with his children. I knew I was not going to be welcome for some time, but I believed we were going to make it and have a happy ending.

Forcing two same-age boys to live and act like brothers was akin to Cain and Abel; it makes them resent each other. This wasn't the easiest of transitions, but I was prepped and ready. I suggested that Alan's son, Stephen, move in with us to ease emotions; initially, he and Bruce had to share a room. It was Oscar and Felix. Bruce was neat and tidy and organized, but Stephen was the opposite. Bruce didn't like anyone touching his stuff. He missed going out for dinner alone; he wanted it to be "just us, like before." Alan's kids were doing the same. The tension was unbelievable and not sexy at all. These were new and uncharted waters for us. Not feelin' groovy.

I cried a lot, and Alan was angry a lot, but we always resolved it at night in each other's arms, in the dark, where we could both always make everything okay. It was going to take time. Feelings are real and can't be faked or forced. I hoped that we'd soon find a way through this situation. If I could do it over, and had I been more evolved, I would have insisted that all involved take part in family therapy. Everyone would have had the opportunity to air their feelings with a neutral arbiter in the form of a therapist. You can't tell children not to feel what they feel, and you can't plead with them to "be nice" because it makes Mommy or Daddy happy. The situation is not the children's problem, and it's important for the adults in the room to be the adults. But love affairs are myopic and can be selfish; there is so much longing and passion, and it doesn't leave much room for angry, upset, and threatened children. I truly longed for harmony and peace. I wanted us to be a real family, and I know Alan wanted the same. Deep inside I knew that one day down the road, this would become a reality. Also, and no small thing, I wanted to be married. I hadn't broached that topic yet.

CHAPTER 7

THREE'S COMPANY

Life isn't about finding yourself. Life is about creating yourself.
—GEORGE BERNARD SHAW

The president of ABC, Fred Silverman, had been looking for a young woman for a new show they were doing. As I would hear it later, Fred said in a production meeting, "I've got the girl—I see her on *The Tonight Show* all the time." The show was *Three's Company*.

It was December 1977. Alan and I were returning from a Christmas holiday in Eleuthera, an island in the Bahamas. Bruce was staying with his father and paternal grandparents. It was the first time Bruce and I had not spent Christmas Day together in his life, but he loved being with his dad, and I knew he would have a good time with all of them. They were fun-loving and irreverent. I always liked my ex-in-laws.

To get home, we were to take an island puddle-jumper to Miami and then a large commercial jet. It was the only way to get off the island. But on the day we were scheduled to leave, the weather suddenly turned dark and ominous. I looked out our window, and the weather was getting increasingly bad, so much so that we considered not flying out that night because of it. The plane was small, a ten-seat commercial Fairchild. We decided to watch the faces of the people disembarking, those who had just flown through the weather. To our relief, they were smiling and laughing; just looking at their faces convinced us it was going to be okay. (After takeoff, I realized they had likely been smiling and laughing from nervous relief.) Twenty minutes into the flight, we were sorry we had made the decision to fly. It became so turbulent that the pilot, who was a few feet in front of us and visible, started screaming into the microphone, "Put your heads between your knees! Put your heads between your knees!"

Oh my god, are we going to crash? Two native ladies sitting opposite us started wailing, "Lord, we're gonna die. Lord, we're gonna die." Gulp. I looked at Alan and told him how much I loved him; he told me we were over the Bermuda Triangle. (His little joke. Thanks, Alan!) I thought of Bruce and agonized. *What will his life be without his mother?*

I became filled with fear at what crashing would feel like. What would it be like in the black ice-cold ocean water? We gripped onto each other, stopping all blood flow with our fear. Baggage from overhead compartments was flying everywhere—that alone could have killed someone. I now get what all the stringent regulations concerning carry-ons are all about. I peeked outside the plane window and could see only dark black angry clouds. Tossing and turning, it felt like we were going to flip upside down. Our plane felt so little and vulnerable. It seemed to take an eternity. Screaming . . . crying people . . . would it ever stop? *Oh, god help us!*

Then as quickly as it had started, we were in clear air, and it all calmed down. And now we were starting our descent to Miami International as though nothing had happened. We landed on the tarmac, and now we were the ones laughing and smiling. A new line of passengers were getting ready to board. I wanted to stop and tell them, but I was frantic to call Bruce. When I reached him, my panic did not match his calm. I was crying and telling him how much I missed him and loved him. He said calmly, "I love you too, Mom." Like, *Geez.*

The next day, safely back in our apartment in Los Angeles, my

Where it all began.

Guys and Dolls where Walter Winchell said, "You're goin' someplace, sister!"

My little pal, Bruce.

My beautiful mother.

My sister Maureen's wedding day with my brothers, Michael and Danny, and my parents.

When Alan got his scholarship to Ryerson.

You can see how much Alan loves his mother.

Stud.

Alan's amazing career in Canada.

American Graffiti—one night's work that changed my life.

The two loves of my life, Alan . . .

. . . and my darling son, Bruce.

The night I was discovered by Johnny Carson.

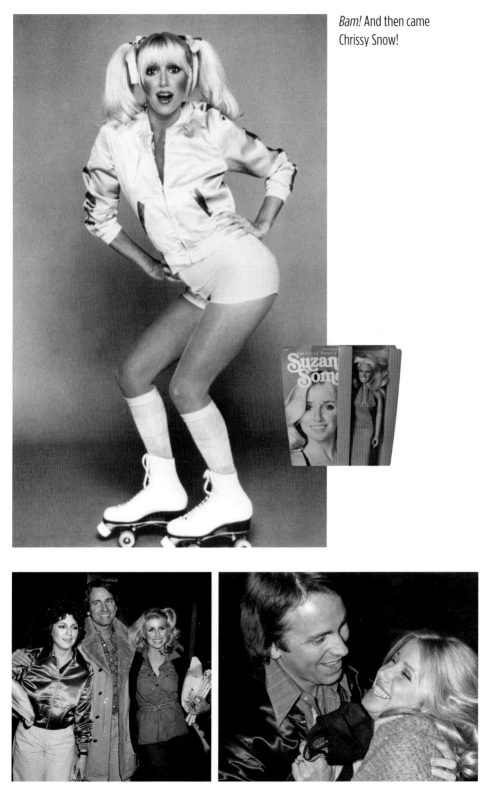

Bam! And then came Chrissy Snow!

The happiest of days during *Three's Company,* with Joyce and John.

The glamorous life.

People's Choice Award for Favorite TV Actress.

Crazy, fun nights at
the iconic Studio 54.

Imagine, me with Fred Astaire!

Thirty-five years of friendship with Andrea and Barry Manilow.

Alan's business partner and our dear friend, Dick Clark.

My talented friend Michael Feinstein.

With Donald Sutherland at the premiere of our movie, *Nothing Personal*.

Happiness.

new L.A. agent called, screaming excitedly, "You have an audition for a show called *Three's Company,* and they seem *really* interested in you." Her decibel level was completely different from my blasé former agent.

I was still so shook up from the prior night's flight that I didn't take it too seriously. I had been on countless auditions at this point, and not much had happened. And she was the excitable type, so I took it with a grain of salt. Calmly, I got ready to go to ABC head-quarters for a show I knew nothing about.

Once I was inside the interview room, there was a somber vibe. I stood in front of a group of men who were staring at me intently. I tried to make jokes, but no one laughed. They just kept staring. They asked me to read a few lines with an actress I would come to know in the future as Joyce DeWitt; she clearly already had a job on the show. Many of the men in the room were the show's producers; the rest were the head honchos at ABC, including its president, Fred Silverman. I didn't know which one he was at that time. After I read, and after they finished staring at me, they thanked me.

I drove off the lot thinking, *Just another interview.*

When I got home, the phone was ringing. My agent was screaming so loudly I couldn't make out what she was saying.

"Stop, stop!" I said. "Calm down. What are you saying?!"

"YOU GOT THE PART of Chrissy Snow on *Three's Company*! It is expected to be the biggest hit of the season. It's going to air on Tuesday nights after *Laverne & Shirley,* the hottest, most successful night of the TV week, and the hottest show on the air. It's a midseason pickup. But if your show gets good ratings, then next season will be twenty-six episodes!"

I held the receiver in shock.

"Oh, and your starting pay is thirty-five hundred dollars— a *week*!"

"Oh my god! Oh my god!" was all I could say over and over.

I'd gotten a great gig—a *series.* It was beyond my wildest dreams. And they were going to pay me! What a thrill!

My agent told me I was to show up the next day at nine a.m. for the first table reading, whatever that was. (I later learned it is literally a reading around a table.)

That first morning I walked euphorically into ABC to meet everyone involved with the show. I just couldn't believe what had happened. I even had my own parking spot in front of the studio. I felt giddy.

I was introduced to John Ritter and reintroduced to Joyce DeWitt, and then the producers formally introduced themselves, as did the production team. Everyone was *much* nicer than they had been in the original interview. The atmosphere was charged. It was as though everyone had a feeling that we were about to be a part of something big.

They were all pros. John Ritter was instantly likable: fun, funny, upbeat, outgoing, and confident. It was clear the producers and crew loved him already. He was the star of their show. Joyce DeWitt, who I had met at the audition, was very friendly, very nice, and very professional. I liked her. She had been scouted by ABC from the UCLA drama department and signed to a contract. This was rarely done, but it assures the network that when the right project comes up, it will have first access. For this privilege, she was most likely getting a monthly paycheck. I was third billed, and frankly I would have taken any deal I was offered. I was thinking only of the incredible opportunity to be on a prime-time network TV show. Remember, this was before cable and there were only three options: ABC, CBS, and NBC.

I felt so out of my element that on that first day I blurted out to everyone listening that I was so excited to be there and then stated (stupidly), "I've never had any formal acting training, so I'm here to learn." The reaction was silence. It was me being honest, but something I probably shouldn't have said. This was big-time TV. This wasn't school or a place to learn. By the time you got here, you needed to know your stuff. What I hadn't realized was what I brought to the table was my *credits;* I was "that girl from *The Tonight Show*." I now had a number-one book on the market. I had cachet as a "kind of" celebrity. I brought value to the show. In fact, I was the only one at that moment who had any visibility. But of course, I didn't see it that way, although thankfully soon I would. What a year!

I saw *Three's Company* as my shot, maybe the only shot I would ever get. Our first season was only a six-week pickup. Would six weeks be enough for me to make a mark? If the show didn't succeed, how could I use this opportunity to keep my career moving onward and upward? I had no management and no "real" agent to speak of—mine had never really been an agent before, and frankly, shortly in, it was clear she was out of her element. Alan was now away half the month in Vancouver shooting his daily afternoon talk show, *The Alan Hamel Show*. For the first time in my life, I had something tangible to use as a springboard to garner more work. How could I do that?

Back then, Farrah Fawcett was the hottest celebrity on TV. She was the star of the megahit *Charlie's Angels*. Her publicist was Jay Bernstein, a flamboyant, showbiz "star-maker," as he referred to himself. He had a cultivated look: perfectly trimmed goatee, professionally shaped and dyed eyebrows, and mirrored sunglasses, and he carried a cane for effect (which had a hidden sword inside). I decided to take a chance and call him to see if he would agree to meet with me. Normally, anyone who has just landed a top spot on a prime-time network sitcom would feel secure enough to know that a meeting request would be received with enthusiasm, but for me it took some courage. I was a newcomer to celebrity, so calling Jay Bernstein was a gutsy thing for me to do. If my tone on the phone call was a bit desperate, it was because that was how I felt.

I met with Jay and explained to him that I saw this show as a springboard for my future career if enough people could be made aware of me being on it. I told him I admired the way he had crafted Farrah's career, and then I made him my pitch:

"I will give you all the money I am making from the first six weeks' pickup, if you will make sure that no matter what happens, success or cancellation, you get my name out there so that everyone will know who I am."

He sat there quietly listening to me. I looked around his office, a shrine to Farrah, with magazine covers on every inch of his walls, interrupted intermittently by photos of Farrah and her then husband, Lee Majors, star of *The Six Million Dollar Man*.

"How much are you being paid?" he asked.

I told him, "They are giving me thirty-five hundred dollars a week." It's not that I didn't need the money—I did, desperately. But I was rolling the dice and believed I had no other way to intrigue him to take me on. It was worth giving up my paychecks if he could pull this off.

Finally Jay spoke. "Well, the first thing we have to do is make sure on season two you get paid a whole lot more than this. But yes, I will take you on. I can do this."

I left his office triumphant. It was a ballsy, creative thing to do, and I felt proud that I had had the idea and pulled it off. Astonishingly, I had gotten to national TV without Alan or Jay and no *real* agent. My excitable agent was so new at it that she had never had a client before me and had never put together a deal. It was a difficult conversation, but I explained to her that I needed to hire Jay and I would be sure she was compensated with her percentage. She was disappointed, but to her credit she took it well; I have always been grateful to her for that. It was incredible that I even found myself in this position of landing a part on a show destined to be a hit. It's virtually impossible to land a hit TV show without proper representation. The people who got me jobs in San Francisco were not managing or culling my career; back then, I was simply and occasionally useful to my kind-of agent to fill a void in a commercial or a backdrop scene in a film.

Years later Jay told me he didn't think I was particularly pretty, and he had no idea if I had any talent, but he had not seen that kind of drive and enthusiasm since he handled Sammy Davis Jr.

The first day, Mickey Ross, one of the show's producers, decided to take me under his wing. Mickey was an old vaudevillian with perfect comedic timing and writing skills that came from that disappearing old school of Jewish comedy writers. They were the funniest of them all. (For examples from today, think Larry David and Jerry Seinfeld.) Mickey had been head writer for Norman Lear's *All in the Family* starring Carroll O'Connor. He also co-created and wrote *The Jeffersons.* This guy was no slouch, so lucky me that he took me on. I got private tutoring from the best. It wasn't simply altruism on his part—it was business. Before this show, the producers—Don Nicholl, Mickey Ross, and Bernie West—had always worked under the tutelage and ownership of Norman Lear. *Three's Company* was their first big solo shot, and they couldn't afford to have a weak link. I looked right, but I needed major direction at first.

I've thought a lot about the generation of children whose parents escaped from or perished in the Holocaust. Why were many of the best comedy writers of that era Jewish? I think it was a sink-or-swim mentality. You saw the humor in life, or else the horrific memories would do you in. The funny part of Mickey was threaded through with a definite underbelly of anger. At the time, I thought of him as old, but good-looking old. It strikes me as funny today that back then he looked a lot like my sexy, gorgeous husband looks today. I digress.

The weekly schedule was five days of rehearsals, eight to ten hours daily, then fittings, photo shoots, press and interviews, and on Friday night there we were, shooting the show. From day one, Mickey worked with me like a coach. His direction was astute, and he taught me simply to *believe everything I was saying.* In a way, it was like when I was a kid playing house, always my favorite game: pretend, and then act accordingly. What Mickey was teaching me felt similar. Sometimes in life you know what you know. A child of an alcoholic learns to size up people and situations. It comes from being adaptable, from having to figure out *What mood is Daddy in tonight?* which is code for *Who do I have to be so he won't be angry at me?* It's fake; it's uncomfortable at the core; but it's survival. Little did I know that it would be an advantage for me in this remarkable position of being on a hit TV show, so I watched, I observed, I listened, I sized up the situation and the scene. I was fascinated and soaked it all in.

I also got to watch the genius of John Ritter, a physical comic rivaled only by the great Dick Van Dyke. His pratfalls were choreographed like a dance; he could flip over the sofa the same way, time after time. I marveled at his extraordinary talent, and I was aware of greatness at work. On the show, he and I found magic together; our scenes were like a Ping-Pong game; he banged it across the table, and I banged it back. It was thrilling to work with someone with this enormous talent. He made me better.

Between Mickey coaching off stage and John's physical ability and perfect comic timing, I was learning from the best. No acting school, no comedy school on the planet, could have taught me what I was learning daily and with such intensity.

I loved it. I loved the rehearsals. I loved the excitement. I loved that I was getting paid to have fun (even if I had to give it away to Jay, it was worth it). Bruce was enrolled in the public school near our house. I was feeling the pull of needing to be home to be a good mother but also the pull of the show demanding so much of my time—the plight of all working mothers.

I'm a sponge when I want to know something. I know when I'm seeing or experiencing the good stuff, whether it's food, an outfit, a song, or a comedy routine and its perfect setup. I know it when I see it, and because I learned early on to be adaptable, I can repeat it once I've seen it done right. With Mickey's guidance, I found the character of Chrissy Snow and morphed into her; I was *her* for those moments.

It was quite exhilarating to know something so completely. I knew when a line was wrong for the character, and I began to protect her fiercely. The writers felt the same way and enjoyed writing for her. We all knew what she would and would not do. I created her moral code: she never lied and would never hurt anyone or anything, for any reason. She was childlike, a woman/child, and she allowed me to have the childhood I had never had growing up. The TV apartment that the three of us lived in was safe and protected. I enjoyed being her immensely.

The first show aired in March 1977, and it was a hit. The Tuesday-night lineup of *Happy Days, Laverne & Shirley,* and *Three's Company* was a powerhouse. At that time people memorized TV schedules. There was no TiVo or even the ability to tape a show off air. The show exploded from the very first week, and clearly from the sky-high ratings, Tuesday night on ABC was *the* night. We were a home run, and it kept up week after week.

Jay Bernstein was doing his job. He was a master at public relations, running all my press interviews, sitting on the sidelines looking menacing, interrupting if it wasn't going my way. His look was intimidating, and every interviewer knew that one wrong move, and Jay would pull the interview. I felt uncomfortable when he behaved this way, but I had asked him to take me on, and he was doing his job, and I did not want to screw things up.

I suspected, but didn't know for sure until years later, that at the beginning he used me as leverage so that the publications that interviewed me could then get to Farrah. But soon I was getting the interviews on my own because of the show's enormous success. By the time the show

Where you come from is not where you must stay, but it doesn't just happen. You have to go for it; work for it. Fix yourself to move forward.

was in its third week, we got an order for the next season. Wow. And by the end of the first year, our ratings had surpassed *Charlie's Angels.*

The show's success changed everything. I had just about emerged from the fog of my past and was leaving behind the low self-esteem that had chased me up till then. Good riddance. I felt triumphant and realized that where you come from is not where you must stay, but it doesn't just happen. You have to go for it; work for it. Fix yourself to move forward.

The money I initially gave to Jay was the best investment I ever made in myself. His massive PR campaign made me the most in-demand star that year for television specials with everyone from John Wayne to Paul Anka to Red Skelton. I even worked with

Minnie Mouse in an animated special called *Totally Minnie,* where I danced and interacted with this cartoon icon. This was the first time Leslie, Alan's daughter, designed my costume. I also worked with Merv Griffin, and we became friends from my frequent appearances on his show, a friendship that remained through the years. I was also meeting greats like Bob Hope and Fred Astaire and Frank Sinatra. By the end of the first year, I was working so much I could hardly breathe, and I was thrilled to be doing so.

In year two, my salary was raised some, and for the first time in my life, real money was coming in. I was no longer in debt. It was the greatest feeling, second only to the pride I felt at having done this on my own. My paycheck was a result of my hard work. For years I used my life experience as a model in raising Bruce and for whatever influence I had with Alan's children. I did not want to make our kids feel entitled by giving them money they hadn't earned. I wanted them to have summer jobs and after-school jobs and feel the thrill of having accomplished on their own.

Too many Hollywood kids are handed luxurious lives and money they didn't earn, and cars they didn't buy. They develop a feeling of entitlement because they have successful parents, as though their parents' success is their own. It rarely works out well. The media and social media are filled with reports of children of celebrities who become drug addicts or are arrested, their mug shots available for all to see, for behavior that shows they felt themselves to be above the law.

This success I had never envisioned was a long time in coming. It started all the way back in high school as Adelaide in *Guys and Dolls* when Walter Winchell singled me out. I got a part here, a part there, a local commercial, a modeling job. It was all part of the journey, the stepping-stones to the big one. I also didn't yet understand that stardom lasts only a moment, but Alan did. He was still doing the show in Canada but was becoming increasingly restless leaving me to fend for myself. It was important to him to see the long range, to have a vision of what this could become down the road.

"I'm not going to return to my show next year," he announced one day. "You're so hot right now, and we should make the most of it. I see a much bigger picture. Jay is a master public relations genius—he and I can work together. You need management, not just PR," he explained. "There are huge business opportunities. You should be a respected brand. Your character is iconic. Chrissy Snow has become the most lovable character on TV. I'm excited about what we can do together."

"How can you do that?" I asked incredulously. "You'll miss doing your show. You're so great at it. Everyone loves your show, it's number one, and you are so famous in Canada!" I protested.

"My heart isn't in it. I keep thinking about you and worrying about you. You can make the right moves right now or very wrong ones. I've been in this business my whole life. I've been on TV and radio for twenty-five years. What's happening to you happens rarely. You've captured the nation. This needs protecting and manag-

> *Sometimes I felt that I wasn't doing a good job with any of it. I was so overwhelmed. What woman hasn't felt the same?*

ing. You say yes to everyone. If you keep doing that, you'll lose your specialness. Don't worry about me. I've talked to just about everyone on TV I ever want to talk to. It excites me to see what we can do with you as a business and a franchise."

We were all adjusting and adapting to this new reality. Bruce had gone from having 100 percent of me to 50 percent, and now this explosive career was taking away even more. I was trying my best to keep him protected, while giving my all to the other facets I was dealing with. It stretched me a lot. Sometimes I felt that I wasn't doing a good job with any of it. I was so overwhelmed. What woman hasn't felt the same?

I had now been in love with Alan Hamel for almost ten years. Ten years! Ironically, Mrs. Kilgore, my therapist, had told me in the beginning, "He's not going to be ready to marry you for ten years."

SUZANNE SOMERS

I was invited to be a guest on *The Dinah Shore Show,* the most popular daytime talk show on television. Dinah's other guests that day were Burt Reynolds and Jane Fonda, both pushing their latest movies. They were the hottest movie stars in the business, and I was the hottest TV star. When I was a kid, the first TV show I had ever watched in color was Dinah's, and here I was sitting next to her. I blurted out one of my unedited observations about Dinah and Burt, who were having a not-so-secret love affair, and Dinah, who was serving cake, shoved it in my face good-naturedly. The close-up of me was a cake face. We all laughed hysterically. The show was raucous and hilarious. Burt Reynolds was darling and funny. Both Alan and I liked him.

After the show, Alan and I decided to continue the merriment and go out to dinner at our favorite restaurant, Le Restaurant. It was located on Melrose Place, which is famous now but was then a quiet little street in the heart of Hollywood. It was an elegant, intimate, expensive place with incredible French cuisine. I was high from just having been on such a fun show and cavorting with its high-profile movie stars.

We slid into the moss-green-velvet-lined booth for two. The atmosphere was soft and hushed. Our table was lit by candles in pink glass, making our complexions look perfect. The plush velvet created a luxurious feeling; in the background was a piano player who was present but not intrusive. He knew his job was to relax the patrons and add to the romantic atmosphere. The waiters were polished and dressed in tuxedos, reminding me of one of our first dates at Fleur de Lys in San Francisco ten years before.

We talked about *Three's Company,* and we marveled at what had happened to us, how this show had reshaped our lives and those of our children. Alan had been a celebrity for most of his adult life, but now I was a major American celebrity, and we were treated royally everywhere we went. It was hard not to enjoy the attention.

Alan ordered a bottle of Dom Pérignon. I never got blasé about it. Not then and not to this day. It was a thrill to experience expensive champagne. The glasses were fine crystal, Baccarat, and perfectly

90

chilled. It tasted so good. We had one glass, then two, before we even got around to ordering delicious rack of lamb with mint sauce.

We were holding hands under the table. I loved him so much. That had never changed from the day we met.

Suddenly he got very quiet. "I want to marry you," he said. His deep, sexy voice was intense.

I felt the room go still. It felt like we were underwater, filtered, like we were the only two who existed. My eyes filled with tears. The moment I had dreamed of was finally here.

"Will you be my wife?" he asked as he searched my eyes.

I put my arms around him and whispered in his ear, "Yes. Oh my god, yes," I said, ecstatic.

CHAPTER 8

JUST MARRIED

And here we are in Heaven
For you are mine at last.

—HARRY WARREN AND MACK GORDON, "AT LAST"

Man, that song, those lyrics, fully tapped into my feelings on our wedding day. I was over the moon.

It was beautiful. We had recently purchased our oceanfront place on Venice Beach, and it made for the most romantic and picturesque wedding locale. It had stormed early in the day, but by five p.m. the sky had turned clear with the most gorgeous sunset I have ever seen: brilliant oranges and blues. We brought in three female singers to be on the balcony overlooking the ocean and singing Gregorian chants, along with Allan Blye, who was Alan's lifelong friend and whose voice was deep, melodic, and moving. The living room was filled with trees and flowers, and we removed all the furniture and made row seating for the small but important group. It was mainly family; the only outside people were from *Three's Company*.

I always found it serendipitous that when Alan called his parents to tell them we had decided to get married, they were both thrilled, and then his father said, "You know, son, I was at the grocery store last week, and when I reached into the potato bin, along with the potatoes I pulled out a gold wedding band. I turned it in to the store manager, and they said if no one claims it, it's yours." His father sent the ring, and it fit my finger perfectly. And astonishingly, on the inside was an engraved initial S—I took it as another sign that Alan and I were meant to be together.

But it wasn't the happiest of days for our children—I'm sure they didn't know what to feel. But I knew that Alan and I needed to take this step to delineate the blurred lines of girlfriend/wife, boyfriend/husband. Being married would solidify things.

So even with mixed emotions, the kids did their best to enjoy the day, and I worked hard to not let any negatives take away anything from us. I was marrying Alan, something I had wanted for ten years. We worked through the worst of times, and finally, *at last,* we looked into each other's eyes and said, "I do."

I could hardly speak; I was overcome with happiness.

Patience and perseverance have a magical effect before
which difficulties disappear and obstacles vanish.
—JOHN QUINCY ADAMS

I kept pinching myself . . . I had married the man of my dreams.
Our wedding turned out to be tabloid heaven: we were on the cover of every magazine, every rag. At times, judging from the photos, it looked like I was marrying John Ritter, because the photographer I hired tried to include John in every photo. He sold them to the *Enquirer,* and then they circulated to other outlets. I had handled the wedding arrangements and didn't realize I needed to make a deal with the photographer *not* to sell the photos. As Alan explained after the fact, if we had decided to make our personal wedding photos public, we would have made big money for them. He was right—I didn't have a clue how this business worked. This was all new territory for me. The vultures were out, conniving,

manipulating, knowing that my rise from obscurity to tremendous fame was so rapid that I would not be savvy about the ramifications.

But the tabloids weren't the only media outlets interested in our wedding. Every day the phone rang with something unbelievable: *60 Minutes,* the most prestigious news-entertainment show on TV, wanted to do a feature piece on me. These pieces were reserved for presidents of countries, kings, business moguls, and top newsmakers. They wanted to position me as the next Farrah Fawcett. Perhaps my collaboration with Jay Bernstein had been a brilliant strategy on my part. I like to think so. Farrah had risen to incredible fame. She was a knockout, just gorgeous, and so hot that she opted out of TV after a year to become a movie star. At that time, if you did movies, you didn't do TV. It's not like that today. Television was looking for the next blond sex symbol, and having the *60 Minutes* crew come to my home so I could be interviewed by Morley Safer indicated that they thought it was me.

When it aired, my career catapulted into even higher gear. Everyone took notice. I wasn't equipped to handle any of it. Magazine covers were what I now did at night after work. I'd be professionally made up, stylists would dress and position me, and wind machines would blow my hair into sex symbol craziness. Night after night, different magazines—everyone wanted me on their cover. It translated into sales to have the hottest star on television on their cover. *People* magazine shot several covers, as did *McCall's* and *TV Guide,* and *Harper's Bazaar* did a cover and a four-page spread on the inside called: "The Business of Being Beautiful." *Star* magazine, with dear friend Robin Leach at the helm, shot six different covers in one night. All in all, I shot fifty-five national magazine covers in the first year. That meant that every week I was on a cover of something, and that didn't include all the ancillary publicity that was everywhere.

And then the big one: *Newsweek*! The most prestigious magazine in America, usually reserved for the hottest political topic of the week, asked to shoot the three of us for their next edition. It had to be done right away. The call came through the *Three's Company* office, and the producers came down to the set to tell us "kids" that we would be shooting *Newsweek* and what incredible prestige it was for our show. That's all they told us. We were ecstatic.

The day of the shoot, Alan was in Canada doing his show— even though he had quit, he had to finish out the season. Hair and makeup arrived, and we cast members were told what we would be wearing. *Newsweek* asked that I wear the classic "Chrissy Snow little teddy," a very low-cut but darling undergarment. We were never told that any one of us would be featured, only that it would be the three of us.

But the photographer kept rearranging us so that I was on top, and John and Joyce were at my feet looking up at me. I was extremely uneasy, and I could tell that both John and Joyce were annoyed. I asked to speak privately with Don Nicholl, one of the producers, offstage. "I'm very uncomfortable," I told him. "This guy is putting me in first place, and it's making John and Joyce angry with me. Can't you do something?" Don feigned ignorance and surprise and assured me that nothing of the sort was happening. In other words, *Don't believe your lying eyes.*

The following week the issue hit the stands. "Sex and TV" was the cover banner. There I was, on top, my teddy unbuttoned baring most of my young breasts and one strap falling off my shoulder, while John was leering lasciviously over one of my shoulders. Joyce was on the bottom and to the side of my feet.

It was an incredible cover. It was phenomenal publicity, for me, for us, for the show. It was shocking. Everyone was talking about it. *Newsweek* had never done a cover like this and it was such a sensation that it was shown all over the nightly news as the changing face of TV.

Oh my god! I thought when I saw it. I had dual feelings: exhilarated, yet fully aware that the placement of the three of us would cause difficulty on set.

If the producers had behaved like stand-up guys, they could have and should have told us up front what *Newsweek* wanted and handled it like pros. They could have said that whatever the means we got recognition, it was still great for the show, that this was the cover *Newsweek* had requested. I later learned that the producers were in on it from the beginning. But they had played dumb with me/us, setting up the bad vibe on set.

How can you take such incredible chemistry as we had and mess with it? Jealousy and resentment are powerful emotions. I had no way of talking to any of my fellow cast members about it. What could I have said or done? I hadn't planned it. I had even tried to stop this cover while it was in motion. So a layer of resentment was added to what was going to become a large shit-pile down the road.

Ego ruins the best deals and friendships—always.

The relationships on the set were never quite the same after that. In time, John pushed it under the rug because he was so secure in his enormous talent, and the two of us were incredible sparring partners. But Joyce withdrew somewhat. If I could imagine walking in her shoes at that time, I'd understand the frustration. She was the one with the promise. She was the one who had the contract and all the training, and then I come along with none of her credentials, and I'm being pushed out front in large part due to Jay Bernstein's magnificent public relations campaign.

Taken in the biggest picture, that cover made our show even more popular. This was the dream of all casts and production teams, a megahit, the biggest show on TV! John and Joyce and I were the show; it was the *three* of us. But Joyce and some of the rest of the cast, and shockingly the producers and the production team, began to resent my breakout. I believe it was in part because at the beginning I announced, "I don't know what I'm doing." My success was perceived as undeserved rather than evidence that I am a quick study. Thank god, I had Alan explaining to me that this wasn't about ego but about maximizing an opportunity, which is why it is called show *business*! Television and all facets of the entertainment world are a *business*.

John, Joyce, and I still played like kids, but as is true on many playgrounds, the kids weren't really getting along.

. . .

On the home front, our own kids were doing a bit better than before. Once Alan and I were married, our kids realized it was a done deal, that we were a united front. Maybe it was going to be okay.

In blending our families, I understood it had to be complicated for Alan's kids to accept me as the new wife, but it's okay for them to like her food. So I made food, great food, as my offering to what I knew was a difficult situation. On Sunday mornings, I would prepare platters of fabulous food: crispy lemon chicken legs; plates of pasta with pine nuts, olive oil, garlic, and lemon; grilled artichokes; and heirloom tomatoes with fresh basil, red onion, and olive oil served with fresh Italian burrata or goat cheese. I would make lemon tarts and hot chocolate cookies. As awful as my father behaved when I was a child, I still never wanted a new father, so I understood the complexities. Had I been a little older and wiser, I would have had an even greater comprehension of my new families' feelings.

I was only nineteen years older than Alan's daughter, Leslie; we were close enough in age that we liked the same music and wore the same kinds of clothes. It might have been easier for her had I been a family friend, but I was her father's wife. I'm sure that had a sting to it.

Stephen, Alan's son, was living with us, and Leslie resided at her mother's home. As I've said, blending families is a very delicate dance, so making sure to get the group gathered together around food was fun, essential, and stabilizing.

We were of the first generation who divorced. For blended families, there were and still are no global rules. We were feeling our way through, always cognizant that emotions were raw and tender. As I've said, no kid, no matter how grown up, wants new parents, no matter how nice. Their loyalty to their parent does not allow for easy acceptance of a new addition.

I did so many things wrong. At first I tried to be another parent. That did *not* work; it was stupid of me. Trying to parent my husband's children was met with resentment. Bruce and Alan were equally uneasy with each other; in Bruce's early life, he had had all of me, but now marriage and my sizzling career cut into that sole focus tremendously. He was fighting for his place in these new uncharted waters. Alan felt great guilt living with my son and not with his own, so having Stephen move in with us would greatly rectify that situation.

WHAT I KNOW NOW

Perspective is one of the gifts that comes later in life along with wisdom. It was perfectly understandable for feelings to be all over the place. Imagine that your father moves out of the home you've all shared as a family, falls in love with another woman, marries her, and then starts living with *her* son. Talk about having your life as you know it ripped out from under you! No one could be mature enough to handle a situation like that. With Bruce, surely his inner child wanted things to be as they once had been: to have his mother back all to himself as it had been for so long. Had I known then what I know now, we all should have had professional help early on to keep the air clear, to allow everyone to vent their feelings, and to give the children respect for their feelings so they could understand they were being heard. Neither Alan nor I was that smart at that time, so we did the best we could.

For Leslie and me it would take many years to find our sweet spot. It finally happened once she graduated from Parsons School of Design, Los Angeles, and was living on her own. Then our relationship became the ground for another family business; it was and is a relationship where she can use her profound creativity, and I have had the pleasure and good fortune to wear hundreds of beautiful creations she's designed for me over the years.

Despite all the work, weekends remained sacred, and as best we could, we reserved them for family. We made wonderful lunches in the kitchen for everyone. The kitchen doors opened right onto the beach, but our house was marked by the paparazzi, so I couldn't easily go outside. I wanted to keep the kids sheltered so as not to give away their privacy. This was all new to me. To keep our privacy and still enjoy our lives, we invited friends over, and it seemed like every Sunday we had a party. A little wine, a little pasta, great music, and hot cookies made for a fabulous and festive afternoon. The kids liked it, and the two boys were starting to enjoy each other.

I loved being married. I loved that we were finally together for life. I loved making a home and a family. But the TV machinery was still rolling; the momentum of being a number-one show had an exhausting and exhilarating pace. I constantly pinched myself at my good fortune, but every moment of mine that the network could commandeer, it did, with photo shoots, magazine covers, TV specials, and New York appearances. Being on a number-one sitcom is huge, and it was an even bigger deal back then.

You can't give yourself away.

One evening I came home late from a *Three's Company* rehearsal and apologized to Alan. "Sorry I'm late. I guested on the Tim Conway special."

"How did that happen?" Alan asked incredulously.

"Well, I ran into Tim in the hallway last week, and he asked if I would stop by and do a guest stint on his TV special. I said yes, of course, I'd be happy to." I'd forgotten about it until his people came to my dressing room for a wardrobe fitting.

"Did you get paid? Did you get billing?" Alan asked, sounding kind of agitated.

"I didn't ask about billing," I said. "But they asked me what kind of gift I would want, so I told them I was collecting my silverware from Tiffany's."

A week later a box arrived from Tiffany's. It had one fork in it.

Alan looked at the fork and said, "You starred on a CBS special for a friggin' fork? I don't believe you, Suzanne. You just don't get it. You got forked, all right! You are the star of the number-one show in

100

America. You alone have become a one-woman media juggernaut. You can't give yourself away. You've earned this recognition. Your number one status is valuable. You should have been paid six figures for that appearance," he said, exasperated.

I felt stupid. "I only worked for an hour," I protested. "It wasn't that big of a deal."

"Doesn't matter," Alan said heatedly. "They're going to use you to promote and advertise their show. They're going to use you to bring in ratings. They must be laughing their asses off. They got you for a fork!"

He was right. I hadn't put together the concept of ratings translating into money. The networks were making huge money from our show's success, and those of us involved had opportunities outside the show on which to capitalize. (By the way, I love Tim Conway and have been dear friends with him and his wife and family for years.)

Alan had a major understanding of a talent's worth, and I had garnered the highest ratings in the advertisers' dream demographic of women eighteen to forty-nine. Alan understood that this had value, and that being on the number-one show on national television also had huge value.

He also understood vision: that the choices you make today need to be thought of in a broader context. How will a momentary success create a long-term success rather than stop at being just the flavor of the month?

Alan left his show in Canada, turning over his seat as host to his longtime friend Alan Thicke (rest in peace, dear Alan, gone too soon), and Suzanne Inc. began. It wasn't formal—I didn't even think about it that way. It seemed a natural progression for us: I trusted Alan with my heart and my life, and I respected the hell out of him. This felt right. I loved having him home. While I went to work at the studio each day, he was at home working the phones, making deals for me and us, our business.

Alan and Jay clashed right from the start. Jay was interested in setting up shorter deals. He wanted me to sign everything, whereas Alan was more methodical.

I thought we could make the Suzanne Somers brand one of the most powerful and trusted in the world. At different times, I'd discussed branding Chrissy Snow with the producers, but they sneeringly dismissed us with "Forget it—all we care about is the show." When I explained to them that marketing Chrissy Snow merchandise, creating a Chrissy movie franchise, and offering a Saturday-morning Chrissy cartoon would bring new viewers to the show, they laughed and dismissed both of us. That's when I realized they were totally ego-driven. If it wasn't their idea, they passed. What's that expression about cutting off your nose to spite your face?

I was offered a three-picture deal with Michael Eisner, head of Disney, at $250,000 per movie, an enormous sum of money at that time (at any time). Jay turned it down without even discussing it with us. Both Alan and I were horrified. Jay said, "With her visibility, she should be getting a million a picture, plus back end." As Alan explained it, these three movies would have been my entrée to the movie world, paving the road to becoming a movie star. One of the movies offered was *Outrageous Fortune,* which went on to box office success with star Bette Midler.

After this, we established new rules. Jay was to run all deals past us and never to turn down a deal without discussion. Anyone could have understood the necessity of this, but Jay was a bit of a control freak, as I was beginning to understand, and he didn't like being usurped.

The situation didn't cause a serious rift between us (yet); it was just a difference of opinion and approach. The three of us were having a great time together—we celebrated every deal with champagne, which meant we were drinking a lot of champagne. Having both Alan and Jay steering the ship was not only a big relief for me but extremely productive.

The show had me so busy, in addition to my roles as mother and running our household, that I never had the time to sit down and think about what was happening or to plan for the future. I needed Alan for that.

. . .

Alan is brilliant. The first deal he made was with Ace Hardware to do a series of commercials for them. They were excited about combining their brand and my enormous visibility. They wanted to be the most successful chain of hardware stores across America.

"I met with the executives and the advertising agency for Ace Hardware today," Alan told me. "They really want you, so I told them what we wanted. Their idea was to put you in coveralls and hold a hammer in their commercials. I explained to them that they would get a lot more attention if they shot you on stage in Las Vegas in a beautiful gown instead. When I told them what I wanted for you, they turned white, but I explained that these flashy commercials would substantially increase their visibility factor and that people would be talking about them."

"How did they react?" I asked.

"They agreed!"

Wow. It all happened fast. We produced a major campaign of Ace Hardware commercials, and they were a home run. All of them were highly produced minimusicals. I danced and sang the tagline: "Ace is the place for the helpful hardware man." You could hardly turn on the TV without seeing one of them. We had several different versions going at the same time. One was like an old Busby Berkeley–style MGM movie, another a huge Christmas-themed commercial where I danced in a line like the Rockettes, except I was the one who was out of step. It was in keeping with Chrissy Snow's "ditsy blonde." Chrissy Snow was glamorous, larger than life, and these commercials presented her as bigger than the TV show. She was a Vegas star. The public clearly enjoyed them, and there was not a hammer in sight in any of them.

Once the visibility factor for Ace Hardware increased by 600 percent, the huge price tag Alan negotiated was not an issue. As Alan said, "They are happy to pay you."

Numerous awards for *Three's Company* started coming our way. John and I were both nominated to be nominated (whatever that means) for our first Emmy Award. Not Joyce. That was uncomfortable. The producers came down to the set, and instead of congratulating us, they asked us not to discuss it. They wanted us to act as though it hadn't happened. Luckily, neither John nor I ended up being nominated that year. We were an acclaimed success, but we were made so by the *people*—the media didn't take the show seriously. And religious groups were always protesting our show because of the sexual undertones. It's laughable by today's standards. The People's Choice Awards came next. I was awarded "Favorite TV Actress." That brought more magazines, more commercial deals. I was flying high.

It was hard to believe what my life had become. I had thought this only happened in dreams.

Unbelievably, the producers of *Three's Company* were not enjoying my outside success. The public loved the character of Chrissy Snow, and these new flashy commercials only added to that fuel. Perhaps the producers felt threatened that I would make trouble because of my outside fame, but that was never my intention. After knocking around for so long trying to make ends meet any way I could, I simply wanted to make the most of this success. Besides, I loved being with the show—it was a joy to come to work each day, and it truly came first for me.

If you want it, you must believe in yourself. If you believe you can, you can, regardless of what you are going after in your life. Passion is the motivator.

I was just happy to be able to hold my own with these two greats, John and Joyce. We had to keep the mood light to create the chemistry that the show depended on. We laughed like kids, we played like kids, and the producers treated us like kids. But fun aside, as I said, it was business. Our weekly reach was gaining in popularity, and every time we were on the air, our value as network commodities grew. By keeping us convinced that we were "the kids," they hoped we would never question the parents' (producers') agenda. Mostly we didn't—we were just glad to have a happy home. Good boys and girls do what they're told. They behave. I didn't know how true these words would be, but I'm getting ahead of myself.

WHAT I KNOW NOW

Training for anything you aspire to do in life is important, a privilege, and a huge opportunity. I would have loved to have the opportunity to study my craft, and in fact that was my goal when I earned a scholarship to college. But as you know, that dream was deferred. Today I say to those who for whatever reason couldn't go to school or get professional training and now believe it's too late to pursue their dream—for those who think it could never happen for them, I am the example. If you want it, you must believe in yourself. (Thank you, again, Mrs. Kilgore.) If you believe you can, you can, regardless of what you're going after in your life. Passion is the motivator. The figure-eight of love, family, and business, in our case, means it never begins and never ends. It's all-encompassing, each component as important as the others. Whatever needs the most attention at that moment is your priority. Then follow your gut, your instincts, and your heart.

CHAPTER 9

FANTASTIC VOYAGE

When you think a grateful thought, there is no
room in your mind for anything else.
—ANONYMOUS

I was on a fast-moving train, and I never wanted to get off.

Our summer hiatus was upon me, and Alan got a call from Paul Anka. He wanted me to star in a big network TV special he was filming in Monte Carlo. *Wow.* Paul is one of the premier entertainer-singer-songwriters of our time; his hits include "My Way," made famous by Frank Sinatra, and the theme song for *The Tonight Show*, to name just a couple.

This deal was negotiated properly, so I didn't get forked again. It was first class all the way. Paul Anka hired the best: Buz Kohan was the writer, the most prestigious TV writer of his time, and Marty Pasetta (director of the Oscars) directed. Alan and I checked into the beautiful Loews Hotel in gorgeous Monte Carlo overlooking the harbor and the Sporting Club, arguably the most glamorous nightclub theater in the world. I stood on our incredible huge wraparound deck and thought to myself that this was about as glamorous a place as anywhere on the planet. I was filled with gratitude for this life I had the privilege of living.

For the special, I was assigned a French choreographer who positioned me along with fifteen chic French dancers while I sang "If My Friends Could See Me Now" dancing down the cobblestone streets of Monte Carlo with Paul. The next day we taped an entire production number to "Gee, How Lucky Can You Get?" and it didn't take much for me to sing these lyrics with total believability. It was a lavish production number including a montage of me modeling French couture fashions one after another. Another dream . . . I had to keep pinching myself.

An unexpected bonus with this gig was meeting Donna Summer. When we met in 1978, she was the queen of disco, and her music was heard all over the world. She was the hottest act in the music industry. We hit it off immediately. I loved her. We joked about being sisters; there was something about her that I related to, besides the similar last name. Both of us had been propelled into the limelight, ready or not, around the same time. She and I were at the top of the charts in our own arenas, and everyone wanted both of us for their specials, TV shows, and magazines to bring in ratings. We would remain friends until her untimely death of lung cancer in May 2012.

The night after the taping, Donna and I had a surreal experience. We performed on the glamorous stage of the Sporting Club, overlooking the beautiful harbor of Monaco. In the audience were the guests of honor, His Royal Highness Prince Rainier and his family along with many other European royalty. Also in attendance was the billionaire shipping magnate Stavros Niarchos, whose huge private yacht was moored in the most prominent spot in the harbor.

After the show honoring Prince Rainier, Paul took all of us to Jimmy's nightclub. Everyone but the prince was there, including Princess Stephanie and her brother, Prince Albert. Stavros Niarchos took a liking to me (an understatement) and declared (they do that in Europe) that "tomorrow I am going to give a party for you on my private yacht." I made it very clear *my husband* and I would love to attend and that I was traveling with sixty people from the show. "Bring them all!" Stavros announced grandly. *Safety in numbers,* I thought, as there were rumors about Stavros's ex-wife mysteriously disappearing, never to be found again. Clearly, the girl from the closet was hanging with a new crowd.

The following night we were to arrive at Stavros's yacht at seven p.m. We all assembled in the lobby at the Loews; getting cars for everyone was a bit of a nightmare, so we arrived about fifteen minutes late.

As our cars pulled up to the private dock, I couldn't help but notice that this dock looked different from the others: polished brass everywhere, clean, comfortable seating, and a definite feeling of luxury. We got out of the car and there it was—the most beautiful ship I had ever seen. (Actually, it was the only one I had ever seen up close.) There was a long gangplank, flanked on either side by white-uniformed attendants. As Alan and I walked to the top of the stairs, I was surprised to see Stavros standing at the top awaiting our arrival. He was wearing a navy blue dinner jacket, an open white shirt, a yellow ascot, and beautifully creased white pants. He kissed my cheeks, saying, "Suzanne. Welcome." Then he shook Alan's hand.

As he walked away, Alan whispered to me, "I bet he wishes I would disappear." We laughed at that one. You got the feeling that Stavros was used to getting what Stavros wanted.

It was quite a heady setting, with white-uniformed waiters carrying silver trays heavy with mounds of caviar, hushed tones, and the tinkling of a piano in the corner. The furniture was all white and plush, big soft pieces like white clouds, I was afraid to sit on one for fear I'd get lost. People began filling up the sumptuous room. Wow! Out of the corner of my eye I saw Ringo Starr, along with a group of royals whose names I didn't know, and our television group, headed by Paul Anka. Were it not for Paul, none of us would have been there in the first place.

Donna Summer arrived. Stavros asked Donna, Alan, and me if we would enjoy a private tour of his ship. When we reached the communications room, he asked me who I wanted to call, saying I could call anyone anywhere in the world. (At that time there were no cell phones and making a call to the States or other countries was not easy.) The only person I wanted to talk with was Bruce, but with everyone listening, it would have felt uncomfortable. Besides, we'd be home in a few days.

Dinner was called, and Stavros roughly grabbed my arm. "You sit with me," he said, then glanced at Alan and added, "You can bring whoever you want."

I looked nervously at Alan and said, "Come with me."

"He's an asshole," Alan said under his breath. He was not liking this "little man" (as he later described him). Stavros was not very tall, maybe five-five at most. But Stavros was not treating my husband with the kind of respect he deserved, and I didn't like it.

Dinner was all things rich: more caviar, duck, champagne, Grand Marnier soufflés. It was all sumptuous and wonderful, but it had been a long day. As dessert was served, I was aware that I needed to go back to our hotel room and get to sleep. We bade Stavros good night and thanked him profusely for a wonderful evening; we said, as one politely does, that if ever he was in Los Angeles, he should be sure and get in touch with us.

Alan and I climbed into our beautiful bed overlooking the gorgeous harbor of Monte Carlo and wrapped ourselves in each other's arms, the place where we always came together at the end of any day, the most wonderful moment of the day, and we fell into a deep, blissful, grateful sleep.

That same year I worked with John Wayne, Bob Hope, Sammy Davis Jr., Jerry Lewis, Rich Little—pretty much everyone in the top entertainment spots.

The next summer hiatus I had the incredible opportunity to star in two major motion pictures. The first movie was *Yesterday's Hero,* a Jackie Collins film, in which I was to star opposite Ian McShane, a very well-known English actor. Alan and I packed up and moved both boys from Los Angeles to London for the summer. The movie was produced by Elliott Kastner, a terrific guy, a real character, and a bit of a bad boy. He had had enormous success as a movie producer, and I was wowed to be working with him. From the very first day in London, I knew this was going to be a fun adventure.

London was exciting, full of energy; I loved the fashion, the nightlife, and the people. Brits have great comedy, and their humor is very dry. Filming in England was very civilized. Every morning James (yes, my driver's name actually was James) picked me up at the Dorchester Hotel in a beautiful wine-colored 1957 Rolls-Royce Silver Wraith. There were only two of these cars in the world, and the other one belonged to the queen. James would drive Alan and me to the countryside while, in the backseat, we sipped tea and crumpets that had been beautifully presented on a silver tray with china cups. Alan and I joked in fake British accents, "Lovely way to start the day, darling."

On an English movie set back then, there was teatime, lunchtime, and then teatime again in the afternoon. The set closed down at a respectable five p.m., when we would be driven back to our hotel, the Dorchester, to have dinner at some lovely restaurant or order room service with the boys. They were having a ball; our two adventurous kids loved exploring London. We would listen to the tales of their exploits each night, hearing their excitement at what they'd seen that day, astonished at their ability to navigate so well in a strange town.

The first week of shooting, Jackie Collins showed up on the set. Her hair was pulled back into a high long ponytail, and she had on lots of perfectly done eye makeup, with eyes and lips beautifully outlined, and a fabulous full-length white lynx coat. Today the coat would be politically incorrect, but back then it was simply stunning. She was stunning, a gorgeous woman with a throaty laugh and naughty sense of humor. Both Alan and I loved her.

This was her first major motion picture, and she was as excited as I was to be involved. We spent many evenings out on the town with Jackie, and sometimes her sister, Joan Collins, would come along. Joan would bring her then husband, Anthony Newley (who I ended up touring summer theaters with the following year. Small world).

Jackie's husband, Oscar Lerman, owned a fabulous nightclub, Tramp, the hottest spot in London at that time, where all the celebrities and high-profile people would meet. That's how I found myself sitting next to Rod Stewart one evening. It was that kind of place.

As you are probably recognizing by this point in our story, there's my recollection of events and there's Alan's. They are always compatible, but he is more of a street fighter. Here's Alan's take on the London experience.

I got a call from Elliott Kastner, a prolific film producer born in the States but who lived in Runnymede in England, where I believe the Magna Carta was signed. He had an offer for Suzanne to star in a movie based on a true story about a British soccer player who was an alcoholic. Suzanne would play a rock singer. We went back and forth a few times on terms. And finally, upon agreement, we hopped a plane and checked into the Dorchester with our two sons, who were around twelve and thirteen. The director was Neil Leifer, a noted and very talented sports photographer and a very nice and funny man with a great smile. His pal was LeRoy Neiman, who did a life-size painting of Suzanne's character that became the logo for the film.

There was a note telling us that James, Elliott's driver, would pick us up at eight-thirty the following morning to drive us to the set. Eight-thirty? In the States, they all start with hair and makeup at five a.m. In the passenger compartment of the limo was a pot of tea and warm crumpets with marmalade and jams. Wow. So far I loved making a film in London. By ten-thirty a.m., Suzanne was on set for her first shot. At eleven-thirty, it was break time for tea. By two, it was lunch. Three-thirty, and it was teatime again. And by five-thirty, we were back in the Rolls with James, headed to the Dorchester with port and cheese.

Our deal was that Suzanne got paid at the end of every week. The end of the week arrives and no check. I asked Elliott when we could expect to get paid, and he gave me one of those answers that started the bullshit light flashing, and one of his eyes suddenly developed a nervous tic. He obviously didn't have the money. "Okay," I told Elliott. "If Suzanne is not paid by Wednesday next week, you can wave goodbye to her at the airport."

Elliott promised we'd get paid, and as a gesture of goodwill, he invited us out to Runnymede for dinner with Tessa Kennedy and the children. James picked us up, and off we went. When we arrived, Tessa, a beautiful and sophisticated designer, met us, and we were seated in the baronial dining room. No Elliott. I asked about Elliott, and Tessa told us that he suddenly had to go to a funeral. Now, I'm willing to believe almost anything, but the idea that someone he knew had just dropped dead and he had to rush to the grave in time to catch the coffin drop, screamed bullshit.

But I didn't really care. Here we were having a brand-new experience in a historical landmark that I had studied in grade school in Canada. In the 1200s, King John, under threat of a civil war, signed the Magna Carta, limiting his power among the noblemen and commoners . . . or something like that.

Dinner was quiet and formal and polite, but still no Elliott. Then he appeared and sat down at the dining table, pulled out his handkerchief, and started polishing the table. No one said anything, and we pretended we were not aware of what was happening. Okay . . . it was weird, very weird. And after trudging out to a rock marker in a field where the Magna Carta was signed (and now I think that that's also possibly bullshit), James returned us to the Dorchester.

Wednesday arrived, and no check, so I hit on Elliott, and he said his best friend Jerry in L.A. was wiring the money. I was to meet him at the bank in the morning. Next morning there was Elliott outside the bank with a large paper sack filled with hundreds. I couldn't open an account or rent a safe deposit box because I was not a resident, and I didn't trust the security at the Dorchester.

So every day I stuffed all the money under my shirt, in my underwear, and in every pocket. I looked like I had gained fifty pounds overnight. And every week thereafter, I kept stuffing. With thousands stuffed into my underwear, I had a very impressive package.

Now we were heading home and going through customs in Los Angeles, and I got the custom form, and one of the questions was "Are you carrying more than ten thousand dollars?" I answered yes and handed it to the customs officer. The guy asked me how much I had. When I told him, and where it was on my body, he laughed and said, "Chrissy, does this guy belong to you?" He said, "Get outta here!"

Before we left London, I told Elliott that Suzanne loved his Rolls-Royce and asked if he would consider giving it to her. He said he had just sold her film for more money than he got for Missouri Breaks *with Marlon Brando, so the answer was yes. We lived in Venice, in L.A., and the first day we drove the Rolls along Ocean Front Walk, with me driving and Suzanne sitting queenlike in the rear, guys screamed, "Asshole!" I grew up being called asshole, so I laughed at that one. But that beautiful car ultimately sat in our garage for three years. Who needed that abuse?*

> Loyalty can't be bought, and neither can smarts. I'm always secure knowing he will take care.

We saw Elliott once more a year later, when he asked us to meet him in his bungalow at the Beverly Hills Hotel. We walked in, and Elliott was sitting on the edge of a chair in his robe with his balls hanging out. He told me he hated my jacket, so on our way out, I hung it in his closet.

Our dear, dear friend Jackie Collins never got paid for her script, and one night at Spago, she threw a glass of water into Elliott's face. That's showbiz!

One year at the Cannes Film Festival, where all the deals for financing and buying films are made, there was a joke circulating. An interviewer asks a French starlet which man, out of all the men at the festival, she would most like to have sex with. She thinks about it for a moment and replies: "George Clooney, Brad Pitt, and Elliott Kastner." The interviewer says he understands Clooney and Pitt, but why Kastner? She replies, "Because everyone I speak with here says fuck Elliott Kastner."

We arrived home, and the beautiful Silver Wraith was in our garage. What a thrill! I grew up with Chevys.

Recently, shockingly, Jackie passed away. She never told any of us she had cancer. She kept it to herself, choosing not to take the present standard-of-care protocol for cancer, a template that has a dismal success rate. She wanted to do it her way, on her terms. She planned every detail of her funeral, put all her things in order, and left this life. I will always miss her. RIP, dear, sweet Jackie.

. . .

After returning from London, we had about a week to unpack and then pack again to move to Toronto for the rest of the summer. I was to star in the movie *Nothing Personal* opposite Donald Sutherland.

We optioned a script by Robert Kaufman, who wrote Love at First Bite, *and produced the feature in Toronto starring Suzanne and Donald Sutherland. The financial guy there was cut from the same cloth as Elliott. Maybe it's genetic.*

He was supposed to send a weekly check to our Los Angeles bank, which he did. But he had a mole in the bank who would take the checks and stick them in a drawer so they never got deposited. I found out after three weeks, then pulled Suzanne off the film. I had the production office make reservations for us to return to Los Angeles with Donald. This little thug freaked, since he had already made a substantial investment in production, and he pushed the desperation button, looking for a white knight. The iconic Sam Arkoff, founder of American International Pictures, picked up the project, and everyone got paid.

When people ask how it works with me and Alan, it's things like this that show it best. He's got my back, no screwing around. Loyalty can't be bought, and neither can smarts. I'm always secure knowing he will take care. It's allowed me to do my work without worrying about backroom shenanigans.

I loved the script for *Nothing Personal*. I played a smart, sexy, sophisticated lawyer, and Donald a professor. Together we are hell-bent on saving seals from slaughter in Newfoundland. Toronto was a great location for Alan, as it was his hometown and he knew everybody. His family was there, including his mother and father; we were able to have Friday-night dinners at his parents' home. That was always special. His mother made the most wonderful foods. My favorite was a rich chicken soup with little handmade ravioli-like dumplings, filled with chopped meat and onions. I could eat ten of them, they were so good, but I resisted the temptation. She would put several of them in the bottom of the bowl, then ladle the hot clear broth and garnish with snipped fresh dill. So good!

Her table was laden with a veritable feast. She was used to cooking for a crowd, having spent most of her adult life cooking nightly for her seventeen live-in boarders: delicious roast chicken dripping in pan juices; sautéed buckwheat with fried onions and garlic; sliced, steamed, and seasoned cabbage; lots of potatoes; and for dessert, honey cake and apple strudel. All homemade, of course.

All mothers of sons want a woman to care for, love, honor, and cherish their boys.

We would leave her home stuffed, which is how she liked it. And then we would lie in our hotel room beds bloated and gassy from overeating, not helped by all the cabbage. My stomach would rumble all night. Alan just plain out farted for what seemed like minutes at a time—something one definitely won't do when first dating. (But on a more serious note, we had not figured out yet that he was gluten intolerant.) It was a symphony that had us laughing hysterically.

The bloating was worth it, though. The food was so good, so authentic, and prepared with such love. His mother was a wonderful person who took me into her family. She loved me, and I know it was because she saw how much I loved her son. I took care of him. That's what all mothers of sons want: a woman to care for, love, honor, and cherish their boys.

Margaret, Alan's mother, worked harder than anyone I've ever known. She was busy day and night running her boardinghouse, taking care of all its people by herself for years and years. She did all the cooking and cleaning, plus she owned a little candy store she worked at every day. Her schedule was impossible, but she did it all cheerfully. That's the immigrant mentality. She felt blessed to have escaped Poland before Hitler could have her rounded up, and she was filled with gratitude to be living in the freedom and safety of Canada.

When she passed away several years later, she was, to our surprise, a millionaire. We were all shocked because she never spent any money. The only luxury I was aware of was her full-length fur coat and matching hat. She wore both in the cold Toronto winters while visiting her four banks (one on each corner) weekly. She saved her money by penny-pinching and never wasting a cent. In her last will, she left a bequest for each of her grandchildren, including my son. I was extremely moved by that action. I never expected it—in fact, it had never entered my mind. Yet it showed her complete acceptance of me and that she considered Bruce one of her own.

Alan's father worked in a sweatshop making pockets for uniforms—for twenty-five years. While we were filming, Bruce got a summer job at a local grocery store, and Stephen worked at his maternal grandfather's tailor shop. I've always believed that children should learn early on to earn their own money, so as to understand the value of hard work and its rewards. On days when the boys weren't working, they hung around the set with us. I don't think it's any coincidence that they've both ended up in the film business. It all just seemed natural to them.

I loved working with Donald Sutherland. We laughed a lot and had only one argument during the entire shoot. While filming the last scene, I wouldn't smoke a joint with him on camera. In retrospect, who cared? But appearances mattered, and I took it seriously.

The movie was distributed by Sam Arkoff. But the company was in transition, so the marketing fell a little flat. The movie did well but wasn't boffo. I didn't get any blame for it, but looking back, I believe I should have done the film I pitched to Mickey Ross and the boys: *The Adventures of Chrissy Snow*.

That's what the public wanted to see from me back then. A lot of actresses could have played the sexy lawyer, but I was the only one who could be Chrissy. I just knew women and girls would flock to movie theaters to see Chrissy on any adventure she took. And think of the merchandising! At that time, no one in Hollywood other than

Farrah Fawcett understood anything about branding and merchandising. But my hands were strapped because my character belonged to the production company, so I had no power to do with her what Alan and I knew could be done. Farrah was smart. She saw her opportunity, and she or Jay Bernstein or both understood the timing, understood her power and her appeal. She ran with it. I admired that. But to do it, she left *Charlie's Angels*. As I've said, I had no desire to do that—I loved being on *Three's Company*. It was the greatest thing that ever happened to me professionally. Look at all the doors it had already opened. We finished filming *Nothing Personal*, and one week later I was back on set for the new season of *Three's Company*.

It had been a heady summer, a heady couple of years. Our life had been turned upside down and inside out, in ways I never would have imagined. We were on a fast track, with no time to breathe. The show was still strong at number one, and I still never went a week without being on a major magazine cover. This was all afterhours work and an indicator that my image sold magazines (or as they say in the business, "tickets"). Magazines at that time carried a lot of weight. There was no Internet, no social media. Everyone got their news from TV, magazines, and newspapers. I was still being written about and talked about in all three media outlets constantly.

I was exhausted but young enough for my body to bounce back quickly. Our multilevel home had five flights of stairs, and scripts were piled on each stair all the way up. I have no idea what I turned down back then. There could have been Academy Award winners on those stairs. I just didn't have time to read any of them, so they kept piling up.

CHAPTER 10

YOU GOTTA HAVE FRIENDS

You control your decisions. You control your
actions. You control your outcome.
—DAVID KEKICH, *MASTER LIFE*

In 1979, I walked into a recording studio to record some voice-overs. Sitting there in front of the console was Barry Manilow, just finishing up a session. We were next in line. He looked at me and said, "Oh, you're the other one they make fun of."

I said, "I know. How come it's always you and me?" And a friendship was forged that has lasted for thirty-seven years. I adore and love Barry. He had taken the country and the world by storm with his megahit "Copacabana." It was beyond brilliant. The album *Even Now* was everywhere—the song was playing in every club, disco, and TV special. No one could sit still when his music came on. I danced to "Copacabana" as Lola, the character in Barry's song, on a Danny Thomas special and again as recently as last year, on *Dancing with the Stars*. My tailbone still remembers! Ha-ha.

Barry was often photographed onstage wearing a ruffled rhumba shirt, and it became his fashion statement. I, on the other hand, had worn a chicken suit when introducing Gladys Knight on *The Suzanne*

Somers Special. That became the photo most used of me. There we were, he in his ruffled rhumba shirt and me in my chicken suit.

We were both at the top of our game nationwide. Barry was and is a musical phenomenon, and I was the number-one female TV star in America. It's comforting to have a close friend who totally understands what you are going through. We both understood the trade-offs. Going out alone is off the table for good. There always has to be someone with you, otherwise you are up for grabs. One of the many things Alan does for me is to provide a "good cop, bad cop" option in these situations. Guess which role he plays? Anyway, I welcomed the trade-off and still do.

> *It's comforting to have a close friend who totally understands what you are going through.*

Celebrity is what you make it. Over the years, I've watched some celebrities in our business change with their fame. I believe it's a result of believing that all the attention they are getting somehow makes them better than others, or that the world revolves around them. That is dangerous thinking. From the beginning, I always saw celebrity as a gift and a privilege. Interacting with the public is part of the deal. You are nothing without them, and you can never forget that.

I am friendly by nature so interacting with fans and others is enjoyable for me. I like people, and I like being around them, but do I want to be grabbed by a stranger or taken advantage of? No. Would you? Celebrity requires respect on both sides.

As I continued to adjust to my career, my celebrity, and its purpose, I found it comforting to be with Barry. I wasn't looking for a special friendship outside the incredible rapport I have always had with Alan, but the celebrity that both Barry and I shared was its own animal. There are no schools or books or classes one can take on Celebrity 101. It's a strange new world that you learn to groove with or not. I have watched so many fall apart, feeling undeserving, who resort to drugs to take away the shyness and then find themselves hooked. So having Barry to bounce experiences off of, and he from me, was invaluable. We are both searchers, fascinated by the human condition; we enjoy discussing what we consider the two big questions in life: *Who am I,* and *what do I want?* Most people go to their graves never knowing the answers to these seemingly simple questions.

I will be forever working on it, and I believe it takes at least a lifetime to answer. Yet I find myself getting closer to my own understanding of what it means. Of course, with each decade, I look back and realize how little I knew in the past decade. Evolution is part of the human experience.

I was evolving into this new life and loving it. I enjoyed celebrity because I like people so much. It's interactive in the best sense of the word. Some of us must come back again and again to finally figure out this thing called life. We humans are comprised of a complexity of emotions that often collide with our intellects. Barry and I have, over the years, had long endless talks about this.

> Who am I, *and what do I want? Most people go to their graves never knowing the answers to these seemingly simple questions.*

We stimulate each other; we make each other laugh. I love to cook for him, and he loves my food. I love his musical suggestions for me, and I take each one seriously. We've promised to produce one another's funerals, because we were both so disappointed at Merv Griffin's funeral. (We both knew Merv would never have put on an event like that, with a bunch of clergy who didn't know him and had never met him but did all the speaking about him.) For all of these reasons, my relationship with Barry became my most important outside relationship. Funny, it was all because of yet another chance meeting, as Bette Midler sang, "You Gotta Have Friends." Not surprisingly, it was a Barry arrangement.

. . .

*G*ood Morning America wanted to do a Mother's Day show featuring the mothers of TV's hottest stars of the moment. They invited Robin Williams's mother, Tom Selleck's mother, and *my* mother; my sweet, very, *very* shy mother. Unfortunately, due to my

> *Evolution is part of the human experience.*

shooting schedule, I was not able to accompany her. Instead, she and my father would make their first trip to New York by themselves, all expenses paid. They would be staying at the Ritz and have dinner at Le Grenouille, the most popular and expensive restaurant in New York. Heady stuff, and a long way away from San Bruno, California.

Mom was so excited and nervous. We discussed her wardrobe and decided on a couple of her most beautiful outfits, chosen as always with her impeccable great taste. I knew—hoped—she would be okay.

The morning of the show, I was lying in bed before getting up to head to the studio, as I heard her being introduced: "This morning our guest is Suzanne Somers's mother, Marion Mahoney." My heart started pounding, and I sat up to see, both excited and nervous for her. She wore her beautiful violet coat, and her great, thick hair was coiffed perfectly. For some women, as their hair grays, it becomes a dead color with an underbelly of dark. But my mother's hair had turned a beautiful white-blond. Most people thought she colored it, but it was all hers and natural. I was glad the makeup department did her right—she looked gorgeous.

All was going well, but I noticed that her eyes looked a bit stunned, like a deer in headlights. She had never spoken publicly before, and the knowledge that millions of people were watching her was overwhelming. David Hartman, the usual host, was ill that day and was replaced by Mike Connors, an affable guy who played Mannix on the series of that name. My mother couldn't believe she was meeting Mannix!

Mike asked the first question: "Did you always know, Mrs. Mahoney, that Suzanne was going to be a star?"

My mother just sat there staring at him, and after what seemed like an eternity, she stammered, "Suzanne was always very obedient."

Mike looked at her, not quite knowing how to respond, so he asked, "Right, but was it inevitable? Did you know early on that her life would take such an incredible turn?"

Once again my mother stammered, "Suzanne was always very obedient."

I could tell she was losing it. I was afraid she was going to faint from fear.

She had memorized that I was obedient, and that was all she could remember under the pressure. Then she blurted out, "I can't do this."

I thought she was going to cry. I pulled the bedsheet up under my chin, saying to the TV set, "Yes, you can, Mom, yes you can."

Mike took her hand and said, "Yes, you can, Marion." But her fear was so palpable, so emotional, that to protect her, they cut to commercial.

My mother was mortified. When I called her, she began to cry that she had let me down. But actually she had touched the hearts of viewers. Here was this pretty, very pure and simple woman who honestly could not take the spotlight. It was endearing, and throughout the day, everyone who called me started the conversation with "Your mother is so sweet!"

We humans are comprised of a complexity of emotions that often collide with our intellects.

My mother's appearance was probably the best thing she could have done for me. No one mentioned Robin Williams's mother or Tom Selleck's mother, just mine. People wrote and talked about her saying, "This is where Suzanne Somers gets her sweetness."

My beautiful sweet mother had saved me in my childhood. While she couldn't keep us safe from the monster who was my father on alcohol, she built me up in ways that were true and honest. She had always believed I could do anything and told me so often. Whether I knew it or not at the time, she had instilled it in my core. Deep down, when you know you have someone who believes in you, you gain an inner strength. It's what got me through. She loved me unconditionally. In looking back, I had quite a support system: Alan, my mother, Bruce, my sister and brother. I didn't know how much I was going to be needing their support a short distance down the road.

Early one morning I woke up to the phone ringing. It was my press agent, Jay Bernstein, and he sounded very anxious: "You're all over the *Enquirer. Playboy* found some nude test shots of you, and they've published them. Now Ace Hardware wants to fire you on a morals clause."

"Fire me? Why?" I asked, bewildered.

"They feel you are no longer the right, clean, wholesome image for them."

I thought back on that horrible trip to Mexico. I thought of the desperation, timidity, and fear that had led me to that waterfall. "But I never shot the actual pictures! I walked away," I protested.

> When you know you have someone who believes in you, you gain an inner strength. It's what got me through.

"Doesn't matter," Jay said. "My guess is that someone sold you out."

I sat at the breakfast table feeling despondent. Here I was at the top of my game, beyond my wildest imaginings, and now I was being brought down by a silly mistake from years ago. I frantically called Alan, who was in Vancouver taping his talk show. As usual, he found the positive. "This isn't the end of the world—we can use it and make it work for you. When they ask why you did it, you tell them the truth. You did it because you were a single teenage mother, with no child support; you had a drunken father. You had to fend for yourself financially, and this was a chance to bail yourself out of debt from your child's doctor's bills."

The phone rang again. It was Jay. "Now ABC and *Three's Company* are in talks as to whether they should fire you." At that time, Vanessa Williams had lost her Miss America crown because someone had dug out some old nude photos of her, so I knew this could be a reality.

"Here's what I think you should do," Jay explained. "I want you to drive downtown to AP"—the Associated Press—"and meet with Vernon Scott." He was a powerful entertainment writer back then. "Explain to him why you did this. If it comes from you and not your people, it will mean more to him."

"Okay," I said. "I'll do it."

I drove to downtown Los Angeles and the Associated Press building and went upstairs. "May I speak with Vernon Scott, please?" I asked the receptionist. My heart was pounding. Jay had called him and told him I was coming, but I didn't know that.

"Suzanne, come on in," said Vernon. He had a nice manner about him. "This is a surprise. I've never had the star of the number one show in America come to me. Normally I have to beg to come to you." I laughed half-heartedly, then dove in.

"Thank you for seeing me. I'm in a heap of trouble, and I thought if I could explain my story, maybe you'd write about it in a way that I don't lose my career."

I sat with Vernon for the next couple of hours. I told him about my childhood and the violence and my father's crazy nightly rages, I told him about getting pregnant as a teenager, and about leaving home because I was so ashamed that I had embarrassed my family. I told him how on my wedding night, my father drunkenly yelled at me, "I always knew you'd get knocked up!" I told him that I had had no help financially, that I had had a scholarship to college but had to leave in the middle of my first year because I was going to have a baby. That I was a Catholic and abortion was not an option, and that I was so glad I had made that decision. I told him of my life with my little boy and that I did any job available to just try and keep the two of us in the basics. I told him how one day I stupidly let my little boy play outside in the driveway of our little rented house with his new toy, and he lost control of it, and it shot out into the street just as a car was coming over the hill. And that the driver ran right over him. That I heard the screeching brakes and then someone pounding on my front door and I remembered picking up his little lifeless head and not knowing if he was dead or alive.

I told him about the ambulance and the ER and being told by the doctor that he had a fifty-fifty chance of survival, and that I had never in my life felt more shame and remorse, and that I would have gladly given my life for his at that moment. That it was the lowest point of my life. I told him I prayed all night for my son to make it; and that when the doctor came out of surgery and told me he was going to live, I broke down in sobs. I told him how they told me to go home to change my clothes because I had been there for twenty-four hours and I was barefoot and covered in blood.

I told Vernon about my son's long struggle to heal, and that when it was all over, I had twenty thousand dollars' worth of doctors' bills, and no insurance from anyone, and was being hounded by bill collectors. And that that was when I got this job in Mexico, and the photographer said I could make fifteen thousand dollars if I took my clothes off. I told him how nervous I was being naked, and that when I finally was chosen to be a Playmate centerfold, I got all the way to the front door of the *Playboy* building and decided not to do it. And here we were today. Now they'd printed those awful test pictures, and Ace Hardware was going to fire me, and ABC and *Three's Company* were right now in meetings about firing me, and it all just didn't seem fair. And then I sobbed. I sobbed in Vernon Scott's office until I was so embarrassed that I stood up, thanked him for listening to me, and left.

I cried all the way home. It had all come flooding back: all the pain, all the fear, all the shit from all the years of hiding in the closet and being the object of town gossip because I had gotten pregnant. The feeling that everyone made fun of me and would again. It didn't seem to matter that I had done the right thing and hadn't taken the pictures, or that it had been a breakthrough to turn it down because I finally thought more of myself. It wouldn't matter that after all I'd gone through, I had made it big. Now I was being brought down, and it was suffocating and just didn't feel fair.

I was all over the news that night. The phrase *morals clause* was repeated over and over. The president of Ace Hardware issued a public statement (I'm paraphrasing) that they were very disappointed in me and that I was not the type of person they wanted to represent their company.

Out of every negative comes a positive.

They were canceling my contract. The advertisers for *Three's Company* threatened to pull out if they kept me on the show. The producers freaked and began the process of cutting me loose. I had become a pariah. I was asked not to come to work. Nobody came to my defense. No one from the show spoke out. I was on my own.

I couldn't wait for Alan to fly home from Vancouver that night. I needed him to hold me. How had this happened? One moment you were on top of the heap, and the next moment you were the garbage.

I had no more tears left. And then Vernon Scott's column came out. I'm paraphrasing the column:

How come we don't take better care of our girls in this country? What did she do that was so wrong? What would you have done in the same position? She was destitute, yet when faced with the opportunity to make the money, she walked away.

And now these people take advantage of her enormous success, and like a meat grinder with no thought of how this affects a career, her son, her family, she is exposed for being something she is not. I spent two hours with her, and I feel nothing but compassion for Miss Somers. She is a fine person who never asked for anybody to take care of her. She did it all by herself and I admire Miss Somers. She deserves another chance.

He explained the entire story, sharing what I had told him in his office. His humanity touches me to this day.

Then the floodgates opened. The public outcry was so enormous that the president of Ace Hardware was forced to make a public apology. He went to Tiffany's and bought me a very expensive pair of diamond earrings. He made nice and made sure the public knew about it, and the advertisers for *Three's Company* all did the same. I was the headline for days afterward. Everyone wanted to interview me about how far I had come.

And *Playboy* apologized and offered me fifty thousand dollars in restitution.

In 1979 Barbara Walters asked me to be one of three guests on her prestigious twice-yearly special, along with Sylvester Stallone and Steven Spielberg (heady company). Being featured on her show was an indicator of success. The awful episode hadn't taken me down—instead it brought me to newer heights. A crazy business, but it did show that a heartfelt belief of mine is right: Out of every negative comes a positive. My embarrassment at having those photos published, and the accompanying public support, catapulted me into a new arena. Clearly Jay Bernstein's advice to pour my heart out had been brilliant.

I went back to work, and strangely no one involved with the show ever talked about it, as if it hadn't happened. But our ratings skyrocketed. It's hard to get any higher than number one, but all this new publicity and focus brought in more and more viewers. *Three's Company* was a blockbuster hit, and I had a lot to do with it. I had survived and come out on top.

But I knew I'd never be the same. The episode gave me an even deeper appreciation of all I had and the knowledge of how easily it could all be taken away. That week the audience gave me a long standing ovation. They wouldn't stop clapping. "We love you, Chrissy!" they chanted. I was deeply moved. The producers stood in the wings smiling big smiles, which is why what happened next was so startling.

CHAPTER 11

FIRED

You've done it before and you can do it now. Redirect the
substantial energy of your frustration and turn it into
positive, effective, unstoppable determination.
—RALPH MARSTON, *THE DAILY MOTIVATOR*

In my fifth year (technically it was the sixth season, but the first season had been only six weeks), my original contract was up and needed renegotiating. In any business, it's standard to renegotiate a new deal when a contract is about to expire. In my case, the pay I had accepted in my original eagerness to have a job, any job, was no longer commensurate with the success I'd had personally and with the show's tremendous success.

Alan and I discussed what we thought would be fair. I was earning a mere 10 percent of what male stars with less popular shows were making, and I wanted to be paid commensurately. At that time, most women were making much less than men in every walk of life. With all the strides women have made since then, that's still too true. But if you do the job well, or in my case if you're selling tickets, you should be paid fairly and equally regardless of what sex you happened to be on the day you were born. In my job, I was selling more tickets than most of the male actors in the TV business.

Alan set up a meeting with the ABC lawyers, himself, and our lawyer. Mickey Ross, my producer and mentor, would also be attending. Mickey clearly felt I was successful because of him. He was also irrationally resentful and jealous of my husband, having decided that Alan was a Svengali and that if he weren't around, I would be much easier to control. It was frankly insulting. I now got how the business worked. Alan had been through this before in Canada, when he was their biggest TV star. He understood how it worked, that big ratings equaled money and profits.

We both felt I deserved parity with actors who had had similar success. Alan kept repeating: "You are a ratings bonanza. With all your outside promotion, you keep bringing in more and more viewers. You bring great value to this show." He was always at work behind the scenes, drumming up the promotion. He loved the game, and while I was at rehearsal, he would take lunch with the right people to promote me and our business. He met regularly with producers who wanted me for their movies.

John and Joyce had no publicity machine—they came to work and gave 100 percent. Occasionally they went to celebrity parties and got paparazzi action, but they were not actively going after promotion. Alan and I were deliberately seeking publicity to make the most of my work, our business. We were working to make my success in the present as strong as possible while also setting the stage for what could happen after the show ended. Most often an actor has a great run on a successful series, and then when it's over, they fade away. There are hundreds of those stories. Alan's theory was that *Three's Company* was a business opportunity and the springboard for a long-term multifaceted career.

On the morning of the negotiation meeting, I was filled with nervousness. I was rocking the boat, yet I believed I deserved what I was asking for.

As Alan walked out the front door, he stopped uncharacteristically and looked back at me, hesitating for a moment. Then he said, "You know, this could all blow up."

I dismissed the thought and said adamantly, "No way—I'm Chrissy Snow. They're not going to want to get rid of Chrissy Snow!"

And off he went.

All morning I sat in my living room, anxiously waiting for Alan to come home. Cell phones hadn't been invented yet. It was a long three hours.

There is a way the front door opens with good news, and then there is a way it opens with bad news. With good news, the door gets slammed, and you hear footsteps running up the stairs excitedly. That didn't happen. I heard the front door open very slowly, then close very slowly. I heard his footsteps slowly, deliberately coming up the three flights of stairs. I met him at the landing, and he looked ashen.

"You're out" was all he said.

I walked into the ABC office, and it was filled with people: the producer Mickey Ross, network guys, and some lawyer dick in a Stetson and cowboy boots. I hate that posturing shit! This asshole was no Roy Rogers. I don't remember if Tony Thomopoulos was there, the president of the network. Hard to believe he was in on this insanity, but he must have been.

I could feel their wrath, it was palpable. I could also feel their trembling anticipation to blurt out that Suzanne Somers was fired, so get out of here. My words, their actions. At least that's how I saw it.

I walked out of that meeting on stun. I couldn't believe that this gang of producers and the network's top management had chosen to recklessly dismantle, sacrifice, and totally destroy the greatest chemistry on TV at that time. Just so they could scare the shit out of other women thinking of asking for salary parity with men.

I don't remember much about my drive home that day. My brain was on fire and screaming. I still couldn't believe the blind stupidity of what had just happened. I knew Suzanne would be decimated, disappointed, angry, and unbelieving. Now to tell Suzanne . . .

As I was pulling into the garage, I realized there was no easy way to tell her that she was out—out, out, out! As I opened the door to our beach house, I felt I had really let her down. I hated every step I took up to the third floor, where she was waiting. But she knew . . . she just knew.

We stared at each other for a long time.

"You're out."

"I'm OUT?"

"You're out."

I held Suzanne and kissed her head. I knew that this gaggle of morons, after all their high-fiving got old, would wonder, What the hell have we done?!

W hat a shock. OUT!

All I had done was ask! I'd had no idea that I was going to be the patsy so that no other woman on TV would get uppity and have the audacity to ask for the same.

The network backed up the producers. Paying me parity would have set a new tone in TV, so best to keep the women in their place. Only the men got high salaries and, in specific cases, ownership percentages. And unlike today, when network TV executives are heavily populated with bright women, in the 1970s there were very few. If this happened today, the producers and the network would be slapped with a lawsuit for conspiring against women. Or at the very least, they would suffer the embarrassment of being sexist, misogynistic pigs.

In retrospect, we'd been warned. The night before the lawyers' meeting, a senior ABC executive with the parent company (a friend of a friend) had called Alan and said, "You didn't hear this from me, but *Laverne & Shirley* just renegotiated and really got the network big time. ABC is 'going to hang a nun in the marketplace' to show all women on their network what will happen to them if they dare to expect and ask for men's money . . . and Suzanne is *it*."

After Alan told me what happened, I was too shocked to cry. He told me not to worry, that we would use this to work *for* us. He had a plan. The press tried to turn Alan Hamel into a Svengali, "the guy who ruined Suzanne Somers's career." Interviewers would ask me if I was angry with him. "Why would I be angry?" I'd answer. "I urged him to do this."

The whole thing was extremely hurtful for me. I had been a professional on the set. I'd helped bring great ratings to the show. I'd always been prepared. But I made one fatal mistake: I'd thought these people cared about me. This was business, baby! Feelings weren't a part of it; my feelings weren't important.

I went from being the darling of TV to the object of the worst publicity campaign ever. It started with the *Hollywood Reporter,* Army Archerd's column; he was a popular Hollywood reporter. "Greedy" was its content. And then it got worse: "Who does she think she is?" was the mantra. The show's spin was that I was "trying to ruin their show," and "Everyone knew that the real star of the show was John Ritter."

One day soon after I was fired I was crossing Rodeo Drive in Beverly Hills and saw the show's wardrobe person walking toward me. He was the one I worked with daily to create Chrissy's look. We had had such a good time together. When he saw me approaching, he did an about-face and crossed the street. Unbelievable. It was like I was an ax murderer or something.

John and Joyce turned on me in a way that shocked me. Their rejection was particularly painful. The producers had made it clear to the cast that they were either with me and against them, or with them and against me. No one from the show would speak to me again, not for decades. That's how petty it all became.

Years later the head of a major independent syndication group told me that in the industry, this event was known as "the dumbest self-inflicted catastrophe in modern television history." This insane, macho, sexist, ego-driven, amateurish, gigantic fuckin' blunder cost the network and producers hundreds of millions of dollars and premature cancellation of the series. That show should have run for ten or twelve years. By firing Suzanne, the number one woman on the number one TV show, they blew through more than one billion dollars in network licensing and back-end syndication.

But for now, after dumping the biggest star on television, this gang of amateurs brought in their PR people to destroy Suzanne in the media for being a "greedy bitch." It was personal: First, we'll fire her, and then we'll make sure she never works again. Heh heh heh . . . toil, trouble, boil and bubble.

*T*hree's Company aired for another three years but with greatly reduced ratings. Viewers wanted the original chemistry. Mickey, with his giant ego, said to the network, "I trained Suzanne Somers, and I can train another blonde like a seal."

To add insult to injury the producers and the network had to humiliate me. It was not enough for this gang to fire me, to destroy me; they also had to make me grovel. They held back the remaining money they owed me for the season, and threatened a lawsuit if I didn't finish out the season. They forced me to show up every Friday and shoot a two-to-three-minute spot to run at the end of that week's episode.

I had to be walked into the studio through the back door by a security guard, who waited and then walked me back out afterward. The badly lit set, behind our original studio, consisted of a wing chair, a floor lamp, and a little table with a telephone. It was eerily silent and quiet except for my one camera. I had to do a one-way conversation with the "kids" back at the apartment, telling them my aunt was still sick and I hoped I'd be home soon. These clips gave the audience the feeling that I was coming back, and the show could use my name in the credits, even though they had a replacement girl living in the apartment now.

But mainly it was to humiliate me, put me in my place. I wasn't allowed access to any of the cast. I was scheduled to arrive when everyone took their lunch break. I knew they all could watch what was going on with the set from their monitors in their dressing rooms and offices; and for sure they were watching the macabre scene taking place.

I dreaded Fridays. I'd wake up and drag myself to the studio. I did my own hair and makeup. Clothes were laid out for me, but with no assistance to make sure they fit and worked for TV, and they weren't the darling outfits I'd been wearing on the show. Each week's appearance was torturous and emotional for me. I was being treated like a criminal by everyone involved: cast, crew, hair, makeup, producers, network executives. Even the lighting was crappy; like they were trying to steal my beauty.

Between the show and the extracurricular publicity and other projects, I had been working nonstop day and night. I went from that to nothing. Nothing! Couldn't get a job. Couldn't get an interview. Shunned. I stopped getting invited to Hollywood events. Not one woman in TV or film backed me up. I was out there alone, the talk of the town. I was a joke.

It was and still is unbelievable; Suzanne was all alone. No one came to her defense. They tried to knock her down, but instead it brought out that fighting Irish in her to overcome and succeed and blow away the crap along with the toxic people.

She never said it, but I will: Where were the women in TV and film? Where were all those women's organizations to stand with Suzanne, a modern suffragette who was looking for parity with men just like the suffragettes were looking for the right to vote? The National Organization for Women. Where were they? Where was Women in Film? Not a peep.

These women's advocacy groups and a dozen others were cherry-picking which women they would support, and "that dumb blonde on that dumb show" didn't deserve their participation. And where were all the female TV and movie stars of the 1970s? Not one phone call. Not one note. Nothing!

We didn't need their support because the real women of America, the ones that Suzanne speaks to, were on her side. Frankly, I had no idea yet where this was going to go.

But . . . Suzanne is a big-time survivor!

When she had no rent money? She sold her clothes.

No money at all? She made a chicken last a week.

Slap her down? Meet a great counterpuncher.

When Suzanne got a job with a lawyer, sure, she knew shorthand and could type a thousand words a minute. But when you looked like twenty-year-old Suzanne, you didn't need credentials to get a job in a nerdy lawyer's office. First day the guy dictated a letter. Suzanne took it down in shorthand, couldn't read it back, grabbed her coat and purse, and sneaked out. She tried being a waitress, now known as a server, but couldn't stack and lost the job. She made clothes for a kids' store, but the work was so detailed and beautiful, she lost money on every sale.

She'd auditioned as a weather girl at a San Francisco TV station, this incredible, gorgeous woman with no bra, a miniskirt, and eyes that would make you cash bad checks. "So it looks like it might be kinda cold over here," she'd said, "but this area looks like it's going to be okay." They laughed at her and said, "Next!" Today all the weather girls look slightly south of escort service ladies. They are beautiful and beautifully styled and ready for a fabulous and elegant night on the town. If they'd hired her, their eleven o'clock news would have skyrocketed.

She never gives up. If something doesn't work, she regroups, reinvents, and tries again. She is a shmoo, an Energizer bunny. Upbeat. Never defeated.

I told her I'd work my ass off to make sure our future would be of our making and that we would not be dependent on anyone else. That she wouldn't stay down for long. That together we would figure out how to make this work for her. That we would control our business, build a solid career bigger than ever, and have fun.

Yes—fun!

A few years after I was fired, I ran into Norman Fell, who had played Mr. Roper on *Three's Company*, at Chinois, a famous Wolfgang Puck restaurant in Venice, California. By the time I left the show, Norman had already gone on to his own spin-off show, so we had no problem—he hadn't been involved with the craziness. When I went over to his table, I was struck by how much he had aged. There was something about his demeanor I found vulnerable, and I realized I was patting his head tenderly. "Norman," I asked, "why do you think they're still so angry with me?"

Norman paused and looked up at me and said: "'Cause you didn't flunk." He was astute: they had wanted me to tank, to fall hard. Sadly, Norman passed away shortly after I saw him. RIP Norman. He was a sweetie.

In 2003 John Ritter called me out of the blue to ask if I would guest star in a dream sequence on his series, *8 Simple Rules*. I was so moved to hear his voice again after all those years of silence, even though he started the phone call with "Look, babe, I forgive you." I kind of choked on that one but decided to let it go. It would open an argument that couldn't be won. He believed what he believed, and I felt misunderstood. I told him that from many letters and comments I had received over the years, the public felt cheated by our unfinished business together. I said that if we announced a real project starring John Ritter and Suzanne Somers, it would be big news and very enthusiastically received. He agreed with me; we would find a project.

Sadly, a month later, September 11, 2003, I got the tragic news that he had died. His tragic and untimely death was a loss not only to his family but to show-business and to the viewing public. Had he been allowed to live, I often imagine what he had yet to achieve. I'm extremely grateful that we had that last contact—it was very healing.

ABC wanted me to fall hard, but I'm a shmoo! I got back up and dusted myself off. Besides, I had been through worse. I remembered the closet. I remembered the words of Mrs. Kilgore: *The worst is over.* I kept repeating that to myself.

Do you know what a shmoo is? My brother Danny got one for Christmas one year. It's a life-size inflated punching doll with a clown face and sand on the bottom to weigh it down. You hit it and it bounces back, you hit it again and it bounces back—again and again. It doesn't matter how many times you hit it, it always bounces back up. Thankfully, I am a shmoo.

In life, when you believe in your gut and your heart that you're right, you can't care what others say or think. And when you have a loyal life partner like Alan, you can become a powerful force that no one can knock down. We had played it straight, played by the rules, but were brought down by people who were having a moment drunk with their power. We decided from that moment on, we would live our life a new way, us against the world. We would never work for anyone ever again. We would use this negative like judo, using forward energy to win.

> I held my head high, and Alan and I supported each other in our resolve to turn this negative into a positive.

I held my head high, and Alan and I supported each other in our resolve to turn this negative into a positive. Arm in arm, we decided we would begin the next phase of our incredible life journey together and that it was going to be fun. We decided not to look back, only forward. Although I didn't know it right then, I was going to bounce back with a brand-new career in Vegas where I would become the talk of the town. But this time in a good way

WHAT I KNOW NOW

Obstacles are opportunities to be moved out of the way. Anyone can be a shmoo. It's about choices. In my case, I could fold, or I could use this awful, unfair experience as rocket-fuel to propel me forward. I needed to take a little time (but not too long) to lick my wounds and heal. Then I would start all over again with the full resolve to win.

CHAPTER 12

VEGAS, BABY!

It's hard to beat someone who won't give up.
—BABE RUTH

It took some time to adjust to no longer being on the show or on TV at all for that matter. Lots of articles were being written about me as a major screw-up, the dumb blonde who was really dumb! Today this notion makes me laugh. But back then I went through so many emotions, and for a time it was difficult to stay upbeat; losing my part on *Three's Company* was a golden opportunity that slipped through my fingers. I had lost all the power I never fully knew I had. I had taken for granted that I was in hot demand, but now clearly TV was off the table. I sat in our beach house filled with self-pity. I was bored, pissed off, hurt, and mad at myself. Who *did* I think I was? *Why had I rocked the boat? Should I have done something else?* (This was the licking-my-wounds phase.) No, I was in the right. But why had something so positive turned so destructive, so quickly?

Then one day sitting in my living room looking out at the ocean—it was a gray, overcast, rainy kind of day—I heard a voice in my head. You know those *voices*? We all have them, but we don't always listen. "It" said, *Why are you focused on what you don't have? Why don't you focus on what you do have?*

The notion stopped me. *What do I have?* I scoured my thoughts and quietly heard the answer: *You have enormous visibility. Everyone in this country and in many parts of the world knows your name.* It was like having my shoulders shaken. *Everyone does know my name.* How could I have been sitting here stupidly wasting this time feeling sorry for myself? My fame, my enormous visibility, was a tangible thing. It had value. It was a tremendous gift, a leg up. It would open the right doors. I was now a curiosity.

"I'd like to play Vegas," I blurted out to Alan.

He jokingly asked if I could sing.

I laughed. "Why don't you tell them I had the lead in *Guys and Dolls* in high school!" Ha ha! But he knew I could sing. I had never stopped singing. I sang around the house, I sang in the shower, I sang in the car, I sang at Big Al's Bar at home. During my years on the series, I had sung with many people on various TV specials, all the greats, and I loved it.

Alan thought it was a great idea, and that a nostalgia would draw people to see me live since I had been ripped out of their TV screens every week. At that time TV was at the center of most people's lives. In today's world, it's difficult to comprehend the meaning of the TV set and the TV schedule. In that era most people memorized what shows were on each evening and their time slots and layouts. They planned their nights and their weeks' activities around their favorite TV programs.

With that in mind, Alan set out for Vegas. His first meeting was with the entertainment director at the Riviera hotel. He was offered a two-week deal at big money. Same thing happened at the Desert Inn; two weeks, big money. They saw the potential for curiosity from the public but didn't want to commit long-term in case I was a bust.

Alan then went to the MGM Grand. The president at that time was Bernie Rothkopf, a gruff guy with a soft heart underneath. "What do you want?" he asked Alan, almost hostile.

"I want a two-year deal for Suzanne Somers."

Bernie answered, "No one gets a two-year deal."

Alan explained that that was what he wanted because he knew me, and even though I had never done this before, if I fell on my ass the first few times, I would eventually succeed. He explained that I succeeded at everything I tried. Something about Alan's confidence and demeanor intrigued Bernie, so they shook hands and made a deal *that day* for two years. Alan said, "I don't care what the money is." As it turned out, the money was very impressive. In fact, it was better money than what I had asked for that got me fired!

I opened in March 1980, and my show was a hit. From day one, the reviews were outstanding, and the people came. They flocked to the MGM. We sold out night after night.

We had put together an extraordinary show, and now we were in charge. Of all of it. No one would be in the position of taking it all away from me, from us, ever again. Alan and I found that we loved working together. He handled all the business, advertising, and marketing; together we handled the creative. I knew what I wanted to do, but Alan had the objective eye for what fit me the best. I trusted him. And why not? He had my best interests at heart. Together we hired the best in the business: choreographers, costumers, musicians, a musical director, and writers. (A lot of them came from Alan's old comedy days in Canada; they loved the opportunity to work with him again.) I loved all of them. They were terrific professionals, true funny men.

I've got to say, never has it been so good for a woman in business as it is for me. The kind of collaboration we have is what all the women in our business want: a true and trusted partner to help navigate the terrain. Maybe I was the first woman in TV to have the gall to ask for parity with the men, but I'm the kind of soft feminist who wants an equal role with the men in my life. I want to work *with* them. I like men. There are things my husband does better than me. He's better with numbers and with the bottom line, strategy, and vision. I want that from him. To know that he's got my back has so much to do with my admiration and respect for him. We each have different strengths.

Women and men are meant to complement each other. One of the great teachers of this concept is John Gray, author of *Men Are from Mars, Women Are from Venus*. It takes an understanding of our differences and accepting each other's strengths to bring out the best in each other. As for a business and love relationship—our figure eight, never ending, never beginning—we realize we both bring something valuable to the table. I believe this is a major reason for the balance Alan and I have found in our relationship. We allow each other to do what we do best without ego. I don't get in his way, and he doesn't get in mine. It all comes from love and wanting the best for each other.

One of our big decisions, in the way Suzanne and I work together, happened after I was introduced to one of the biggest female stars in Hollywood. She wanted to work with me "the way you work with Suzanne." (Do I also have bed privileges?)

I told Suzanne. And that night in bed in the dark and after some silence I heard:

"Al?"

Whenever I hear "Al" in the dark, I know I'm in for a special announcement.

"Yes?"

"I don't think there's any room in our relationship for her . . . !"

I was never going to work with this woman even though it would have been interesting. Suzanne was my one and only.

Back to Vegas: we had a ball, night after night. This was a life I never knew existed, and it fit both Alan and me perfectly. We were the toast of the town. It was glamorous. Billboards promoting my show were all over the Vegas Strip, including on the highways leading in. You couldn't miss them, and it became the new show everyone had to see.

In Suzanne's words: "This is the most fun I have ever had . . . EVER!!" She was fulfilling her childhood dream of becoming a big star on stage. Her mother was sitting in the front row, proudly smiling up at her. I was happy for her. This was the early 1980s. Now, thirty-six years later, she still loves performing live on stage. Last week she played to a sold-out crowd of five thousand enthusiastic admirers, who kept her on stage with an extended standing ovation.

We met everyone who worked in Vegas. We were invited to Sinatra's dressing room after his closing shows on Sunday nights. I was awestruck. We met all the greats, and we stayed up late going to other shows on the Strip. Soon the pain of losing *Three's Company* was a thing of the past. I realized that being fired only made me bigger in the eyes of the public (as Alan had told me it would). I had garnered so much publicity by the time of my leaving, even though so much of it was negative, that the cumulative effect was powerful. I learned that all publicity is good publicity (as long as you haven't murdered anyone ☺). Negative PR hurts and stings personally in the moment, but as time passes, the public often remembers only that you exist and should be paid attention to in a big way.

Out of necessity, we forged something that might not have happened without the firing. We were on our own. Suddenly working for ourselves had the upside of allowing us to arrange our schedule around our family. We would book two weeks on and then be off for two weeks. The weeks we were in Vegas, we would fly our children in to be with us on weekends. They loved the life. As you can imagine, being backstage with all these amazing talents was very exciting for our teens. When they were in school, we worked; when they were on break or summer vacation, we either took them with us or stayed home.

We tried to keep our home life as normal as possible. All during the *Three's Company* years, I rarely went to Hollywood events on weekends, choosing instead to spend time at home and be a mother. We still invited close family friends and relatives for Sunday afternoon lunches, and these were very special days for all of us, where we got to connect. Our blended family was working. Feelings were still tender, but we gave everyone their space and time to adjust, we didn't push or force it, and we were making progress. In the summers, we took the show on the road, performing mostly back east. Bruce and Stephen loved being part of the crew. Leslie was very involved in her art and design at Parsons School of Design. Even though the boys were young, they were good roadies and were having fun. We had become a family business. And we were happy.

> *In life, you can't look back. The longer I live, the more I realize that it all happens as is supposed to be. That there is a perfection in each moment and in each lesson. We learn as we go along; we screw up and succeed when we are ready.*

I was honored to be named Vegas Female Entertainer of the Year by Ron Delpit, who coordinated the voting each year. The male entertainer of that year was Frank Sinatra. Imagine how I felt sharing this incredible award with the greatest entertainer of all time! I had come a long way.

I let all the anger and pain of the firing fade. I deliberately let it all go. I wouldn't and couldn't let it affect me negatively any longer. I began to be grateful once again for all that Mickey Ross and the others on set had taught me. He had been a great teacher during the time that we were meant to be together. In life, you can't look back. The longer I live, the more I realize that it all happens as is supposed to be. That there is a perfection in each moment and in each lesson. We learn as we go along; we screw up and succeed when we are ready. The people in our lives are there for a reason. Mickey was a great teacher not only for the comedy he taught me to "hear" but for the emotional work I needed to learn to move forward as a person.

The Vegas years!

With Tanya, the elephant.

On stage with
my dad at the
Las Vegas Hilton.

I loved my
chicken suit!

Feeling *hot, hot, hot*
with my dancers!

Fabulous designs by Leslie Hamel.

One of the great honors of my career was entertaining our troops.

My *fabulous* ladies from twenty-five years on shopping channels.

Receiving my star with Les Moonves, Barry, and Alan.

The family on Phil Donahue's show for my book *Keeping Secrets*.

My other great husband, Patrick Duffy, from *Step by Step*.

My Broadway musical, *The Blonde in the Thunderbird*.

Family is everything—after the Malibu fire.

Sex in the City 2 premiere.

With the fabulous Dr. Oz.

One of my incredible book tours.
Al always has my back.

Left: Back in Vegas!

Right: *Dancing with the Stars!*

Alan with Stephen and our grandson.

Our talented and beautiful daughter, Leslie.

We have the best time with our grandkids!

My son, Bruce, and his beautiful wife, Caroline.

Bruce . . . didn't he grow up great?

Uber talented and superhot, Tom Ford.

Shared so many laughs with Merv Griffin.

The iconic Dick Van Dyke.

The world's sweetest man, Don Rickles.

My seventieth birthday at Big Al's Bar.

And the love goes
on and on. . . .

He hurt me, but I chose not to own it. Mickey was one more person I had to forgive to move on in my life. To fly, I needed to gain perspective and see it all for what it was. My time with him was brief but ultimately an exquisite life lesson. I grew as a result and became more as a person; rather than stay angry, I became grateful for the show and for Mickey, both of which gave me the greatest platform of my life, one that lasts until today.

People still stop and tell me how much they loved me on *Three's Company* and that they still watch it in reruns today. That piece of my life's work will never go away because in today's world, content has found a permanent home on and through the Internet.

Our life after *Three's Company* had turned into a whirlwind of activity. I had no idea of the future, that my career was going to broaden in a way I never imagined, that I would meet kings, princes, and presidents, that I would become a global health advocate selling millions of books worldwide and meet amazing people from all walks of life. But what made it so satisfying was the greatest of all these amazing things that happened: I was married to the love of my life, the most perfect husband and partner I could have hoped for.

> First they ignore you, then they laugh at you,
> then they fight you, and then you win.
> —MAHATMA GANDHI

One day, Alan received a phone call from Henri Lewin, president of the Hilton Las Vegas. As Alan tells it . . .

Henri told me he had a bomb on his hands called The Moulin Rouge, *which had a cast of sixty. Every night there were more people on stage than in the audience, and they were dying big time and bleeding money. Aside from paying for the nightly production, he was paying a big royalty to the French family that owned the original Moulin Rouge in Paris. He asked if we would meet him at the hotel and see the show. So we boarded the Hilton jet, and an hour later, we were with Henri in his office.*

That night we saw the show; it was predictable but great. Lots of feathers and headdresses and half-naked beauties roamed the stage, with live fire and French music and great lighting. I really enjoy extravaganzas with great-looking showgirls.

Henri, in his German accent, asked, "So . . . ?"

I suggested Suzanne open and close the show—do her personal cabaret act in the middle of The Moulin Rouge. *We'd launch a gigantic promotional campaign with dozens of billboards, TV spots, TV appearances, and loads of print—plus my own secret promotional campaign. "It'll cost a fortune, but it'll work, I promise."*

Henri asked how I was so sure, and I told him there was no way I was going to miss the opportunity to work with spectacularly beautiful women prancing around half naked every night. Plus, the formula was simple: a big star, a big show, the right price—it had to work.

A lan loves being around beautiful women. We have a look-but-don't-touch rule, and I've never worried. Sounds cocky, but truly he only has eyes for me. He got his serial dating out of his system in all the years before me. When you are "Mr. Canada," the women are plentiful.

When we married, I told Suzanne that I love women, all women. I told her I didn't want to be one of those husbands who sees a beautiful woman and has to take furtive glances when his wife is not looking. I told her I want to openly admire interesting-looking women and I promised her I would only look and not touch. Suzanne was cool with that. Opening night came, and every one of the sixteen hundred seats was sold out. The audience was already lining up for the midnight show, the line snaking around the slots and tables in the casino. Henri kept asking me about my secret promotional campaign, so I met him for a drink and divulged what I had done. My campaign was based on the thinking that everyone flying into Vegas asks their cab driver what's hot in town. I figured that every cab likely picked up dozens of passengers. What better way to spread the word than through the grass roots?

I jumped in a cab and told the cabbie to take me to Caesars. On the way, I told him I'd just seen the greatest show in Vegas, and I'd seen them all: Suzanne Somers was incredible! At Caesars, I jumped into another cab, and on the way to the Riviera, I told that cabbie about Suzanne's must-see show. At the Riviera, I jumped into another cab and did it again on my way to the Desert Inn. I kept doing it until the next cabbie told me, "Wow—someone else earlier this evening told me the same thing." Fortunately, he didn't remember it was me.

Suzanne did two two-hour shows a night, seven nights a week, for over two years, and every show was sold out. That's 1,600 seats x 2 x 7 = 22,400 tickets sold every week. It was the first time the Hilton had opened its balcony for seating since Elvis played the room. And as far as I know, Suzanne holds the record for selling more tickets than any other performer. After two years, she sold over two million tickets. (I may be challenged on that one, but 22,400 tickets every week is huge.)

We occupied Elvis's dressing room, and although Henri offered to replace everything, we opted for keeping it the way it was when Elvis lived there.

Elvis's former dressing room had orange shag carpets, a smoky gold mirror behind the bar, and orange leather bar stools. My dressing area was all mirrored. Night after night I would fix and fuss with my hair and makeup, always aware that Elvis had sat in the same chair two decades before me.

On opening night, there was a knock on the door, and in walked Colonel Parker, Elvis's lifelong manager. We spent two hours together and recognized a kindred spirit in each other. Later we'd spend dozens of wonderful evenings together, the Colonel spinning tales of managing Elvis and me loving it. He told me things I'd never heard or read about his life with Elvis, and they will go to the grave with me.

I told him about my secret promotional campaign, and he told me about his time as a carny working the dancing chickens tent. Was I impressed that he had trained chickens? Not quite. When the tent was full, about ten people, he would switch off the light, a spot would hit the chicken cage, and cowboy music would play. Within seconds, the chickens would start dancing, first slowly and then frantically. How? That switch also turned on a hot plate under the cage floor. PETA would have a field day with the dancing chickens today.

Chickens aside, it was a heady time. The hotel was doing so well, the word no never came up whenever we wanted anything for ourselves or for the show. Whenever we needed the Hilton jet—no problem. Suzanne could fly to San Francisco to have lunch with her mother if she chose. If we wanted to take the kids out to cruise around Lake Mead during the day, the Hilton yacht was ours.

Suzanne arrived onstage each night on a life-size train at the Hilton. When we did the show in Reno, she arrived on a 747. Big star, big show. People got their money's worth and loved it.

I loved being the star of *The Moulin Rouge,* and it was an extravaganza. I entered onstage on a life-size train caboose in a sexy white suit with a short skirt slit up to there, a fitted broad shoulder-padded jacket, pin-striped in silver bugle beads, wearing a big white hat with the same pinstripes and a white fox muff designed by Ret Turner. It was a real throwback to the old MGM 1940s movie musicals. At the "train station" were forty dancers, men and women all costumed in the look of the times. Two male dancers helped me off the caboose, and we danced and leaped and jumped in the style of old Hollywood.

For the next number, I appeared at the top of sixty stairs in a gorgeous floor-length gown of nude beads with a feather design; it was based on a costume of Gypsy Rose Lee. (Coincidentally, we had just purchased Gypsy Rose Lee's Beverly Hills estate.) The stairs were lined by fabulous-looking boys all in white top hats and tails, with arms outstretched to me as I sang "I Love Paris" and danced all the way down. The show kept unfolding, one fabulous number after another, and thirty minutes into the production I tap-danced onstage to "Boogie Woogie Bugle Boy" and spent the next thirty minutes onstage doing my cabaret act. I was all by myself singing and talking, then bringing a guy onstage and singing to him. We ended with a production number to "Sweet Georgia Brown," tap-dancing while jumping rope and dribbling a basketball. It was quite a feat. No surprise, I was in the best shape of my life.

The finale of *The Moulin Rouge* was me riding on one of the dearest friends I have ever known, Tanya, a nine-year-old elephant. She was a smart and beautiful animal, huge and gentle. Both Alan and I loved her so much that on our afternoons off we would go visit her. She was well cared for by her owner-trainer Yenda Schmaha, who provided a large barn for Tanya all to herself, with toys such as big tractor tires and a shower where she could wet herself down as often as she wanted. When we would visit her at home, she would run around her large corral like an excited kid. She would roll her tires at us and run through her shower. She could, and did, smile; it was so endearing.

When Tanya and I did the finale together, I wore a long red bugle-beaded gown, with a huge jeweled headdress, and Tanya had a matching saddle and headdress. I usually ran a little late getting into this costume, but Tanya was punctual. She would come over to my dressing room, squeeze through the door, and walk around impatiently until I was ready. We would ride up to the stage in the oversize elevator together. It all seemed very natural to me.

She was so human that it was easy to forget that she wasn't. When the elevator door opened, we were usually five minutes early, so I would talk to the dancers while Tanya waited at the curtain's edge for our music cue. She was so astute that when the time was getting near to our entrance, she would come over to me and impatiently dance in place. She'd get down on one knee so I could easily get on top of her. Then with no prodding, she would take me to the wing and wait for our cue. I was supposed to tap her when it was time to go, but it was never necessary. She knew the precise moment we were to make our entrance.

She would prance onstage, doing one big circle. Then she would gently and gracefully rear up on her hind legs, smile a big smile at the delighted audience, and gently, gently, gently, come down on one knee so I could easily slide off and take my bow. She would take her place behind me and let me have the applause. When the curtain closed, Tanya and I took the oversize elevator back down and returned to our side-by-side dressing rooms. While I removed my makeup and costumes, she was having her headdress and saddle removed, anxious for her big treat. She would wiggle through my dressing room door, knowing that all the cut-up fruit we ordered every night for the coffee table was hers. In literally one swoop, she would inhale the fruit.

Then Yenda, her trainer, along with Alan and me, would quietly ride up the elevator that led to the back parking lot, where her large custom truck was waiting for her. Tanya's trainer would always first allow her to romp in big circles in the parking lot, where she would run like an excited kid. When it was enough, Yenda would call her, and she would obediently slow down and waddle up the ramp to her truck. We would yell goodbye to her and then, exhausted, drive to our individual homes. It was usually around three a.m.

Imagine having a true relationship with an elephant! Two years after I left *The Moulin Rouge,* Alan and I stopped by the Hilton to see if Tanya remembered us. It was two a.m. when I climbed down the back stairs to visit. As I got close to her dressing room, I remember feeling nervous. What if she had forgotten me? I'd be so heartbroken. As I got closer, I called out "Tanya!" I rounded the corner, and she stood there and looked at me and Alan and started flapping her ears. We both went inside and rubbed the sweet spot under her neck. She nuzzled and cooed and rubbed her face against mine, and when I pulled back and looked at her, she had tears coming from her eyes. It was one of the most special moments of my life to have connected with this being; she is a girl I will never forget.

After the first year, we grew weary of living in a hotel room. The Hilton management was very generous and kept adding rooms to our suite to make it more homelike, but to me home is about a kitchen and the ability to cook our meals. We also had a cat named Fweddy (like Freddy with a lisp), who did not like living in a strange hotel room and was simultaneously going into heat or whatever you call it when your male cat starts howling. I'd always had outdoor female cats and knew when it was their time of the month by the night screams I would hear out the window.

But a male trapped in a hotel room who was acting like he was in heat was challenging. He started spraying everything, and our hotel suite smelled awful. We finally gave him his own room, where we turned on the TV to *National Geographic,* and Fweddy would lie there all day watching (and probably dreaming) of being with other animals or hunting them at least. So he settled in, and occasionally we'd order smoked salmon from room service for him. It was all we could do for the moment, but the whole thing was wrong. And smelly.

We decided to buy a house. I loved the Vegas life, so why not become Nevada residents and live in a real home? After several days of looking, we settled on an old run-down shack on a large piece of property, which was a few acres, about thirty-five minutes from the Vegas Strip. It appeared to be on flat ground but was actually elevated so that at night the lights of the city twinkled below us in the distance. We would have no neighbors, just a herd of wild horses that would occasionally come to our wall, led by a large, muscular stud. He would stand in place staring at us, then thunder off into the desert. It would be quiet and serene and exactly what we were looking for. We decided to enlarge and rebuild the shack as a cool adobe-style ranch. An adobe house would be the perfect place to display my small collection of turn-of-the-century Native American children's moccasins. Collecting is interesting because you don't plan on it—something just speaks to you. Over the years, I had found three pairs of turn-of-the-century Native American moccasins, and when we spent vacation weekends in Santa Fe, I would find another and then another. They went with the Navajo rugs I had been collecting since my teen years. It started when I was living in Sausalito; I had bought two Navajo Germantown rugs on layaway (this was before credit cards), paying them off with ten dollars here and there. I didn't know anything about the history of the rugs or the shoes, I just was taken by each piece, and a collection was born.

Alan and I are always so in sync, and building this home together was an exercise in compatibility. I've heard that decorating, building, and money are the areas where couples fight the most, but not us—we built on each other's ideas. I'd say, "How about placing the bedroom here?" and Alan would respond, "Great idea, and let's put an elevated sitting/fireplace room over in this corner." That turned out to be a great idea. That sexy little cushioned area with ottomans and a fireplace became a great place to wind down after the show on many nights. Some nights we would fall asleep there wrapped in each other's arms, covered by the Navajo blanket that was normally thrown casually on the sofa's back.

We ordered authentic latias and vigas (large, stripped-down pine logs) to be used as ceiling braces and for aesthetics. The walls were hand-rubbed unpainted adobe plaster, and the floors were hand-made twelve-inch-square terra-cotta tiles. The look was authentic, simple, and to my eye very beautiful. I re-covered our old pieces of furniture in off-white muslin, and the finished effect was plain and cool and very desert. I knew not to fight the desert, so instead of plants that would always be dying of thirst, we placed beautiful cacti (some ceiling height) in gorgeous large terra-cotta planters. Every room had an authentic kiva fireplace with gas lighters, but real logs. Having a fire at night in most of the rooms created a beautiful glow and warmth. I loved it.

Our job as parents is to guide and protect.

We planned five bedrooms with baths so that our children could come when they weren't in school. Leslie was now eighteen and flourishing at design school. They said she was their most outstandingly talented student. (I agree.) Bruce, fifteen, was going to Thacher School in Ojai outside Los Angeles and loving it. And Stephen, sixteen, was attending Ojai School in the same area.

When you are a performer in any aspect of show business, your family life gets disrupted. How do you maintain control and handle all of it? We felt that boarding school would keep the boys safe. They'd get a great education, we'd always know where they were, and it would keep them out of trouble. Los Angeles was then and still is a difficult place to raise children. Around this time, the book *Less Than Zero* about the drug culture in L.A. was an incredible success because it struck a nerve, forcing parents to see a reality to which they had conveniently been blinded; it was a visual road map to the damage drugs were doing to kids. It also became a movie starring Robert Downey Jr. I knew of parents who smoked dope with their teens trying to be "cool friends," instead, blurring the lines between parent and child. This is never a good idea. Our job as parents is to guide and protect. So much potential was (and probably still is) lost to drugs. In L.A. the pace is fast, and the parents are often show-business-oriented and self-involved. With drugs so rampant, we wanted to protect our kids from that as best we could. It turned out to be a wise decision.

School provided a rich environment for the boys. Bruce took to academics and also became a whiz at computer technology, which was new at the time, plus he started a radio show for locals called the *Bruce and Becky Breakfast Show* (Becky being his then girlfriend) and was taking care of the campus horses. Stephen learned about hydroponics and grew his first organic garden as an extracurricular activity, with incredible tomatoes.

Alan found a local contractor to interpret Bob Easton's architectural plans and assembled a crew. Construction workers were willing to come out that far because at the end of the day, every day, Alan would turn up and pay some of the workers in cash. As Alan said, "This is Vegas, baby!" Money talks but cash screams, as my vice-president of production, Roger Ball (our everything guy and friend who now has been with us for thirty-five years), always says when he wants to get things done on the road.

To my astonishment, we finished building our romantic adobe

ranch house in three months. Once we were walled in, we could begin a real life in Vegas. When you are a performer in Vegas, everybody comes to see you; now we had plenty of room for friends and family.

I am domestic by nature. I love making a home, making meals, and providing stability for my family. Cooking has never been a chore for me but rather a stimulating hobby. I love hearing the yums from my family as they savor their first bites. Now I had my first vegetable garden, ten chickens who laid fresh eggs in the henhouse daily, and two geese, Jake and Minnie, who hung out at the pond. Food was fresh and plentiful. Fig trees and peach trees were already on the property. We could go out during the day and gather eggs, figs, peaches, and whatever vegetables were perfect that day. It was a beautiful life.

Jake the goose had a major crush on Alan. Every morning we would wake around eleven or noon (morning in Vegas time), and Jake would be at the window staring, waiting for us. When Alan went to the kitchen to make his incredible coffee, he would follow him on the outside parallel with the hallway. Then Jake would patiently stand outside and wait for Alan to come to him and stroke his long neck. Jake would affectionately nuzzle and coo, a truly lovely thing to watch. It's an insight into who Alan is to see how animals respond to him. The guy who is fiercely protective and ready to take on anyone who dared come after any of us in his family was a counter to this guy whom animals sensed as gentle, safe, loving, and caring. Animals know things. We once took a driving trip through the French countryside, and we stopped to look at cows in a field. They were drawn to him like he was a cow whisperer. The wild horses near our home sensed his gentleness, too; we had lots of wild rabbits on the land, and one became tame and domesticated because of his affection for Alan.

It was glorious to live in the peace and serenity of this beautiful authentic adobe ranch on the outskirts of town. The house was perfect for us in every way, providing a balance from the excitement of the Strip. Our glamorous and lucrative Vegas life could now be peaceful as well.

. . .

I was still appearing nightly in the fabulous *Moulin Rouge*. Word of mouth for our show was incredible, and soon stars from every facet of the business were showing up to see what was going on.

One night Michelle Pfeiffer came to see the show. There is always some point in my act, still to this day, where I lie on the piano and sing one of those heart-wrenching songs that make you want to slash your wrists. The night Michelle came, we comped her with a seat at "the Frank Sinatra table" (that's the table you always keep vacant in case Frank Sinatra drops by). The next year, 1989, the movie *The Fabulous Baker Boys* came out. I went to see it and there was Michelle Pfeiffer lying on the piano singing a torch song. I took it as flattery.

Respect is paramount in a relationship.

We had entered a new phase. Had *Three's Company* continued, I doubt I would ever have explored this arena. It's always difficult to see the perfection of the moment in the moment. It's like having your nose pressed against a mirror, impossible to have perspective and see clearly. I loved being a Vegas headliner; I loved everything about it. The show was always such fun, a great way to entertain guests and family and meet new friends and stars from every part of the business. It was all good. And no small thing, I was my own boss.

WHAT I KNOW NOW

Alan and I became a perfect working team. We operated with great respect for each other and still do. Ours is a work/love relationship that never ends and never begins, like a figure eight, a constant intertwining of the two dimensions. I cannot downplay the feeling of comfort you have when your partner in life, love, and business is your best friend, your most trusted confidant, the person who has your back. I was and am fiercely protective of him, as he was and is of me. Respect is paramount in a relationship. With respect, you listen to each other and take each other's point of view seriously. We each have the other's best interests always in mind and always at hand.

After two and a half glorious years as the star of *The Moulin Rouge*, two shows a night seven days a week, I began to physically wear out. We went to Henri Lewin, the president and head of entertainment at the Hilton, and told him I needed a day off. The schedule was grueling. I lived like an athlete: no drinking after the show, getting enough sleep (from four a.m. to eleven a.m.), and eating fresh home-grown food, yet my usual weight of 127 had dropped to 98 pounds. I was skinny, and not in a good way. I started to wear shorts under my gowns to look fatter. I was tired. Two two-hour shows nightly, seven nights a week, is hard on the body. I needed some time off, and as difficult as it was to say goodbye to all the kids and crew with *The Moulin Rouge*, I knew it was in my best interest to leave while I was still on fire.

After two and a half years, it was time to move on. Henri couldn't understand why we would leave.

I told him in the German accent I always adopted when talking with him that I was tired of looking at dozens of statuesque naked women every night. But if I went into serious withdrawal, I might have to come back for a night or two to say hi to the girls. He loved that and wished us well.

My time off was rather short-lived because the phone kept ringing. One day it was the entertainment director of the Desert Inn. As Alan tells it:

When I made my Vegas deal for Suzanne at the MGM Grand, the "boys" were running the town, and it was great. The hotels really understood the gamblers' needs and met them. High rollers were given complimentary RFB (room, food, beverage): the biggest suites, limos, fabulous gourmet food 24/7, jets, privacy, and hookers. High rollers got everything and any-

thing they wanted. These hotels didn't care about making money on the rooms, the restaurants, and the spas; all they cared about was the drop in the casino.

The Desert Inn was also traditionally a high roller hotel, but around this time, its ownership changed. The "boys" man was replaced by an accountant from Chicago, a bean counter. Now, I have nothing against accountants, but they don't know how to make money—they know how to save money. The first thing this guy does is post an announcement in Sammy Davis Jr.'s dressing room that "henceforth, the star will not be allowed to order dinner from any of the restaurants in the hotel." Instead, the star had to use the employee cafeteria. This was unheard of in Las Vegas. The star of the show should be treated like a star and given all the accoutrements to support that image and make them happy while playing the hotel. Sammy took a bar of soap, scrolled "Fuck You, Asshole" on the makeup mirror, and walked.

That night the accountant phoned me at ten p.m., in a panic that his first move to save money had crashed. Could Suzanne open the following night? I suggested to this man that he rescind his directive for stars vis-à-vis the hotel restaurants, and he agreed it was a dumb idea. I admire a person who can stand back and acknowledge they made an error and correct it, which is what he did. And we did open for him the following night for a two-week run.

Headlining at the Desert Inn was such a success, we decided to put together a whole new show, the biggest production on the Strip. Up to this point, Ann-Margret had owned the genre of big production numbers and flashy costumes. I had done that as star of *The Moulin Rouge*, but this would be a complete solo turn. I was excited.

While we were in production, we kept working other gigs, and to our delight, we got a call that summer to perform at the Sporting Club in Monte Carlo, a command performance for Prince Rainier. The promoters wanted "full Americana," and we had just the show for them. We brought great-looking Hollywood dancers dressed in Busby Berkeley–style costumes who tap-danced onto the stage to "Boogie Woogie Bugle Boy." The Europeans loved it.

The Sporting Club was owned by Prince Rainier, as was everything in Monaco. It was truly his country. I had never met Prince Rainier, though he had attended the Paul Anka show I had done with Donna Summer earlier. He must have liked me, to bring me back solo. I knew and understood that I was there at his request and blessing; nothing happened in Monaco without him knowing and approving it. I was told before the show, "Do not look at the prince. Do not call the prince up onto the stage. Do not acknowledge him in any way." *Okay.* Too bad, I could have had some fun with him.

A dear friend of mine, the legendary French singer-actress Line Renaud, was in the audience. We had met during my *Moulin Rouge* days in Vegas; she had been the star of the original Moulin Rouge in Paris, and she came to see the American version. She and I hit it off immediately.

And now once again she was in my audience, so I called her up onto the stage knowing she would understand how to roll and would love the fun of it. She is beloved in France in the way that George Burns and Bob Hope were beloved in our country at that time. The audience loved it as she sashayed her way up to the stage. I spoke bad French, and she spoke English with a heavy accent. We sang "It Had to Be You" and laughed our way through it. The show ended with a rousing standing ovation from all the royals in the audience. I sneaked a peek at the prince and could see he was enjoying himself.

After the show, I was changing into street clothes when there was a knock at my dressing room door. My wardrobe assistant opened it thinking it would be one of the crew with a question, but instead it was two rather menacing-looking security police. "The prince would like *you* (meaning me) to join him for a cocktail in the showroom."

I was stunned. I was not expecting this. Of course I could not comply. The invitation was pointedly for me only and not for Alan, so I stammered nervously, "Please tell His Majesty I would love to, but my husband and I have plans—"

Alan interrupted, "Miss Somers would love to join His Majesty."

I looked at him strangely, and he asked them to wait outside. "What are you doing?" I whispered, shocked.

"Are you kidding?" he said. "This is great!"

Some husbands wouldn't like the idea of their wife being whisked off with a glamorous *unmarried* prince with a penchant for famous blond American women. But that was not part of Alan's MO. He knew what we had.

I grabbed my beautiful black Azzedine Alaïa gown, thinking, *This is crazy,* and was escorted to the glamorous showroom by the prince's two security guards.

As we walked toward the entrance, my childhood and the life I once lived flashed before me. I was on my way to have a cocktail with Prince Rainier of Monaco. When I entered the beautiful show-room (the same room in which I had first seen Stavros Niarchos), I was taken aback when the audience stood and applauded me. I felt like Eliza Doolittle. My heart was pounding as the prince stood regally and beautifully in his white tie and tails. "Please have a seat," he said graciously, as he pulled out the chair next to him. He was clearly a gentleman. He complimented me on my show. His English was flawless. But of course, he had been married to Grace Kelly.

Across the table were his daughter Princess Stephanie and his son Prince Albert. I was surprised to realize that the prince was nervous and a little shy with me, as if he didn't know what to say next. I've always been uncomfortable with awkward silences, and I noticed on his program there were a bunch of handwritten numbers in columns. So with my usual lack-of-an-edit-machine, as Alan always calls it, I blurted out, "What are you doing, counting heads?"

He laughed from his belly and poured me a glass of champagne. "You're very funny and charming," he said, laughing some more. Two gulps of champagne, and the warmth of the alcohol calmed me down, and I began to feel somewhat comfortable. As comfortable as one could feel sitting next to a prince who ran and owned a country.

Unbeknownst to me, his daughter Stephanie was a regular watcher of *Three's Company,* so she started telling me how much she loved the show. Her father shot her a look, as though he wanted her to bow out and keep quiet. She went back to her champagne. Living in the public eye, to the degree these people were scrutinized, must be akin to living in a fishbowl.

As I took another sip of the delicious, chilled champagne, I noticed that the stage on which I had performed had been lowered hydraulically and was now a dance floor filled with finely dressed couples doing the rhumba. As the couples twirled and swayed, I noticed Alan right smack-dab in the middle, twirling and swaying, except he was alone—with a video camera. Signs posted everywhere in the casino stated clearly, in no uncertain terms, that we were not allowed to take photos, and there was Alan videotaping me with the prince and his family! An absolute no-no in the Principality of Monaco. Back and forth he swayed to the rhumba band, smiling and laughing with the camera firmly over his eye, catching my eye as often as he could.

I tried to remain composed making small talk with the prince, but I was extremely distracted. Then suddenly two security guards grabbed Alan by the neck and dragged him off the dance floor. I lost sight of him. The royals kept dancing, but somewhere in that crowd of swaying people, my husband was being dragged off to who knew where. I stuttered to the prince, "Ummm, I—umm, have to—ummm, get back now." I extended my hand to him and his children. "Thank you very much, so lovely, wonderful . . ." My voice trailed off as I was saying, "Such a pleasure."

I hurriedly left and ran to find my husband, who by now could be at the bottom of the beautiful harbor outside. The prince must have thought I was nuts, but my heart was pounding. I felt like Cinderella who had stayed too long at the ball and now my beautiful black Alaïa gown was going to turn into a housedress and poof, all of this would have been a dream. *Where can he be? Is he in jail?*

My thoughts were racing. *What should I do?* I thought of my lawyer in Los Angeles. Could he find Alan and make sure he was safe, not handcuffed to a jailhouse door somewhere or worse?

I ran full speed backstage, lifting my gown to my thighs so I could move faster. I swung open the dressing room door out of breath, and there was Alan, smiling, in fine shape. Later that evening in our Hôtel de Paris suite (owned by the prince), we watched the footage. There it was, recorded forever, me and the prince, laughing and smiling, the camera swaying back and forth to the beat of the rhumba. The swaying only added to the intrigue, and then suddenly the video went all crazy and wonky, as he was being dragged off the dance floor. Astonishingly, no one confiscated the footage, and we have it, this magical, crazy night, forever saved.

After the Desert Inn, our next venue was Caesars Palace. The first time I was in this showroom, I saw Frank Sinatra. Now I was headlining it. Leslie, who had by now graduated from Parsons, had been well prepared for her new career. We were very proud when she graduated at the top of her class. She is so talented, and our new show was an opportunity for her to go all-out, putting her sense of style and design to work in a way that only Bob Mackie, Ret Turner, and Ray Aghayan had had the opportunity to do with Cher, Diana Ross, Tina Turner, and others. Leslie was now designing everything I wore, both for personal appearances and on-stage. She enjoyed the compliments and the rave reviews she garnered. I was proud to wear her beautiful costumes.

We were/are such a good team, never in each other's way, allowing each of us to do what we do best in every venture. We have space to create, without criticism, knowing that the other knows what they are doing. It's how we've thrived.

We hired Walter Painter, the hottest choreographer of the time, to give us the biggest and the best. We decided to open the show with a throwback Latin number, done to the song "Hot, Hot, Hot!" Leslie designed a large fruit hat à la Carmen Miranda and a twenty-five-foot-long rhumba skirt with multicolored ruffles. This was wrapped around a colorful leotard that was all legs; halfway through the number the skirt was ripped off. The guys were shirtless, with tight rhumba pants, and my girl dancers were in pared-down versions of my costume. I danced down ten stairs accompanied by an eighteen-piece orchestra, and from there the show took off like a bullet train. One extravaganza followed another, broken by a quiet section in the middle where I lay on the piano wearing an electric blue gown of such extraordinary beauty I still can't get over it.

Man, were we having fun.

By now, it was the late 1980s. I had been doing thirty-five weeks a year in Las Vegas for nine years with few breaks. Opening night at Caesars was very exciting. Everyone showed up: family, friends, press. It was the most prestigious hotel and showroom in Vegas, best known as "Sinatra's room." It seated nine hundred, all white leather, sexy booths, first class all the way. After the show, my sister, Maureen, hosted an incredible after-party, and everyone had a wonderful time.

It's amazing what true listening can do for the soul as well as for seeing others' pain and finding true compassion.

Around three a.m. we drove home, and I filled the bathtub for the two of us with hot water and Epsom salts, a ritual we love doing together. The calming effects of the salts and the release of muscle tension guarantee a deep, relaxing sleep. It's hard to come down after experiencing such a high as opening a new show. We were happy and tired and flopped into bed exhausted but triumphant, wrapped in each other's arms, recounting the wonderful night before falling into a deep sleep.

This moment of the day is always my favorite time, when it's just the two of us, as close as two people can be. We hold each other tight, and he tells me how much he loves me; on this night as he drifted into sleep, he was telling me how proud he was. I was proud of the two of us. We were/are such a good team, never in each other's way, allowing each of us to do what we do best in every venture. We have space to create, without criticism, knowing that the other knows what they are doing. It's how we've thrived. This was no exception. We had a vision, and the execution was flawless. I have such deep admiration for Alan. I know that any time he takes a stand and digs in his heels in disagreement with me, it is because he's a visionary. I've learned to trust that.

WHAT I KNOW NOW

With each passing decade, we gain in wisdom and perspective along with an ability to see the big picture more clearly, and it is a blessing. Perspective evolves and this clarity allows for contentment and a lack of angst, another reason every day with him is a joy and a gift. There is no tension between us—we worked through most of that in the early years of our relationship and marriage. Back then we fought it out, cried it out, and in doing so, we eventually heard each other. We also went to family therapy together with our children, which was incredibly healing and connecting. Therapy allows all the things unsaid to be spoken in a safe environment with a neutral arbitrator to keep the sessions from becoming an attack fest. It's amazing what true listening can do for the soul as well as for seeing others' pain and finding true compassion. Therapy was the best thing we have ever done for all of us. I strongly urge anyone who is suffering or searching to take advantage of this incredible tool.

The next evening we drove to the theater, my blond hair full and wild, already wearing piles of stage makeup, ready to get on stage and hit it out of the park again. We had put together an incredible show. Everything was first rate, and I truly felt that it was by far the best show I had done to date. But when I walked out on stage, it was not to my usual packed house but to a half-filled showroom. What had happened?

Though my press had up to now been good in Vegas, the beat reporters were brutal about my new show. One in particular went after me for everything: what I said, how I sang, and how I looked.

The comments were nasty and personal—in this instance, not all publicity was good publicity. The poor start of the show was a bellwether for its run. For the first time since I began working Vegas, attendance dropped off.

When I told my friend Barry what was going on, he said, "How can they miss you if you won't go away?" I'll never forget it.

I had had a good run. He was right. It was time to pack it in.

CHAPTER 13

THE ROAD LESS TRAVELED

If you do not change direction, you may end up where you are heading.

—LAO TZU

Timing is everything, and just as ticket sales started to drop in Vegas, I got a call from David Salzman at Lorimar to come back to TV. They were trying a new experiment, first-run syndication. *Three's Company* was prime-time *network;* syndication meant we would be on at a different time on a different channel in every city. It was not optimum. I wouldn't have the heft of a big network behind the marketing and advertising; instead, I would need to schmooze station managers from city to city to give the show a great time slot. It would be a lot of work and effort, but if it worked, it would forge new ground.

The show was called *She's the Sheriff.* I would play the local sheriff in Lake Tahoe, a widow with two small children. When I saw my costume, my first thought was *Oh my god, I hate it.* There's nothing less flattering on a curvy woman than man pants. But with careful tailoring, we got the outfit looking kinda sexy: all beige, shirt and tie, big black belt with holster, and a big mother of a gun. The lady was packing! The home set was a jailhouse with a cell and two desks, one for me, and one for my right-hand man. We added a third

165

desk for Don Knotts, who was reviving his character from Mayberry as the officer who was nervous and couldn't shoot straight. The cast was wonderful and talented, and Don Knotts was a doll. Of course, I was fond of him already from working with him on *Three's Company* when he took over the part of the landlord. He was a pro.

Pros come to work and give their all, and that was Don. What most people don't know is that by this time Don was virtually blind due to macular degeneration. He only had 2 percent peripheral vision. He had a person by his side we called his walker, and she would count out steps for him: "Mr. Knotts, it's ten steps to the desk and six steps to the cell." Imagine. In addition to memorizing his lines, he had to memorize and count steps, so as not to trip, and he did it brilliantly . . . at eighty! Watching him navigate and struggle and never complain made me appreciate all I had. Don always had a smile on his face.

Around this same time, my darling, sweet mother woke up one morning with the lights out, virtually blind. For some people, macular degeneration comes on slowly, allowing the victim to adjust and get used to it. For my mother, it was instant. She could no longer see. I felt so bad for her. She was depressed and scared. I had read a book by Louise Hay on death, dying, and symbolism, and she related blindness to those who wouldn't or couldn't see their reality as it was. Accurate or not, my mother had allowed the alcoholic craziness to exist for so long, "seeing but not seeing" what it was doing to her and to us and I often wonder if this is how it manifested.

On the other hand, in the alternative medical world, macular degeneration is understood to arise from a lack of hydrochloric acid in the stomach. We make less as we age, and when you don't have sufficient HCl, your food doesn't digest properly, so you aren't able to extract the nutrients from your food no matter how excellent your diet. Nutrients are the fuel that keeps our parts running, so it makes sense that the eyes might take the hit. But I digress.

I asked Don Knotts if he would speak to my mother about blindness. He did, and he said something to her that changed her life and attitude. "Marion," he said, "a blind person would love to see what we see." Wow. Simple. He taught her gratitude for what she *had* rather than sadness for what she *no longer had*. From that time on, my mother coped beautifully with her blindness. I was very proud of her. And I thanked Don for this enormous gift.

Rest in peace, Don. I miss him. He was one of the good guys.

She's the Sheriff was my first TV series since *Three's Company*. The studio audience was primed and ready to see Chrissy Snow come back to life. Before the show, I came out to thunderous and long applause. They kept cheering and screaming.

They couldn't wait for the show to start. Once the director called action, you could feel the energy leave the room. My character, Hildy Granger, was nothing like Chrissy Snow. She was a sheriff with no funny lines in a crappy-looking outfit; she was the "responsibility" role, the one who had to do the right thing in every scene. No laughs. No fun. The audience clapped at the end, but it was limp, lukewarm. I knew we had a flop.

The show ran for two years but with very little fanfare. I loved the cast, but the show was a chore for me. It's hard to get worked up every week when you know the special spark is just not there. The writing wasn't the strongest—the money just wasn't there for A-list writers—and our producer had a nasty habit of going home on Thursday nights after our dress rehearsal and rewriting the entire show. No kidding, some show days, Fridays, I was presented an entirely new script. I took to taping notes all over the furniture, something I had never done before, but I had to because memorization within minutes was impossible. At the end of the second season, David Salzman, head of Lorimar, called with "some bad news." When he told me it was canceled, I said, "I'm so glad."

I think he was hurt. "Glad?" he asked.

"Yes," I said. "Nothing about this show and character ever felt like the best fit. I'm sorry, but it just never felt right for me."

TV was no longer the glue to our life, work, or happiness. I understood the dynamics of our business now in a way I had not the first time around. All emotion was removed. It was about business, the bottom line, and nothing more. It didn't matter if the network execs liked you. They weren't there to do you any favors. They wanted ratings, because ratings equal revenue. It was as simple as that. You tried something, and you either won or lost.

It had always been a roll of the dice, but now it was different for me: I would move on when something was not working. I would have no heartaches, only gratitude that I got another shot. Just being cast in the starring role was an indicator that a lot of money people felt the investment was worth it. So much goes into a successful TV series, things the viewing public does not think about, like demographics, and the sales team's enthusiasm. First-run syndication was a lot of work because the sales team had to schmooze each individual market, which at that time meant actually flying to each city to do promotion (whereas a network show ran promotion to the whole country at one time).

Next, Alan and I decided to take our show on the road. At that time there were theaters all over the country. During school break, we went on the summer circuit back east and played theaters in the round. Bruce and Stephen worked the show doing whatever job was needed. We all loved it. The road is fun if you are not missing anyone. Having the boys with us made it like a family circus.

One night on stage, I heard new backup singers echoing some rather horrible sounds to my songs. Turned out the boys had set up microphones backstage and decided to surprise me by being my backup. The song was "I Want to Be Happy," and I heard discordant "Happy, happy, happy"—made-up backup vocals. I put a stop to that immediately, but it was funny.

The road is great fun, and the money is good, but expenses are high, and it's certainly not as financially rewarding as a hit TV show. Late one night we were driving home from the airport, dog tired from one-nighters three weeks in a row, in a different city every night. I yawned and said, "We need to find other ways to make money. I love doing this, but it's exhausting. What else can we do to bring in money?"

Alan said, "You mean passive income?"

I said, "Whatever." I didn't know what passive income was at that moment.

Enter the ThighMaster!

In the late 1980s, a guy I knew casually called me up with a fitness product for Suzanne. This guy was not in the fitness business but was part of a film development company with two or three partners who also had no film credits. As I understood it, they were financed by a wealthy divorcée whose ex was a major person in the film business who perhaps wanted to "show him." I don't know and don't much care.

He pulled out this steel and plastic upper-body device that was all gray, called the V Toner. Why? Because it was V shaped, and if you used it, your upper body would get shaped like a V.

Suzanne put it between her knees and squeezed. "Is this good for your thighs as well?"

He said, "Yes, but it's an upper-body device." I asked him to leave it with us.

We fiddled with it for a while and decided it was a great product that really worked, even if not for what it was intended. Women are often unhappy or concerned with three body parts: thighs, butts, and breasts. We could help them with all in one pop. We registered the name ThighMaster, gave it blue and red colors, and went into business with this film group.

One night I was in my dressing room at home and admiring my new nude-colored perfectly designed Manolo Blahnik high-heeled shoes. They had the right heel, the right arch, and the perfect toe; the kind of shoe that makes your legs look great. They cost five hundred dollars. It was a lot of money for shoes, especially back then.

I thought, *Alan is going to think I am so dumb that I spent five hundred dollars on a pair of perfectly plain shoes. He won't get it.* So I looked in the mirror, and I was wearing my bra and panties, and I had a mischievous idea. I walked to Alan's office wearing the Manolos and the sexy underwear and said to him sexily, "How do you like my new shoes?"

He looked me up and down lasciviously and said, "Great legs." Was it manipulative of me? Absolutely. I know my man. That exact scenario became the commercial that sold ten million ThighMasters: the camera started on my Manolos, then panned up my legs with Alan in a voice-over saying those exact words. With the success of ThighMaster that continues even today, that five hundred dollars was the best money I ever spent on anything.

> *We give each other a lot of attention . . . I always tell him how beautiful he is.*

One year we were traveling to Paris, and the French customs agent looked at my passport, then at me, back to my passport, and then back at me. I thought, *Oh, no. What's going on?* Finally, he said to me in a heavy French accent, "ThighMasteur?" It was a global success.

WHAT I KNOW NOW

The opinion of my husband is one thing I find so delicious about our relationship. After all these years, I love that I can walk down our long hallway in our bedroom to his office wearing my high heels and the dress I'm thinking of wearing that evening to get his opinion. He always tells me the truth, but when it's a winner, it's in his eyes. It's a look he has only for me, and it's one of the things about us that makes life so fun and compatible. We give each other a lot of attention and don't really need it from the outside. It's a great confidence builder, making aging a nonissue. He doesn't see the flaws! I always tell him how beautiful he is (and he is), and I see in his eyes he likes it. Another of the many reasons we love being together all the time.

> The best and most beautiful things in the world cannot be seen or even touched. They must be felt with the heart.
> —HELEN KELLER

With the success of our road show and the Vegas act, Alan and I felt the timing could be right to do a big TV special. It was standard in that era that if your star was bright enough, a network would finance an entire hour of entertainment featuring you. The head of TV specials at CBS at the time was a cool guy by the name of Bernie Sofronski, who was also an acquaintance of Alan's. *Three's Company*, although it was an ABC show, had leased space at the CBS facilities on Fairfax for rehearsing and taping episodes. As a result, I often ran into Bernie in the CBS hallways, and he was always very nice.

Alan took a meeting with him and he said it was the shortest pitch he's ever given.

I said to him, "So Bernie, this will be the shortest pitch you have ever heard and one you will buy immediately."

Bernie started his stopwatch and replied, "Go!"

"Suzanne Somers and six thousand sailors on an aircraft carrier."

Bernie stopped the watch at three and a half seconds and said, "Sold."

Alan and I laughed that night over dinner. Alan always says when the deal is done, talk about the weather. Bernie gave Alan a green light on the spot, unheard of today, and we were off and running. We knew how to put together a fabulous show, and I couldn't wait to get working on this, as it was a mission of the heart for me. I have always been pro-military, so my first choice was to try and pick up where Bob Hope had left off. I knew these were big shoes to fill, but I felt the opportunity to entertain military was not only exciting but good for the country. Vietnam vets had been poorly supported when they returned home from that horrible war. To try to "right a wrong," I wanted to shine a big, bright, positive light on these heroes.

We met with Captain Dan Pederson, commander of the USS *Ranger,* and he agreed to give us carte blanche for the necessary days on his ship, including the use of his landing strip to put up a stage and seating for six thousand. We would have two fighter bombers on each side of the stage and sailors hanging from all parts of it. There were going to be sailors on every deck, as far up as the eye could see, enthusiastically cheering. It was going to be a thrilling sight.

This was my first time back on prime-time TV since my firing, so it was quite the big deal, and I was excited. I knew we were going to kill it: I was primed, ready, and relaxed because my business and career no longer depended on achieving network success. Fortunately, with focus and a lot of effort, Alan and I had moved on in our business, taken control of ourselves and our careers. We were independent and enjoying our life. But being back on prime-time network TV was in a category of its own, and it would be a very good thing if the show was well received.

I was lucky enough to be featured on the cover of *People* magazine, promoting the special and wearing my "Take Back Your Mink" costume, a black corset from the *Guys and Dolls* production number (the sex symbol returns), and I could feel the anticipation. My comeback was making news, and ironically the press was welcoming me like the shamed daughter that the family decided to take back into the fold.

The day of the actual show was tremendously exciting. The energy on the aircraft carrier was palpable. The sailors and military brass all wore their dress blues, and I have to say there is nothing sexier or more impressive than dress uniforms. There were no women on the ship, so it was just me and my line of gorgeous, sexy female dancers, and the sailors who were all revved up. The ship was pulsating, and everyone was impatient for the show to begin. Testosterone was oozing from everywhere, as though it were the fuel that was running the ship.

My guest stars were Marie Osmond (still a friend today), Gladys Knight and the Pips, and Flip Wilson. It was one fabulous costume change after another, big production numbers, and frankly you can't miss when you do a striptease to "Take Back Your Mink" on an aircraft carrier with six thousand guys! All the girls behind me had on black satin gowns that broke away to do the number. One moment we were dressed in gowns, hats, gloves, and minks, and the next we had thrown all of it away.

Next I wore a beautiful nude beaded gown so I could sit on a stool and sing Sam Cooke's "You Send Me." At times the camera would lock in on a sailor mouthing the words with dreamy eyes, surely remembering something from his life back home that made him want to put his arm around his best girl. I was their girl for the hour, and I took good care of them. I brought one darling sailor on stage to sing to him and also Captain Pederson, a guy who looked more like a movie star than any movie star.

The show was shot live, which was considered risky and un-doable because everyone knew that all shows were made in the editing room, but we wanted live and live only. Besides, we had been doing live for the past several years by this point, and it just seemed natural to us: you rehearsed, and then you got one shot at it. It allows for spontaneity and lets you fully capture the response from the audience. It was the right call; the show was a powerhouse from start to finish. I ended with Betty Grable's "Bye, Bye Baby" in full dress whites, then changed to a long, red beaded gown to sing, with only a harmonica as accompaniment, "God Bless America." As the camera panned from the sailors' faces to the blue light dusk, the overhead shot reminded the home audience that we were at sea.

The show's ratings went through the roof. I loved entertaining the military. I signed up with the USO and agreed to do more shows for them. We were a perfect fit. My uncles and father were former military. My brother Dan was former military. I grew up in a patriotic home, and many of my relatives were cops and firemen (Irish family). So uniforms were something I respected.

It was an incredible experience on the USS *Ranger.* Captain Pederson was the consummate host and professional. I loved everyone we met on the ship, and before we departed, I was gifted my own flight jacket—a treasure I still have—and numerous medals and ribbons.

As soon as the *Ranger* special aired, CBS was on the phone wanting next season's special. We were thrilled. Our next show would be shot at Ramstein Air Force Base in Germany. This time it would be me and ten thousand GIs. We also agreed to do shows at every military base in Germany in association with the USO. I was jazzed. There is no better audience than the military, especially a group that hasn't been home for a while; they were pumped, ready and grateful for all things American.

Whereas our experience on the USS *Ranger* was flawless relative to execution, Ramstein Air Force Base was another matter (no offense to the Air Force). Its general had received bomb threats to our production from the Baader-Meinhof gang, a terrorist organization hell-bent on ending the Western way of life. Suddenly all our carefully made plans were discarded. The entire production was to be brought inside.

We had less than twenty-four hours to pull it all together. If we did not deliver a show, Alan and I were at financial risk of having to pay for everything out of pocket. A network is not going to pay for a show that didn't happen. The stress was intense.

The general at Ramstein threw us a curve at the last minute when he ordered us to move the show inside the hangar. Now we had to light an enormous area but had brought only enough lights to shoot with natural lighting. I called technical facilities all over Europe, and sensing we were up against the wall, they quoted prices that made my sphincter snap shut. We got all our lights, I wrote checks and paid in cash, feeling grateful, pissed off, and vulnerable at the same time.

. . .

Show day came, and it was going beautifully. I look out at this beautiful sea of young and handsome men, take a pause, and say, "And the nuns in Catholic school said I'd never get to heaven!" As the men laughed, the Pointer Sisters strutted onto the stage to sing "I'm So Excited" and the troops went wild. Next Jonathan Winters meandered onstage with a propeller in his hand. I asked him what he was carrying, and off he went talking about a fictitious crash, but he lived through it, he said, because he held on to the propeller. It was genius. The guys loved him; he was irreverent, completely unscripted, and slightly naughty but not inappropriate, a master of timing.

Just after Susan Anton and I finished up "Blondes Aren't Dumb" the number ended and unfortunately so did the lights. We lost all electricity! Right in the middle of the show.

We were finally back and shooting when suddenly all went dark. The power load had melted a generator. I pulled out two bottles of killer cognac, poured shots for everyone (except Suzanne), and we got a little blotto. Yes, alcohol definitely has a place of honor when everything turns to shit. When a production is over budget and shit keeps happening, it feels good to stomp around muttering "Shit, shit, shit, shit!"

But being up close with Jonathan Winters, the master of comedy, made it all worth it. He had boarded the plane in L.A. dressed as a general and stayed in character all the time we were on location.

Five hours later they finally got generators and the lights working, but by now we had lost all but a few of our audience. Worse, we had only about twenty minutes of show in the can. We had forty minutes more to go. But the show must go on, and by two in the morning we finished the show and a grueling day.

No time to celebrate. Next morning very early our team was on cleanup and breakdown of the stage and all the set pieces. We wanted to leave it as we found it. Me, my girls, the band, and the crew were loaded onto a bus to start the USO part of the tour. We drove from one base to the next; we'd sleep on the bus, get off, run out, do an hour show, get back in the bus, and sleep some more. We did three to five shows a day. Then we were told the Baader-Meinhof gang was on our tail. More stress. To say we were tired was an understatement. Stress and jet lag were working against us. Finally we were near the end of the tour.

We pulled into the second-to-last base, and a band of MPs came over to us: "Miss Somers, we have every reason to believe the Baader-Meinhof gang is going to blow up this hangar tonight. We've had bomb-sniffing dogs patrolling the perimeter of the tent, but, Miss Somers, if the bomb goes off, I want you to look for anyone wearing a yellow armband, and we'll get you out first. Have a good show, Miss Somers."

Trust your gut.

I took a deep breath and locked eyes with Alan, who was standing guard next to the stage, always there, my rock. He looked extremely concerned. I smiled nervously at him and walked out in front of the audience of all men. My legs felt shaky, like they were made of Jell-O, so wobbly and numb I couldn't feel the ground. Somehow the performer in me came through, and we put on a great show.

Driving back to our hotel afterward, I sat quietly in the backseat of the military car with security escorts flanking all sides of us. I was exhausted. The last show would be at a base near the Berlin Wall the next day. I quietly said to Alan, "I've never canceled a show in my life, but I don't feel good about going to the base near the Berlin Wall tomorrow. I'm tired and scared."

We canceled. The next day I heard from the PR person that a bomb went off where we would have been performing.

WHAT I KNOW NOW

Trust your gut. It's that voice inside all of us, giving advice. Is it a "higher-self"? Some people are very tuned in to that inner voice, and some people are deaf. My inner voice never lies to me or lets me down. It's only when I can't hear it because I'm not tuning in or I ignore it that I get in trouble.

Performing for soldiers gets under your skin; it's addicting. Military personnel are very good people, appreciative, well mannered, polite, and honorable. You know they have your back, they'll take care of you. A lot of the men we interacted with were still kids chronologically but old souls beyond their years; they had to be. Terrorism was just taking hold in Europe, and our men and women needed to be on guard at all times. Little did we know what was to come in years ahead.

To honor the USO and our commitment to it, we decided to take the show to the many military bases in South Korea, including those in the north and the demilitarized zone. I wanted to go to Panmunjom. By the way, Panmunjom, the village, no longer exists because it was destroyed during the war but it gained lasting fame as the site where the Korean Armistice Agreement was negotiated. I had seen photos of that historical day so many times and was looking forward to feeling the energy and history in that room.

Our drive from Seoul to the DMZ took a couple of hours. We rounded the corner, and there it was before us, Panmunjom, that famous hut where history happened. We were told sternly, "Do not look at the enemy. Do not make eye contact with the enemy. Do not do anything that could be construed as aggression."

The first impression as you enter the area is an eerie silence. The U.S. side is predictable. The North Korean side was lavish and lush, with white palatial buildings; large, broad, grand staircases; and hundreds of workers quietly tending flowers. But when you turned the corner, the palatial buildings turned out not to be buildings at all—just big movie flats, providing fake photo optics.

Alan and I entered the hut. I had an eerie feeling. No one was laughing or smiling; the tension was still in the building. The room was safe *unless* something erupted, and then all the blurred lines would come tumbling down. I sat on our side, had my photo taken, looked around, and felt the history. Then we had to go on to visit soldiers and bring them some cheer.

Performing for soldiers in cold, windy outposts poses challenges, but you make do. As long as we had any way of setting up sound and a stage, we did our best to put on a show. If not, I got a microphone and talked and took pictures with them. We ate in their mess halls and pooped in their little outhouses. We roughed it, and it was appreciated.

Guys get lonely sitting in these desolate outposts, yet they must remain constantly vigilant. While we were there, we heard about a tree that was dying, and everyone was upset about it. When I asked why, I was told that it meant the water source for the tree had been cut off and that most likely meant a tunnel had been constructed underneath. Sure enough, they found an underground tunnel big enough to move large tanks.

We visited all the bases: Army, Marines, and Air Force. (The Air Force had the best food.) We brought as much cheer, joy, and home as we could. I know it helped. One night we were flying low in a Chinook helicopter, and I noticed a red light on the dashboard. "What's that?" I asked the pilot. "Well, ma'am, that means a missile from the North is pointed right at us, but if we fly low enough, they can't hit us." We were flying at two hundred feet. Then he said, "As long as we stay below four hundred feet, we're okay." Gulp.

We were taken to a lonely outpost for photos with men who would not be able to attend the evening's show. It was on top of a cold desolate hill, and inside the mess hall was an old poster with BOB HOPE written on it. He had been the last one to visit. I crossed out BOB HOPE and wrote in SUZANNE SOMERS. I felt privileged to be there. We went outside to look at the view, and right across the DMZ were North Korean soldiers pointing their AKs right at us. I remembered I had been told not to look at them. We got out of there.

The DMZ has a dangerous feeling about it. Along the roadsides, soldiers pop out of the bushes in full battle paint with twigs and leaves stuck in their helmets. It's disconcerting. You feel like you're in a war movie. After the show, as we drove away from these incredible men and women, all so committed to doing the job they had been given, I felt fortunate indeed that these people have our backs. Alan had his arm around me supportively. All I could think as we left was *God bless America.*

What I also felt leaving the DMZ was gratitude for having the opportunity to give back. Coming from nothing and now living a privileged life, it felt like the right thing to do. These wonderful people who put their lives on the line for our freedom and liberty deserved the little bit of cheer we could bring. Something I learned through these appearances, unbeknownst to me at the time, would take me in a whole new direction of giving back.

CHAPTER 14

NO MORE SECRETS

There is no end to education. It is not that you read a book, pass an examination, and finish with education. The whole of life, from the moment you are born to the moment you die, is a process of learning.

—JIDDU KRISHNAMURTI

When you follow the flow and don't resist, life takes you on the most interesting journey. I wasn't looking for another career to add to all I was already doing. I was quite happy with where I was and where we were.

It was 1988, and we had been married for eleven years. Each day more and more fulfilling than the last. The kids were all doing so well. Bruce had graduated from Berkeley and was about to start the graduate program at UCLA film school. Leslie

> *When you follow the flow and don't resist, life takes you on the most interesting journey.*

was hand-painting jeans and selling them out of her house. Eventually a pair ended up on the cover of *People* magazine, worn by Madonna, the hottest star of the moment. That really put Leslie on the map. We were so happy for her. Stephen was going to Parsons in Paris and starting a life in France, where he would reside for the next ten years and eventually marry a wonderful French woman.

When your kids are doing well you can relax. There's a saying that as parents, we are as happy as our least happy child. We had happy children at this point, so we felt comfortable in the life we had created together.

Alan and I love taking long driving trips; we load up the car with water and our luggage and take off. Often we head toward New Mexico, usually Santa Fe. I think it's one of the most interesting cities in America. We've explored Santa Fe bit by bit over the years, but this time I wanted to go deep into the past and feel real Native America up close. I had always been drawn to the Native American culture. From prior experience, we knew that the drive from L.A. to Santa Fe is world class, hours of desolate and beautiful highways; these are hot, windows-open, feet-hanging-out-the-window kind of trips, sometimes with music, sometimes in silence. We're comfortable being alone and silent together.

> *When your kids are doing well you can relax. There's a saying that as parents, we are as happy as our least happy child.*

These are the times when the mind lets down its guard. You can relax. You think about things differently, and in 1988 there was no such thing as a cell phone, so no office interruptions. Phones can intrude on these special times if you let them; today we're all so used to being connected, it's hard to conceive of not being able to take a peek to see if something is going on. On this trip, our only connection to the outside world was the radio—not even GPS. We used a map. Imagine!

Over the years, I'd made friends with Forrest Fenn, and he was now one of my dearest buddies; I jokingly referred to him as my boyfriend. He has been one of my great teachers in the art and archaeology world. He is the unofficial mayor of Santa Fe. These days he is especially known for the buried treasure he has put in the ground—somewhere, for some lucky and adventurous person to discover and keep. He says the treasure consists of a few million dollars' worth of gold, silver, jewels, diamonds, rare coins, and other artifacts that he collected in his lifetime. Over the years, I have personally seen him fill this treasure chest many times; I can tell you for a fact it contains a fortune. But he is the real national treasure, the Will Rogers of our time.

Whenever Alan and I visit Santa Fe, Forrest is always our tour guide, introducing us to shop and gallery owners, plus restaurants that only the locals know

We're comfortable being alone and silent together.

about. Santa Fe has a way of life most Americans don't know exists. It's the land of Tom Ford, who grew up there and keeps his roots. Ali MacGraw makes Santa Fe her home. Val Kilmer, Gene Hackman, and Shirley MacLaine all live or lived there. You get the picture. It's a very special place.

On this crisp autumn morning, I wanted to wander around the Anasazi ruins and the famous ancient cliff dwellings of Bandelier. We made our way out to this historic place, where whole lives and cultures once abounded, with structure, moral codes, and attention to beauty and nature. The cliff homes or "condos," as I call them, are enchanting. You are aware, even in the stillness, that people were here. The evidence is everywhere, in the petroglyphs at the backs of their caves and the fire marks on the walls, indicating their need for light and warmth.

As Alan roamed the cliffs above me, I settled into one cave and was struck by the energy inside. I imagined four or five people had slept here, but people were smaller then, so maybe more than that. There was a ledge outside overlooking a vista that hadn't been touched for thousands of years, and there I sat, all morning, with the warm sun beating down on me.

I was mesmerized.

That night around three a.m., I awakened from a deep sleep, sat up, and leaned over the bed to grab a yellow legal tablet I had brought with me and a pen. I'd never done this before. I started writing . . . and writing . . . and writing. Around eight a.m., Alan woke up and said, "What are you doing?"

I answered quietly, "I don't know."

And then I read it back to him. And I sobbed.

I didn't realize it, but I had written what would become the first sixty pages of my book *Keeping Secrets*. Mrs. Kilgore had opened the door, and clearly I was now ready to understand, feel, and remember all of it. I thought with my success I was finished with this story; I thought I had left behind that little girl in the closet. But to finally understand the perfection of life and the gifts inherent in the negatives, there was something else I needed to do. I needed to tell my story and use my celebrity, my louder voice, to help others. I wanted to pull someone else out of their own personal closet, whatever that meant in their lives. I didn't know this was my motivation then, only that I needed to tell my story.

> We learn when
> we are ready.

To do so, I had to go back, all the way back. I opened my emotions and wrote and wrote. It was like a movie running before my mind, the terror, the violence, the shame, the fear. Overwhelming fear. I could hear it, smell it, feel it. I was terrorized once again just by the thoughts. Alan had known, but he had never really known. Like his terrible injury as a child, we tend to repress pain. It's a survival mechanism, until we are ready to learn from it. Yes, I had dealt with my low self-esteem with Mrs. Kilgore but that was just one aspect of healing. The real story had remained locked inside me until this moment.

As I read aloud to Alan he was very moved and held me tight. "You must keep writing. This is important." And I did. I wrote nonstop for the next year. By hand. I was literally cutting and pasting, scratching out, using Wite-Out to delete. This is so antiquated from the way I write today. But it was good because the process of writing longhand is slow, and I had the chance to truly *feel* and embrace all of it. Also I had enough acquired wisdom to see it from a perspective I would never have had as a child or a young woman. We learn when we are ready.

. . .

As a child, my life had been all about fear and powerlessness. As an adult with life experience, I could see it through different eyes. And it was sad. So sad. My poor, shy, sweet mother tried so hard to keep us looking normal to the outside world. We were all so good at keeping secrets, but I had learned that this was not the path to health in any facet of life: We are as sick as our secrets.

As a family, we made up stories to protect ourselves from others knowing the real truth. This was where I learned to put on a happy face and pretend to the outside world that all was good or great. Man, what awful training for living and surviving. This was training for learning to be unrealistic, to pretend, to lie. When we got the courage to call the police, my father would answer the door and explain it away as "overemotional children." He could be a charmer when he wanted to be.

But I also saw my father from a place of great compassion. He was a merchant marine loading bombs in the bowels of a ship. He often said if they got hit, he knew there was no way out for him. He was in Nagasaki when the unthinkable happened. When he came home in 1946, I was conceived to prove he had made it. But by then the demons were such that only booze could take them away. All his pent-up emotions came out as anger and violence. He couldn't have a couple of drinks. He drank alcoholically; he drank to get drunk. It's not normal to get drunk. Most people realize when they've had enough or had too much. For an alcoholic like my father, no amount was too much. He drank till it was gone or he was gone.

We are as sick as our secrets.

That he quit after all those decades of drunkenness is commendable. It's one thing to give up the substance; it's another to emerge from the fog having your emotions laid out bare naked, to be forced (as a sober person) to feel all the feelings he tried so hard to shut out. That takes real strength and courage, and I have deep admiration for him for doing this. He was forced to remember the pain he inflicted on himself and his family; he had to live with the fact that we didn't like him much at that point (which changed, by the way). I realized I was writing the book to find forgiveness, both for him and for me, to let us both off the hook. Forgiveness is key to happiness. And the choices we make matter.

Forgiveness is a process. It takes time. Page by page, I saw it all more clearly. I saw why my sister and then my brother and finally my younger brother and myself all found our individual ways to take the pain away.

WHAT I KNOW NOW

We all do the best we can. My father did the best he could. I accept that he had a terrible disease over which he was powerless. I've learned in life that no one can judge another. No one is better than another. We all make mistakes. We all make bad choices. We all succeed and fail, and we each have our own solitary individual journey. The journey is the gift. Who can cast the first stone?

> Before you start pointing fingers . . . make
> sure your hands are clean!
> —BOB MARLEY

One day I was finished. It took me a year and a half, but I finished the book. I sat on the floor of my hotel suite and looked at the thousand handwritten pages I had been dragging around with me all these months. The relief, the feeling of accomplishment, the growth, the freedom I felt at having faced it, felt it, looked at it honestly, and forgiven it, him, everything—these were all swirling around inside me. If there is such a thing as an evolutionary scale, I was moved up a couple of notches. I had grown as a person writing this book. I would never be the same. I understood another level of myself and felt good with it. I also felt true love for my father. I got it. I got him. I understood. It was all going to be okay. And I would never again hold anything against him. He had made it out of a living hell. I admired him.

I was now working at the MGM Grand Hotel in Reno. I had taken a residency, much as I had at the Las Vegas Hilton when starring in *The Moulin Rouge*. A residency is a contract for full-time work and to do an agreed-upon number of shows. I had signed on for a year. I was the star of *Hello Hollywood, Hello*. It was a perfect setup for me: I would write my book all day and then go onstage at night in a big extravaganza, with feathers and beautiful girls.

Forgiveness is key to happiness. And the choices we make matter.

Afterward, when Alan and I returned to our hotel room, we were greeted by our cat, Chrissy Snow, a beautiful white long-haired Persian. When you live in a hotel room, having a pet is a big deal. It's the only thing that says home, and it is extremely comforting. I'd take a bath while Alan sat with me, and Chrissy sat on the sink and stared at both of us. (What do cats think about?) Alan lit candles and put on soft music. Sometimes we'd have a glass of wine. Then we'd get into bed, and I would read to him that day's work. Alan was so supportive of me and the project (and every project). I had done this at his urging, and every night he was left aghast realizing what had happened to me and my family growing up. I was grateful we had found each other, that life had turned out so sweet.

I sold the manuscript to Warner Books. My new publisher was Larry Kirshbaum, and my editor was Nancy Neiman. We were a great team, and they were very excited about this book. No celebrity at that time had ever written such a raw and honest account of herself. It's not easy writing your own story because the people involved never see the story quite the same as you do. It causes tension. My shy mother was upset with me for "airing the dirty family laundry." We had tense flare-ups about it. I said heatedly one day, "That's what you've always done—pretend what's happening isn't happening!"

I didn't want to hurt anyone, but I also hadn't planned to write this story. It wrote itself, including the first sixty pages, which were like automatic writing. What possessed me to wake up and grab a legal tablet and write? I felt directed.

Keeping Secrets came out and shot to number one. It stayed on the bestseller list for weeks. We licensed it to ABC as a movie.

And my life as an author began. It was 1989.

The concept of the "adult child of an alcoholic" was just starting to be recognized, and my book had a lot to do with it. Millions who, like me, had never drunk alcoholically, were finding in adulthood that their emotions just weren't right. Destructive behaviors, like shopping and spending money you didn't have to take away pain you didn't know you had, and being a pleaser, were getting in the way of living happily. These destructive traits were part of the disease. You'd do anything to take the pain away (for the moment).

Before therapy, I had unknowingly needed to re-create the heart-pounding crisis of fear and tension of those violent nights because I had become addicted to the craziness. I didn't feel complete without it. Exhaustion and sadness from the events of the previous night were a part of who I was, who we all were. The nondrinking child of an alcoholic gets kudos: "Everyone in your family is drunk but not you." Right, I didn't drink, but I was just as sick. Crisis creating was my form of alcoholism; I just didn't use alcohol as the catalyst.

When I moved out of my father's home and no longer experienced the nightly violence, I felt an empty hole inside me that needed filling. I filled it by doing stupid things like spending the rent money. I had to have constant crisis. Whenever I could say those magic words, "I'll take it!" I felt happy, and the pain was gone. But then, of course, it would be followed by another deeper panic of *How do I pay for it?* This is the sick merry-go-round of screwed-up emotions of the adult child of the alcoholic. We look okay, but we aren't.

To survive you do what you have to do to make yourself feel well: alcohol, drugs, shopping, sex, or food. Take your pick. They are all the same thing. They all lead to destruction, which is the point. You feel worthless, and this is how you prove it to yourself.

I went on every talk show. It was hard not to get emotional on each show. There were a lot of tears.

And then letters started pouring in: "You wrote my story." "I finally figured out what has been wrong with me all my life." "I had the same father." "I finally feel free." I wrote it for me, but it was turning out to be for them also.

Two TV shows asked my family to be on as a family. The first was *Oprah*—she treated us so well. The second was *The Phil Donahue Show*. His show was very popular and prestigious. I was very nervous. I knew Phil from having appeared on his show several times before. Before the taping, I took him aside and said seriously, "Phil, this is my family."

He said, "I know."

"No, you don't. This is my family." I looked at him sternly, like, *Don't screw with them.* It took great courage for my mother, father, sister Maureen, brother Dan, brother Michael, and me to sit down before America.

Then Phil Donahue opened his show with "Well, this family had a major drinking problem. Meet the Mahoneys."

I died inside. Maureen and Dan had been sober for several years. My sister looked glowing and beautiful, and Dan was ready with his twinkling eyes and quick humor. Michael was still drinking and

> To survive you do what you have to do to make yourself feel well: alcohol, drugs, shopping, sex, or food. Take your pick. They are all the same thing. They all lead to destruction, which is the point. You feel worthless, and this is how you prove it to yourself.

using; little did we know that in a few years, it would take his life. But today he showed up, nervous and unable to really speak, but he showed up. My mother was beautiful but once again so nervous being on TV. This time she memorized what she was going to say, and she pulled it off with her sweetness. She was endearing.

Phil Donahue opened the questioning by going directly to my father: "So, your name being Mahoney might have something to do with your drinking problem, right?" Without skipping a beat, my father shot back, "Yeah, and my grandmother's name was Donahue!" The audience roared with laughter, and the show got off to a great start. He won their hearts.

The show was an unabashed success. It was an important one. It brought the secret out and into the light. Others related. So many people to this day tell me how this book freed them and unlocked their demons. Afterward Alan and I and the whole family went out for lunch at Tavern on the Green in Central Park and had a celebration. We had made it as a family, and our story was now going to help so many others.

Having a bestselling book had a major ripple effect. Requests for lectures came in, from large groups and small groups. A new career as a lecturer emerged for me, thanks to Alan's creativity, one I had never entertained. Ironically, he had said something to me years before, the first time I ever did my Vegas act. That night we were lying in bed recounting the evening, and he said prophetically: "I see a day when all you will do is speak." I sat up and looked at him as if he were crazy, yet here we were today on the lecture circuit.

Now he got to work booking me. There is no prep for lecturing, no "lecture school." You are either good at it or you aren't. You succeed and fail in front of people.

My very first lecture was before an audience of approximately eight hundred people and was funded by a recovery house program. I came equipped with a memorized script and a stack of index cards.

Halfway through, I saw people leaving, people uninterested, cough-ing, frankly . . . bored. After it was over, I wanted to go home and never speak again. But Alan had already booked several dates, and I couldn't renege.

The next lecture I decided to go it without notes. After all, in nightclubs I was used to speaking off the cuff. I treated all audiences as though we were having a telephone chat, as if the whole audience were one person.

What a difference. I spoke from my heart; I spoke my truth.

Speaking is a privilege; a whole lot of people give up their time to come hear what you will say. They hope they will walk away with a better understanding of the subject and themselves. My job was to make sure I inspired with a clear cohesive message.

Alan soon had me set up as the national spokeswoman for Adult Children of Alcoholics (ACOA). He booked lectures; I spoke to adults and children alike, including young children at Alatot meetings.

One group of children asked me to come speak to them. After-ward there was a reception line where they could hug me or touch me or tell me something. Out of the corner of my eye, I saw a little boy who kept moving to the back of the line.

Finally everyone was gone except him. He shyly looked at the floor. "Do you want to talk to me?" I asked.

He shuffled his feet and looked away and finally, quietly, shyly, said, "I wish I could hit my father over the head with a tennis racket like you did."

I knelt and put my arms around him. I said softly, "You are lucky because you are here. You have someone to talk to and other friends who are going through the same thing. And because of that, you won't ever have to do something as awful as I did."

Alan and I locked eyes. Poor little boy. I never forgot him. If I wrote the book only for him, it was worthwhile.

As the national spokesperson of Adult Children of Alcoholics, I could be a voice for all those who had never been heard. I also sat on the board of the American Psychiatric Association, the first layperson to do so.

This was an important time in my life. But as with all of life's breakthroughs, after I had explored, dissected, found forgiveness, and gratitude, I wanted to move on.

What was next?

CHAPTER 15

REINVENTION

This is a new year. A new beginning. And things will change.

—TAYLOR SWIFT

The beauty of the career I have been privileged to have is that you never know what tomorrow will bring. One day the phone rings, and your life changes. All the plans you made get turned upside down, topsy-turvy. I love the saying, "If you want to make God laugh, tell her your plans!"

Alan and I were in New York finishing up a book promotion tour, and the phone rang. It was Michael David, a prolific Broadway producer, who asked to meet with us. He came to our hotel room to woo Alan and me into taking on the project of starring in *Annie Get Your Gun*. I would be Annie, and the commitment would be for one and a half years, not including rehearsals.

There were a few complications. First, the two remaining daughters of Irving Berlin had not allowed anyone to do this incredible musical since Debbie Reynolds in the 1950s. They flew to New York from Paris to meet with me to see if I was an appropriate choice.

The rehearsal room was bare and unadorned and looked like a scene in movies. Sitting on fold-up chairs were the two Berlin sisters and the Rodgers and Hammerstein lawyers who handled the Irving

Berlin estate. They were there to look me over, and after an hour they all went out of the room. They gave their approval to Michael David and left.

Over the next couple of weeks, everyone involved had a lot of back-and-forth phone calls to structure the deal so everyone would walk away feeling satisfied. Alan always says in every deal, everyone should feel they won something. I would be obliged to open the musical in Japan, work my way across America playing regional theaters, and then finally appear on Broadway, with a minimum of a six-month run and a year and a half commitment or longer. Alan of course would go with me. It was a huge commitment, not only in terms of time but also in life on the road and all that that entails; crappy hotels, crappy road food, and the gypsy life; it's the way of the road. I'm a homebody, I like a calm life, and I love to prepare our meals and enjoy our evenings, so this would be a big "give" on our part. Broadway doesn't pay television money, and it is expected that much of your joy comes from the thrill of being in the theater. We were both enthusiastic but also apprehensive.

Finally our lawyers and their lawyers all agreed. We would sign the papers in their office the next morning and then take off like a rocket. But then . . . the phone rang.

It was Tom Miller and Bob Boyett of megatelevision series fame. Think *Bosom Buddies, Happy Days, Full House, Perfect Strangers, Mork & Mindy, Laverne & Shirley,* and *Family Matters.* They had had one hit after another, and on that phone call they offered me the starring part opposite Patrick Duffy to begin a new series for ABC called *Step by Step.* The production was to begin immediately. ABC by now had new management—the boys who had so gleefully ousted me were all gone. Anyway, what a delicious position to be in: having to choose between a prime-time TV series and a Broadway show. I could tour for a year or film for what could turn out to be several years. My decision had to be made that night.

We passed on *Annie Get Your Gun.*

Soon I had a parking spot at the famed Warner Bros. studio, a starring role, a great dressing room, happy people, and the big prize: Patrick Duffy. It was a joy to come to work every day to be with this uncomplicated, funny, talented, nice guy.

The show was about two divorced people who fall in love and get married. Both have children; he had three, and I had three. It mimicked my real life—I understood all too well the complications of blending families and the emotions that run so high. But unlike in real life, in a situation comedy the issues are material for big laughs.

Tom and Bob were extraordinary producers. We went on the air in the fall of 1990, and the public loved the show. It was family entertainment, clean and wholesome.

The underlying theme was that Patrick (Frank) was always trying to have sex with me (Carol), but every time they got near the big moment, a kid would burst through the door or have a nightmare or have a problem. Patrick and I got along splendidly. He had a great wife, and the four of us would socialize and became great friends, remaining so to this day.

The show was renewed for a second year and before our summer hiatus was over, Tom Miller and Bob Boyett called to tell me that my salary would be raised to match Patrick's. No lawyers, no negotiating, no issues, no hard feelings. They offered an incredible sum, which was so lovely of them (and smart).

Once again I was on the covers of magazines regularly and in demand for outside projects. I played the good, cool, sexy, hot mom. My kids came first, and I was fiercely protective not only of my kids but of his as well. I think the series spoke to all the blended families who were now out there. They could watch and be entertained and relieved that they were not alone in their circumstance.

Step by Step was marketed globally. It was a big hit in France, and in Italy it was renamed *Una bionda per papà*. The voice-over dubbing made me sound like a domineering balabusta. One summer Alan and I were vacationing in Italy and we took a side trip to Ravello, a charming village with cobblestone streets, lots of churches, and outdoor markets. I noticed people looking at me and couldn't understand it. Then kids started following me and calling me *Carole* (with a heavy Italian accent). We walked faster and faster, and the group of kids grew to about thirty or forty, all yelling "*Carole, Carole.*" Then they started running, so we started running. Finally we ducked into a small restaurant, and I said to the owner, "May I hide here for a minute? I'm being chased."

The owner looked at me and stated excitedly, "*Carole!*"

Then I realized *Step by Step* was a big hit in Italy, and they were all calling me by my show name, Carol. The amazing power of television.

Step by Step stayed on the air for seven seasons. It was a genuine hit, always at the top of the ratings for Friday night—family night—television.

Our life had settled into a manageable routine. During the week, I filmed *Step by Step,* while Alan was at his home office taking meetings, proposing new projects and deals, and manning phone calls and offers. He is so good at instigating projects, I call him my "idea man." His brain never stops. Sometimes he's far out there, and other times his ideas are so solid it's breathtaking. On weekends, we either went on the road to do a lecture or maybe a gig with my nightclub act. So to say our plate was full was an understatement. It was hard work, but we were together and having fun. I couldn't and probably wouldn't do any touring without Alan. I love the work, but the thought of being alone in a hotel room somewhere was not appealing.

Another thing happened in the seven years I was on *Step by Step.* The children in the large cast needed to work rehearsals around their school schedules, so I had a lot of free time in my dressing room. I am a productive person, so I started writing another book. This one was called *Wednesday's Children,* about children of abuse who made it out. I interviewed countless people who had endured terrible childhoods to explore what strength they found in themselves to survive and go on to productive lives.

I am fascinated by the qualities of those who survive and of those who are done in by trauma, like my brother Michael. I remember Michael as the most beautiful child; I used to take care of him and would proudly push him around the neighborhood in his stroller showing him off, he was so bright and darling. But over the years, as we all left home and he remained alone with our dad, his life turned dark. I remember with horror my own nights in that house, so I can only imagine what it was like for Michael. I at least had had my brother and sister to comfort me.

Michael essentially stopped talking; yes, he spoke a word now and then, but it was as if his voice were stuck deep inside him. His eyes were always downcast; he was a child with no self-esteem, and I am sure he was the butt of the "worthless" diatribe that spewed from my father during his drunkenness. At twelve, Michael started using drugs. He had a lot of emotional pain and acted out in ways that turned people off. No one really understood drug addiction at that time. He was just considered a bad kid, rather than someone who was screaming for help and to be heard. I was so mired in trying to survive as a single teenage mother that I wasn't able to help Michael. I wish I could have. We do the best we can with the information we have at the time. I couldn't realize he was so troubled—I was too young and too overwhelmed with my own problems just trying to get through each day.

Looking back, I can see that all the signs were there. Finally his drug addiction and alcoholism took their toll, and at age forty-six his heart exploded. But it wasn't a lost life, he made a true family with his second wife and raised his four sons. At his funeral, I was deeply moved by how his children talked about him. His oldest son spoke simply but eloquently: "My dad was the type of father that would get up at four in the morning to drive us to our wrestling match." That said volumes. I was happy for Michael that he had found such love and support in his life.

Around this time, while at Berkeley, my son, Bruce, met the love of his life, the wonderful Caroline Arminio. On his twenty-first birthday, I gave him a surprise party at Trader Vic's, a hip restaurant in San Francisco. That night I saw this beautiful young woman, Caroline, with gorgeous skin, long luxurious chestnut hair, and spectacular, expressive brown eyes. I could see she only had eyes for

Bruce. Bruce had another girlfriend then. The next day I mentioned to Bruce, "That Caroline girl last night sure likes you." He said, "Oh, she'd never be with me." He was wrong, and they ended up together. I like to think I had a hand in setting it up.

After graduation, they remained together while he attended UCLA film school and began living together. Caroline was and is a great girl. It was not up to me, but she was who I had hoped he would choose, and sure enough, she would go on to become his wife. Not only is she a knockout, she is an amazing cook. She fills in all the gaps for Bruce and gives him the attention he deserves. They make a life together that continues to bring joy to him, them, and all of us today.

Stephen, living in Paris, had met Olivia, his future wife. Leslie was combing through flea markets looking for used jeans to hand-paint and had created quite a successful business. Her designs were now in high-end hip stores like Maxfield Bleu. She designed the incredible matador suit for Madonna for her Mitsubishi commercial, which aired in the States and in Japan. As always, it was a perfect design: black matador bolero jacket and pants with a big jeweled M on the back. In one of the iconic Madonna's best-known posters, she stands with her back to the camera with the large jeweled M as the focal point, along with her short platinum blond hair. The commercial caused quite the sensation. Leslie designed for various rock 'n' roll groups and continued to be my chief costumer, making clothes and costumes so hip and sexy and beautiful that they got applause whenever I walked out on stage in a new outfit.

What a privilege to be married to your best friend, your lover, your business partner.

Alan and I loved our wonderful life together. We spent weekends at our Palm Springs home doing the stuff of life, cooking and spending time with our children, family, and friends. It's amazing that we never get tired of being together. What a privilege to be married to your best friend, your lover, your business partner. Love, sex, and business were and are all part of the rhythm of our lives together.

We might wake up in the middle of the night and discuss the show, or a business deal, or have incredible sex. It's all delicious. It never gets old—it's always sexy.

Our relationship is romantic; I have always loved to get all dressed up and go out on a date with Alan. I love the way he looks at me when I emerge from my dressing room; his eyes say everything, and he never forgets to admire. He usually says something like "my beauty." I don't care what anyone else thinks about how I look, I just like to know my husband thinks I'm beautiful. He tells me all the time, just as he tells me how much he loves me many times every day.

> *We all have problems, but our problems are our opportunities.*

When we go out on a date, I often wear my favorite Richard Tyler black cocktail dress, based on the lace-trimmed slip Elizabeth Taylor wore in the movie *Cat on a Hot Tin Roof*. Richard made mine out of men's thin wool suiting fabric, in black, with black lace trim around the décolleté and tiny spaghetti straps.

On this Christmas in 1991, Alan gave me a perfect pair of beautiful antique diamond earrings that are still my favorites. They are what I always wear on special occasions, really lovely, small but exquisite. With a dab of Chanel No. 5 behind my ears, wearing my diamond earrings and my favorite little black dress, we go out to our favorite restaurant in Palm Springs, Le Vallauris. We go there regularly and have been enthusiastic customers for the past forty-plus years. It's a throwback of a place with a jazz trio, a cool bar, and authentic fabulous French food. We love it. Once I like something, I never get tired of it.

The next year I wrote another book in my dressing room called *After the Fall*. I was like so many women who have had problems, and I've always used my problems to learn and win; that's what I was doing with my writing. My problems became my gift. In writing my books, I found clarity. We all have problems, but our problems are our opportunities. I seem to have an inordinate need to flush them out, learn from them, and then write about them. Each of my problems has propelled me forward as an opportunity to learn and grow. Mrs. Kilgore had told me on that last visit that the worst was over, so this became a great coping mechanism for me. No matter what happened in my life, nothing would ever be as bad as those horror-filled nights in the closet. It freed me and gave me gratitude.

The next problem was unexplained weight gain, so I began writing about that. Everyone was having trouble with weight. I devised a protocol I had learned about while summer-vacationing in the South of France: you lose weight by eating. This was before the South Beach Diet. It was science-based, and people took to it. No one likes to diet. The body needs fuel but the right kind of fuel. My books on this subject, my Somersizing plan, each sold over a million copies; I was proud of them. My publisher said to Alan one day, "Suzanne's books are keeping us afloat." The books just kept coming out of me. I am paired with a great publisher, Crown, who were and are so supportive that they pretty much gave me carte blanche to write whatever was on my mind each year. They called it the "Woody Allen deal": Woody's studio allows him the same kind of freedom in making his movies.

> *The moment when you feel you are tapping out in what you are doing at present is the perfect time to change directions and turn right or left. You take with you what is still working but change it into another form.*

My Somersize books were a great outlet, allowing me to create recipes, and soon, while promoting them, I was teaching cooking on TV. Ironically, my dream of making a living cooking had found an outlet. I loved doing cooking demos, so soon another new business emerged: Somersize food!

In life, reinvention is the name of the game. The moment when you feel you are tapping out in what you are doing at present is the perfect time to change directions and turn right or left. You take with you what is still working but change it into another form.

One day Alan said to me, "I think you should go on HSN, the Home Shopping Network."

"What?" I asked. I thought he was crazy, but as usual he was a visionary, and it turned out to be a great idea. Little did I know that we would spend the next seventeen years on HSN. The loose, free-form, ad-libbed nature of the work fit my personality perfectly. I loved talking to the women. It was truly interactive TV. They would tell me what was on their wish lists, and I was able in most cases to provide it for them.

Use your problems to work for you. Don't let obstacles that seem overwhelming do you in. Use them; they're your great asset.

We are entrepreneurs, and entrepreneurs are self-starters. Frankly, entrepreneurs are also unemployed. We don't have employers who set up profit-sharing plans or IRAs or provide health care and paid vacations and bonuses. We're on our own—for everything. To succeed, you need at least one great idea and the knowhow to bring it to fruition. Then to fully exploit this great idea, you need to play long ball over months, years, and maybe a lifetime. You have to be impatient, yet patient enough to mellow out the great idea. This means thinking about it day after day, and if after a time (a month maybe) you still feel it's a great idea, you act on it.

Who knew I'd become the queen of the Home Shopping Network? It all started with a negative: way back when I was fired from *Three's Company* Alan and I decided to go it on our own. The shmoo! So much of my writing is to be a cheerleader for all my readers to use the negative; use your problems to work *for* you. Don't let obstacles that seem overwhelming do you in. Use them; they're your great asset. Our choice to do it our way freed Alan and me to have fun, take risks, and reinvent. It was the best choice we could have made.

Writing my books and then appearing on the Home Shopping

Network allowed me to continue to grow and explore all that I might become and do with my time on this earth.

One night after I finished filming *Step by Step,* for the last scene I had been wearing gold satin pajamas. After the show, we were going directly to the airport to fly the red-eye to Tampa, since my first show on HSN was to start there at eight a.m. It was a grueling schedule. I said to Alan, "I wish I could wear these pajamas on the plane." He said, "Do it."

I thought, *Yeah, why not?* To civilize it, I tied a caramel-colored cashmere sweater around my waist (frankly making it a great-looking outfit), and I know I was the most comfortable person on the plane that night. When we arrived, my luggage was lost so I had no choice but to wear the pajamas on the air. The phone lit up. The ladies wanted the PJs! We started a business, and on our first show we sold twenty thousand pairs of satin pajamas.

At this point, we brought our talented daughter, Leslie, into the picture as our fashion designer. She had already achieved much notoriety designing for Madonna. She hooked up with a vendor who took her designs to a manufacturer in China, and two months later we were in the pajama business. They became a signature look for my ladies, or Suzanne's Ladies as they'd come to be called. And they were the catalyst for what became a dynamite fashion line. Leslie was and is the most talented designer I've ever worked with, and I've worked with the best.

As for jewelry, we started at HSN with a line they provided to us; they wanted me to sell run-of-the-mill HSN product. I tried it a couple of times, but it wasn't right for me. I had good taste, and as a woman, I know what *we* want. I told a vendor that I believed all women, me included, would love to have estate jewelry, the kind that once only the wealthiest women in the world could afford. In other words: fabulous fakes.

I turned over design of the jewelry to my cool stepdaughter Leslie, who is in the vanguard of all the hippest and coolest things, and that is what the collection looked like. We had the most beautiful jewelry made exclusively for my line; emeralds and diamonds, diamond bracelets, matching earrings, big fabulous real-looking rings. They were spectacular. So now the fashion line had an additional component, the right jewelry to go with the outfit. It was a slam dunk.

Many of my wealthy friends in Hollywood asked me if they could have some. It wasn't inexpensive. A fabulous fake diamond necklace set in 18k over metal, hinged and pronged exactly like the real thing, would sell in the three-hundred-dollar range. But it was an investment. We sold out—couldn't keep them in stock. The collection was a smashing, phenomenal success. In fact, all our jewelry and fashion collections for the next seventeen years were colossal successes. During those years, we added new categories: small kitchen appliances, organic food, both packaged and fresh, candy, bedding, fitness, and beauty.

Great relationships are those where you both give each other a lot of attention. It's what everyone wants: to be noticed, loved, appreciated. It takes two.

But best of all was my audience. At HSN I developed a relationship with the women viewers that was a true bonding. I loved talking with them, respected them, learned from them, and listened to them. I talked to them the way I talked to my girlfriends. One woman called me on the air one night and said, "You are the best friend I've ever had." It's part of being human, connecting and caring for each other.

I would talk to them about Alan. The women loved seeing us so happy, and they loved him—he was sexy and cool and hip. Remember, he *came* from television and knew how to work a camera. But mostly they liked the way he liked me. I didn't want any other man, and they could see it. From the very beginning, up until today, he has loved me, and I know it. Lucky me. I don't know what I did to be so adored, but I don't question it. I just take it in and love it. I truly believe great relationships are those where you both give each other a lot of attention. It's what everyone wants: to be noticed, loved, appreciated. It takes two.

. . .

What started as a shopping business became much more, and it lasts to today—One day I finished a phone call on air and lightheartedly said to my viewing audience, we should all get together sometime, maybe a cruise. And that started the phone ringing. The women *loved* the idea. So in my constant reinvention, now we had Suzanne Somers Cruises. We took the largest ship Carnival had and sold it out in twenty hours.

I was sitting in the green room at HSN joking around with Jim England, the president of our company, and I heard Suzanne say on TV something about "all getting together." What did she mean by "getting together" with thousands or even millions of women?

Carnival told me that the cruise sold out in twenty hours, and if they had had more people answering phones, it would have happened in ten. That had never happened before in their history.

Suzanne told her ladies to wear their satin pajamas to the ship and lots of Suzanne jewelry. And they did. It was incredible to see twenty-two hundred ladies all dressed in different PJ colors wearing loads of jewelry laughing and boarding the ship. None of them had ever met, to my knowledge, but they behaved like they belonged to a secret club. They had Suzanne in common, and they loved Suzanne . . . still do.

Truth is powerful— when you tell the truth you can't lose.

I learned a lot on that five-day cruise. First of all, women seem to have a herding instinct. They immediately formed groups to party, and party they did day and night. When Suzanne turned up, they laughed and danced and screamed and had the best time. Jim and I sat in the penthouse looking down at this scene, and I thought if it were guys on this cruise drinking heavily, they'd be beating the crap out of one another and tossing each other overboard.

The one weirdness was the shoplifters in our midst. On most decks, we had Suzanne stores and watched as women checking out the goods would put on a pair of our sunglasses and walk away. The same thing happened with jewelry and some fashion pieces. I never intervened because I didn't want to alter the great spirit of the cruise, but I was disappointed.

Suzanne performed her Vegas show for the women, gave a couple of lectures, and did a couple of cooking demos. She flitted through the hordes of happy ladies hugging and giggling until suddenly we were back in Miami. It was a wild bonding experience and a successful cruise.

Through the years, I taught my "ladies" everything I knew and was learning on my life's journey. I taught them all the tricks I had learned in my years of being in the business, like the value of a cool haircut, and nude pointy-toed heels with toe cleavage to make their legs look longer and sexier. I taught them how to cook and offered them useful cooking tools. It became a club of sorts, and in fact the women referred to themselves as Suzanne's Ladies. I liked them, and they liked me. I told them the truth. Truth is powerful—when you tell the truth you can't lose.

CHAPTER 16

THERE'S ALWAYS MORE TO LEARN

As we express our gratitude, we must never forget that the highest appreciation is not to utter words, but to live by them.
—JOHN F. KENNEDY

So much had happened in the years since Alan and I first met and started dating. Our life was full, rich, and blessed. I loved my husband, I loved my family, and I loved my work. That's about as great as it gets.

All of you who are mothers know that once your kids go off to college, you lose control and don't have a pulse on their daily lives anymore. Bruce always had nice friends, but who were they now? He graduated from Berkeley and married Caroline. Today my dear sweet daughter-in-law, after twenty-four years of working her way up, is now the president of our company.

> *You can't force love, you can't force another person to feel the way you want them to feel.*

Leslie married Frank, a beautiful bodybuilder from France, who was Monsieur France Jr. (Mr. France Jr.). Stephen married Olivia, the gorgeous woman from Paris. She was born in the countryside, a small village called Mirmande, and lived a beautiful country life until she got restless, moved to Paris, and ended up marrying an American by way of Canada.

Soon all our kids started having kids. Bruce's first baby was Camelia, and I had the privilege of being in the delivery room when she was born. The baby was born cesarean, and as Bruce was caressing Caroline's head and face, the doctor said to me "Suzanne, would you like to meet your granddaughter?" I put my finger in her teeny hand, and the moment I touched her, she grabbed back. I always tell Camelia it was an E.T. moment; a special and bonding event that rarely happens between two people.

Kids don't know blood—they only know love.

Soon after that, sweet Violet was born to Bruce and Caroline. Leslie and Frank gave birth to Daisy. (Ironically, at the same time on *Step by Step,* I was giving birth to a TV daughter, Lily!) We had a bouquet of beautiful flowers now in our family garden.

Stephen had three boys, and today we have a total of six grandchildren.

I now understand the photos that grandparents pull out, but I resist the urge. Having grandchildren is a gift that keeps on giving—it's a new love affair. Our family had come so far. Blending families takes a lot of patience. I learned to stop trying and to let it be. We all must come to it on our own, when the time is right.

It's important to be the grown-up in the room, but growing up takes a long time. Along the way, there are stupid little flare-ups. It's hard to remember what they are now; emotions are complex when children are involved. As a family, we had worked through difficulty in these treacherous waters, but it was worth it, and grandchildren are the equalizers. They are the opportunity to start fresh. Kids don't know blood—they only know love. Today we are all in love with one another, and it's the greatest.

During the *Three's Company* years, we purchased our beloved home in Palm Springs to protect ourselves from the paparazzi so we could enjoy normalcy. Our life then and now is at the ocean and in the desert. Palm Springs is still our home, and today it serves as a family compound and the place we nurture ourselves. At this writing we have been living there for forty years. This is where I have my famous organic vegetable garden, one of the joys of my life.

Television called me back several more times. I spent two years on *Candid Camera*. Next, I did *The Suzanne Show,* a daily talk show taped at Universal Studios. At one of those tapings, I got the phone call we all dread; my father had died. *We all know death is part of life, but we are never ready.*

By now both of Alan's parents had passed, and we realized this was a train that wouldn't stop rolling. I was so deeply grateful that I had found peace, forgiveness, resolution, and true love with my father. It would be awful to not have made that effort. The people I know who struggle most with a loved one's death are those who have unfinished business with their parents. I had nothing left to work out with him, and as a result, our last years together were always fun.

When I was still performing in Vegas, my mother and father came often and would sit in one of the VIP booths. One night I brought my dad onstage and sang to him, "You Made Me Love You." The audience loved the piece and us. One of my favorite photos is of my father with two six-feet-plus showgirls wearing feathers

> *The people I know who struggle most with a loved one's death are those who have unfinished business with their parents.*

and little else. He is in the middle and not very tall. When he put his arms around their naked waists, he let out a fun but shocked howl. "Oh Jesus!" he said. The photographer clicked at that moment, and there it was. I saw what people had always said about him; funny, charming, quick wit, likable. I would miss him.

So now I had peace in my life. The worst was over. My dad and I found resolution. I had great love in my life. Everything was great, right?

Not so fast . . . here comes life.

I had no idea the shmoo was going to have to pop back up again. Why did I have to keep learning lessons? I get the whole concept that lessons are opportunities—it's been a running theme in my life. But learning the hard way over and over isn't what you'd call fun. Learning one's life lessons is an agitating and difficult experience. Every time I've gotten cocky and think I have life by the tail, think I have it all figured out and tidy, reality pops up and hits me in the face.

By 1998, our neighborhood in Venice had changed. The town had been discovered. Our beach house on the sand was marked as ours, and just as it was getting beautiful at sundown each night, we had to close the drapes, so people couldn't camp right in front and stare at us or, worse, take photographs.

> *Learning one's life lessons is an agitating and difficult experience.*

Believe me, I am not one of those celebrities who complains about how terrible life is with all the attention. Whenever I hear that from someone, I want to say, "Oh p-leeeease!" Those who achieve celebrity are damn lucky—it's a privilege, and it's fun if you make it so. But we couldn't hang out in Venice incognito as we originally had. Our kids were grown, out of the house, so that year we bought a great beach house in Malibu.

There's no place like Malibu. Blue, blue water, and a quiet yet sophisticated village. It's populated with showbiz types who don't want to be part of the crazy energy of Hollywood yet want to remain close enough not to be out of it entirely.

Our house was a small, sexy, romantic place, right on the water but high on stilts above the beach. Our evenings were spent outside on the deck. I made Provençal chicken, a yummy concoction slow-cooked in butter, pan juices, wine, and fresh rosemary. I served it in a shallow bowl with loads of hot rich sauce, soft-cooked garlic cloves, and a crusty French baguette. The idea was to smash a garlic clove on the bread, swoosh the bread around in the buttery sauce, top it with a piece of succulent chicken, and wash it down with cold white wine. Then do it again and again, until it's all gone. Moonlit nights were the best for this dinner. I tried to plan it for when the moon was high and full and sparkling on the water; it was simply dreamy. Then we'd roll into bed with crisp white sheets, the door and windows wide open, wrapped in each other's arms, listening to the waves crashing, and fall into a grateful sleep.

I remember the first day we walked into this blissful bedroom with the realtor; I said something weird: "Boy, if you ever had to be sick this would be a great room to recuperate."

You never think it will happen to you. You never think you're going to go for your routine mammogram and have the doctor say those dreaded words: "You have cancer."

That's how it happened for me. As I was getting dressed after my yearly breast exam, the doctor tapped on my dressing room door and said, "You've got lumps and bumps all over the place. I just bought a new ultrasound machine, paid a half million bucks for it. Why don't we have you take an exam on it?"

We all spend our lives feeling invincible. Then those three words, you have cancer, shatter your safety.

I hesitated. I had rehearsal later that day, getting ready for a Vegas stint the following week. "Well . . . okay."

That's when they found it; a fairly large tumor, 2.4 centimeters, against the chest wall of my right breast.

The air went out of the room: I felt a strange stillness that blocks out sound, like being underwater.

Alan and I drove home in silence, both of us lost in thought. We all spend our lives feeling invincible. Then those three words, *you have cancer,* shatter your safety. My thoughts went to places I had never entertained. *I'm not here forever.* This life, this incredible journey, this ride I'd been living, was changing.

We arrived home and went about our usual routine, putting things away, arranging rehearsal clothes for later that day, keeping busy, still not talking.

"Want to go for a walk on the beach?" I asked quietly. We put on our warm jackets, wrapped our arms around each other, and walked out onto the sand. It was a windy day, cold

You can handle this.

and overcast. We held tightly to each other, both lost in thought. We walked like that for maybe a mile until I heard "that voice" whispering in my head, and it stopped me: *You can handle this.* It repeated itself, this time more loudly: *You can handle this.* It was what I needed to hear. What is "that voice"? Is it our higher self? Is it God? Is it our intelligence? I heard it and heard the truth in it. I stopped and looked at Alan and said calmly, "I can handle this. I'm going to be okay."

"Suzanne, you have breast cancer," said the doctor.

My first reaction was "Holy shit!" Then in a speechless moment, our lifetime flashed by in a millisecond. I kept hearing those words over and over and over.

How could this be? Where did it come from? Not that I thought this was the end. It was just my first moment of contemplating our mortality. And I mean our. I'm sure that from the outside, our relationship smacks of codependency. But what's wrong with depending on someone else, though? Shouldn't you be able to depend on those you love most? In many, really nice ways, we are codependent, we rely on one another. Some might regard our dependence as a negative, we see it as an asset as we're mostly interdependent. We had often talked about going out together, but there was no plan afoot.

We walked along the beach that day holding each other and feeling vulnerable. We are vulnerable! But then I thought of all the devastating things that Suzanne had overcome in her life and realized that cancer was just going to be one more. We can beat this thing. . . . We can do it! We WILL do it!

We knew that traditional, standard-of-care treatment was not going to be for Suzanne. The concept of poisoning the body to near death in the hope of destroying the cancer and then hoping for the person to return to robust health was crazy. Suzanne would do it her way. When she revealed her plan to the doctor, he said to her, "You will die." What a terrible way to sell someone into a treatment that has a very poor record of success. And for what reason? Follow the money, folks.

"Will this cure me?" I asked the doctor. "I mean, pounding me with poison is a big deal. So can you guarantee that if I do this, I will be cured?"

The doctor hesitated. "Well, it will shrink the tumor, and then radiation should burn out the leftovers. Then the tamoxifen will ablate your hormone production, so there's no more fuel left to reignite the cell proliferation [cancer]."

Are you kidding me? Cut, burn, poison . . .

You play a part in every drama of your life. What had I done in my diet and lifestyle that I now played host to this terrible disease? I saw the answer: I had not taken nutrition seriously. All my life I had been an incredible baker. I loved making scrumptious cakes, pies, cookies, soufflés, and chocolate mousse. I wasn't a fast-food junkie, but early on I didn't yet have the knowledge and information that sugar is cancer's fuel. Sugar is addictive and makes you crave other foods that are not good for your health. Later, as I wrote in my Somersize books, I greatly reduced sugar and white flour in my diet, but what about all the years leading up to it? I hadn't thought much about sugar.

At one point I had replaced sugar with chemical sugar substitutes, thinking that was the healthy thing to do. But the body doesn't recognize the difference between real sugar and fake sugar. And artificial sweeteners can do horrendous damage to the body. They are known carcinogens. Talk about throwing kerosene on the fire! My body (like all bodies) wanted the highest-quality fuel: fruits, healthy vegetables, healthy fats, and organic protein.

Then came another major problem: on my various TV shows, there had been long tables laden with doughnuts and chemical nonfood nibbles like cheese-somethings, Ho Hos, chips, candy, cupcakes. How many of these foreign molecules did I mindlessly down without thinking? My liver must have been groaning and saying nooo! How much of that contributed to the tumor growth?

Then there was the childhood stress: what does hiding in a closet night after night trembling in fear do to you? For a good portion of my adult life, too, I had been greatly stressed. What had that done?

During this time, I sought the help of a medium. I know it sounds weird, but I was desperate for clarity. A trusted friend referred me and said that this person had the ability to tap into the energy from life-after. *Why not?* I thought. On the phone to this person, I didn't say anything about the diagnosis, but amazingly, he blurted out: "You can handle this. When you were a child, you couldn't handle it, so you encapsulated it—you *entombed* it until a time in your life when you could handle it."

I took this as a sign that stuff happens to you in life when you can handle it. That's what "that voice" had been saying to me when I was walking on the beach. Now I understood. I was ready to grow from this experience. Little was I to know the gift cancer would turn out to be, but I get ahead of myself.

Stuff happens to you in life when you can handle it.

For my next visit to the doctor's office I was ready and strengthened for the conversation I was going to have with him.

"I'm not going to take chemical poison, and I'm not going to take tamoxifen. I find the idea of ablating my hormones not sound. They are there for a reason. My hormones are already in the beginning stages of imbalance, and their decline is very debilitating, and now you want to take away what's left? No."

"But you could die!"

"It doesn't feel right to me. With all due respect, I really think I'll die if I do what you say."

We went back and forth like this. I also called many doctor friends who I had talked with while writing my Somersizing books, which were all about the hormone insulin. Every doctor was emphatic: "You must do radiation."

Against my better judgment, I decided to take the radiation treatment.

And so we started. The tumor was removed, in a barbaric surgery that I will never forget. I was told it would be just a simple procedure and that it was "going to hurt a little." They asked Alan to stay out, and they'd come and get him when it was over.

I was taken to a pre-op room where four wires were inserted in my breast to form a "basket" around the tumor, so the doctor would not be working blind. Imagine! Wires were threaded into sensitive breast tissue, as if they were hemming a dress. It was done without anesthetic, and still to this day I can't figure out why a painkiller wasn't deemed necessary. I almost passed out from the pain. Three nurses held me down so I couldn't wriggle and scream and make the "basket" uneven.

Why didn't they tell me in advance that this would really hurt? What kind of doctoring is that? If I could have punched him in the face or scratched his eyes out to make him stop, I would have, but the nurses were holding me down. What an arrogant, insensitive, cruel thing to do to someone. I had been tricked into this one, and I was so angry.

I was sweating from the pain, water dripping off my body. I felt like I had been in a concentration camp experiment. Later, I angrily told the doctors that I did not appreciate being tricked into something that painful without prior discussion. When I demanded a reason, they explained it was all about money. This hospital took care of women who often could not afford their treatments, so it was a judgment call on the part of the hospital to reduce costs. I wasn't given a choice—this was just the way they did it. Poor women get lousy treatment, as I learned firsthand. It's not right, and it's not fair.

Then the radiation treatments commenced: daily zaps of harmful radiation. Nothing about it felt right. I would leave the clinic drained of all energy. I would sleep all the way home and then immediately drop into bed in our beautiful little bedroom with the ocean view. I remembered what I had said when we first bought the house: "If you had to be sick, this would be a good place for it." I must have known, innately, that I would be lying in this bed so ill and so sick from the radiation assault. It violently disturbed my stomach, causing me to vomit daily and lie in a fetal position.

Life does go on. I would spring forward, and I would look to the future.

The skin on my chest blackened, bubbling up like charred steak on a grill. I wondered if I (and my skin) would ever be the same. Looking down to see my once-beautiful breasts now reduced to one and a half breasts took some adjustment. I would have to deal with all that.

Suzanne got talked into radiation. Two of her doctors said, "Oh, it's a walk in the park." That's their pitch line. Maybe there's a commission on radiation as well. Radiation is brutal. It is definitely not a walk in the park.

Every morning for thirty-six mornings, except Sundays, I drove Suzanne to the radiation clinic, where she lay on the table. They focused the radiation gun on the part of her breast that had had the tumor and blasted away. There is something ugly to me about a guy in a white coat filling your body with radiation. Doesn't radiation give you cancer? Didn't all those people at Hiroshima and Nagasaki who were not incinerated get cancer from the radiation? When I asked him about that, he bragged about the accuracy of his machine and how it is focused only on a very small area to ensure no loose cancer cells that the surgeon missed will roam around. But he was so terrified of the radiation that he dashed out of the room and closed what appeared to be a solid lead door before he activated the radiation gun.

Suzanne kept saying to the doctor and the nurse that it felt like she was being burned inside, and she pointed to a place in the middle of her chest. The doctor got very defensive; he gave all kinds of bullshit reasons why this could never happen. He said what Suzanne was feeling had nothing whatever to do with radiation. Later, one of the nurses whispered to Suzanne that her sister had had the exact same experience and in fact was burned internally from the radiation.

After each session, we would get into the car to drive home, and within two minutes, Suzanne was in a deep, deep sleep beside me. I felt so badly for her. There was little I could do other than look after her, make her comfortable, and hold her a lot.

She spent her days in our small bedroom in the beach house staring out at the ocean. Thankfully, this eighteen-hundred-foot house turned out to be perfect for her recovery. It also became our favorite place we ever lived. It was our little love nest, where I could speak with Suzanne from anywhere in the house, and she would hear me, without the help of an intercom.

One day I was lying in my bed by the ocean holding my stomach and writhing in pain from the morning's radiation. For the first time, I felt sorry for myself. *Why me?* I don't usually resort to self-pity. Then suddenly something out of the corner of my eye caught my attention: a huge whale leaped from the sea! I called Alan to make sure that I wasn't seeing an apparition. We both watched this huge gray whale leap out of the sea three times until it was no longer in my line of sight. It was so beautiful and enchanting and exciting that I started to cry. I took it for the metaphor it was: life goes on. Nature had sent me the most motivating sign I had ever received. I decided right then and there that the message was pure and real: Life does go on. I would spring forward, and I would look to the future.

I decided cancer was a gift from which I would learn. From that moment I would eat as though my life depended upon it, which it does. I would change my life in every way. I had been working too hard and writing my books well into the early mornings because the house was quiet, no phones ringing, no interruptions. But I was staying up regularly until three and four a.m. I'd get into bed afterward and then have trouble sleeping.

Sleep is a game changer. If you don't sleep seven to eight hours a night, the repair work the body depends upon for life and health can't happen. I was pushing my body to do the impossible. But no more. I was going to eat, sleep, and think like an athlete. A great athlete thinks to win. I would win. This would be a blip, a lesson, and I knew that somehow in the future I would be able to use this experience to help others.

Suzanne is an inveterate researcher. The Internet was made for her. When she was first diagnosed, she learned to navigate her way through reams of research and pluck out the information that was relevant. Interestingly, for some time prior to her cancer, she had been collecting research on doctors and oncologists who were treating and controlling cancer without the use of drugs or radiation. Perhaps her subconscious knew that cancer was in her future and she was simply being proactive. By the time she heard the three words, Suzanne was ready to go to war. I have watched her do it many times, and I'm certain that the genesis of this survival tactic was in her childhood.

We were now beyond that first wave of discovery and moving into stage two, when we were ready to take it on big time. The concept of "crap in, crap out" is what we believe created this cancer. Today Suzanne and I really love shopping at Erewhon, Whole Foods, and Clark's. They all offer a generous selection of organic food. One of them also provides the option to purchase "conventionally grown" food, meaning food that has been sprayed with unbelievably toxic chemicals. Suzanne has often said that shopping habits would change dramatically if, for example, in the apple section the shopper had a choice between organic apples and apples sprayed with poison. But conventionally grown *sounds okay to most people, and it's usually slightly less costly.*

When we travel, I bring a small suitcase filled with organic food, plus a small coffee maker and a couple of pounds of fair-trade organic coffee. My job every morning, whether we are at home or on the road, is to make a great cup of coffee for Suzanne.

She sits propped up in bed waiting with great anticipation for me to serve up what she calls "the greatest cup of coffee in the world." I fake nervousness at the side of our bed as she picks up the coffee and whiffs the fragrance. Then comes the moment of truth: the taste test.

Would today be thumbs-up or thumbs-down?

Maybe it doesn't sound like a big deal, but I cannot tell you how I enjoy my morning cup of coffee. I had never had coffee before I met Alan. My parents drank coffee, but it was beyond awful. They were from the Depression era, and frugality was part of their MO, so they would reuse coffee grounds for a day or two to make them last longer. Yuck!

Alan makes the best coffee I have ever tasted anywhere, but it's about more than the coffee. It's the ritual. It's about tenderness and affection. It's a little joke between us that I rate each day's coffee. It starts at a ten, but there are days when it hits thirteen! We start every day with this little laugh.

Eleven years later I would become the first American woman to legally regrow my breast using my own stem cells and my fat.

I had heard about Dr. Kotaro Yoshimura of the University of Tokyo—he had successfully regrown the breasts of over four hundred Japanese women using their own stem cells. In 2011 I took a chance and called him. Lucky for me he had heard of me and my books. We talked for a long time that day and had several subsequent calls; he graciously agreed to come to America and teach the procedure to my friend Dr. Joel Aronowitz, who was involved with stem cells and research. The goal was to obtain permission from the FDA to qualify for a clinical trial to regrow my breast. It took three years for the permission to be granted, and as soon as we received it, we went to work to make it happen.

A problem became an opportunity.

The morning of the surgery was very exciting. It was about more than my becoming whole again; it was about a breakthrough for all women. At present, women in my position are offered implants or a TRAM flap (which often has very disappointing results and is generally unattractive, with much scarring and a long painful recovery).

To do the surgery, they removed fat from my stomach (boo-hoo), spun out the stem cells, discarded the weak ones, kept the strong ones, and injected those strong cells back into my removed fat. That fat was then injected into my once-cancerous breast (kind of like a turkey baster) until it was the same size as the other one. Early on I had adjusted to losing half of my breast, figuring that being alive was the better option. But to become whole again would be a great experience.

Take care of each other, compliment each other, and listen to each other.

The surgery was a fantastic success. I awoke and looked down and saw myself perfectly back together. Once again I had two beautiful breasts, and they were all me. Beautiful, soft, and real. Nothing plastic or foreign. Luckily the original surgery had preserved my nipple and skin, so my result was perfect restoration.

In the operating room, my daughter-in-law Caroline oversaw a film crew to record this historic event. Eventually, it was all over the Internet (look it up on YouTube), and Dr. Oz had me on as well as the doctors involved to discuss the cutting-edge procedure. It was a huge step forward for women. Since then over a thousand women have been able to take advantage of this incredible procedure.

Once again, a problem became an opportunity.

For about ten years, I had two fabulous different-size breasts to enjoy. We had "big guy" and "little guy," and we were able to laugh at them. I had one for every mood. But then Suzanne arranged to be the first woman in America to legally, under the aegis of the FDA, regrow her smaller one using her own stem cells. It took me a while to get used to this new member of our family, but it's so perfect now in shape and size and feel, I have to really think hard to remember which one went under the knife. And I was so proud that she did it her way; no chemo, no harsh after-care drugs, no implants.

Then everywhere we went, Suzanne would show her new breast—to anyone. We'd be out for dinner and an acquaintance would come over to say hello, and before I knew it, she and the friend were in the ladies' room,

and Suzanne was proudly showing her breast. After two weeks of this, I fi-
nally said to Suzanne that she had to stop showing it to everyone. Besides,
I like to think that her breasts are mine alone. I know how that sounds,
but screw it. I think one of the reasons we've lasted so long is that she's full
of surprises like this. I still can't figure out why I love to stare at them and
consider them my pals who are always there and never disappoint me.
Thank God for making breasts.

WHAT I KNOW NOW

It's the little things in life that make or break a relationship. It's
the special attention paid to each other. It's learning to do little
favors for each other, and understanding that what you put into a
relationship is what you get back. It's a simple formula: take care of
each other, compliment each other, and listen to each other. And
whoever makes the best coffee gets to serve it to the other in bed
in the morning!

CHAPTER 17

LIFE GOES ON

Perseverance is not a long race; it is many
short races one after the other.
—WALTER ELLIOT, SCOTTISH POLITICIAN

I was back, healthy and happy, putting cancer behind me. I re-
fined my diet, so that I was eating delicious real food. I ate lots
of healthy organic fats, butter, cream, full-fat cream cheese, sour
cream, olive oil, coconut oil, and flax oil; I ate quality grass-fed
proteins and no chemical foods. I took no drugs, not even over-the-
counter ones. I greened my home, getting
rid of toxic cleaning chemicals. I took it all
very seriously.

*Life got better
after cancer, and
it was pretty
great before.*

I realized I was in control of my health
by the choices I made and the thoughts I
was thinking. I know it all matters. I live
in gratitude for getting this second chance. I had fully learned how
precious life is, that each day is to be enjoyed. I appreciated my
loving husband and family even more than before. If this is what
growing up is about, then bring it on. To my surprise, life got better after cancer, and it was pretty great before. I learned from the

experience and would eventually write books that taught people about the value of making healthy choices for a long, quality-rich life.

What I loved most was how in sync Alan was with me and my message. I wanted him to be in peak health forever. He had taught me so much in our life together. His wisdom and perspective are profound. He sees life through a bird's eye that is evolved ten years beyond mine; I respect it and grab at it to learn and grow. It was through him that I learned about using negatives to move forward. He taught me everything I know about business, branding, and using my asset (fame) as a springboard to create business opportunities as an entrepreneur, and I loved it. So I was happy to be able to teach him about achieving true and optimal health and about revering and respecting the human body; and that we only have one body and how foolish not to take perfect care of it. He was and is a responsive and passionate student.

When Suzanne lectures to executive business groups and to Ernst & Young entrepreneurs, she stresses that although we are driven to succeed in business and often work sixty hours a week, missing meals, and getting jacked up on a steady flow of strong coffee, will destroy your body. By taking that course, shit will eventually happen. The body will say, "Sorry, pal, I've tried to keep up with you now for years, but you've abused me by eating crap and missing sleep and creating stress, and now it's payback time. You feel like crap, and you did it to yourself, so now you're going to have to give your body more attention than your business."

You may try to rectify by gobbling down the latest miracle pharmaceuticals—to sleep, to give you fake energy, to correct your out-of-control thyroid and cortisol. Or you may try some dumbass diet program to lose all the weight you've added to your once lean body by ingesting the most dangerous toxins on the planet. Or you may just give up because this mountain is too high to climb. And now unfortunately, you're too far gone, so you feel like a big schmuck.

. . .

Isn't that uplifting?

Health is all we have, yet our choices belie that fact. We seem to take a great-working body for granted, and that is a dangerous mind-set. It takes a long time to wise up.

When I got ill, we were running businesses, manufacturing many products for HSN. It was time-consuming on several levels. We loved our little Malibu beach house, and the kids and babies would all come over for Sunday dinners, often cookouts on the beach. We had a great business, I didn't want to be working on the road as I had for so long. I had had my wake-up call and was listening. From here on in, I was going to make taking care of myself my priority. Now I accepted only isolated theater and nightclub dates, occasionally a week here and there in Vegas. I appreciated that our life was pretty perfect. Except I had a new problem—I couldn't sleep.

From my research for the books I was writing, I knew sleep was vitally important for optimal health, but now suddenly I found that I couldn't sleep. What was wrong? I'd fall asleep as soon as I dropped onto the bed, but then I'd wake up all sweaty.

I was bitchy, too. When you don't sleep for nights on end, you're just not in the best mood. My leg itched fiercely, and I was gaining weight again. My sex drive, which was normally off the charts, was nonexistent. Finally, I could relax, enjoy my hard-won health, and luxuriate with sensual time with my husband in this amazing little house—and I wasn't in the mood! I could do it, but frankly I'd rather have a smoothie. I was angry—what a rotten trick.

Alan was compassionate but impatient and perplexed. This was not who I'd been all these years. I'd always been this happy, smiling, upbeat person who saw the glass half full. Now I felt dark. We both were frustrated. You see, at that time, no one ever talked about menopause!

First cancer and now menopause, and it was to go on for three years! Finally, one night Alan said in a serious tone, "Suzanne, a marriage can only take so much of this!"

Oh my god, I thought. We always take it out on the person closest to us. Had I been that bitchy? It snapped me back to reality. "I'm so sorry, Alan. I don't mean to be this way. I will figure this out."

I went from doctor to doctor and was offered sleeping pills, antidepressants, cholesterol-lowering pills, and diuretics. All the doctors had to offer was drugs and more drugs. One doc said to me, "The drug companies know best, dear!" *Are you kidding me?* I finally said to one doctor. "Are you joking? Is this the best you can offer women?" I left his office determined to figure out how to turn the problem of menopause into an asset. That was what I had always done with every problem.

> *We always take it out on the person closest to us.*

I suddenly became aware of how many pills my friends were taking: pills to go to sleep, pills to wake up, pills to lose weight, pills to take away menopausal symptoms, pills to get erections. No one was doing or feeling well, but doctors were providing the "solutions" to mask their patients' problems and symptoms with pills, pills, and more pills until they became walking, talking, confused messes.

Not for me—I didn't want to be drugged up. We are kept alive much longer today through technology: MRIs, CAT scans, sophisticated blood tests, antibiotics, even excellent sewage disposal. All these things have prolonged life, but what about its quality? I wanted quality back.

Finally I heard about the endocrinologist Dr. Diana Schwarzbein in Santa Barbara. I sent in my blood work, then drove like a maniac on my appointment day. As she looked at my lab results, she said, "You poor thing—you must feel awful."

I said, "I do. I feel awful—I feel like I don't want to be here anymore. But I love my life. I have everything to live for."

She explained that I had virtually no progesterone left (the feel-good hormone) and almost no estrogen. I was like a car running without gas and oil. We humans are made up of biochemicals and molecules, and a woman's chemical makeup is particularly complex.

"We're going to get you right," she said, "but it's going to take some time. I can't give you all that you need immediately, or you'll literally go crazy. It took a long time for you to drain out and lose your hormones, and we have to dose you back up gradually."

I didn't know it then, but this day would be a life-changer for me, the beginning of a huge new reinvention. The day I began to learn about bioidentical hormone replacement was the day I got on track to get my life back. Using natural bioidentical hormone replacement, week by week I eventually got "me" back. I didn't itch, I didn't sweat, and my weight was normalized. My sex drive came back—I was in the mood again, in our sexy beach house; I had a hot sexy husband and was happy to reclaim this lost part of me. I didn't have cancer, and I was living a healthy lifestyle. I felt good all the time, I was upbeat, and I had great clarity. By changing my diet and my thoughts, fixing my sleep, and replacing missing hormones, I dodged a bullet.

I had never realized the profound effect of hormones on human health and well-being. And I never realized so little was known about menopause. Researching natural bioidentical hormone replacement, I learned that the body recognizes hormonal balance as valuable (as in, this is how we perpetuate the species). On the other hand, a hormonal imbalance signals to the brain that this person is no longer valuable (can't make a baby). So nature's objective is to move out the unhealthy nonreproductive ones to make room for the healthy reproductive ones. In my cancer scenario, I was what is called estrogen dominant. This actually means I stopped producing sufficient progesterone. When your progesterone production slows or stops you are set up for cancer.

Aha! Possibly that's why so many women get breast and other cancers around menopause—nature is trying to move us aside. And most likely that's a reason I got cancer.

But hormonally balanced women of menopausal age are crucial to the wisdom pool. When allowed to live longer and healthier, we are an asset to the planet. We are the matriarchs. We have perspective.

Yet without hormones, we often can't think straight or remain healthy. So many women enter menopause and spend the rest of their lives white-knuckling, dealing with debilitating symptoms. As I learned everything I could about replacement, I quickly realized that the pharmaceutical hormone business is designed to keep women essentially *bandaged*. Synthetic hormones don't fix the problem, because they don't replace the missing hormones, and they aren't *human* hormones. They're not a solution, just a way to calm women down. And women get fat on this protocol. Women not knowing or understanding how it works figure it's just a shitty midlife trade-off.

The Women's Health Initiative of 2002 declared (and I'm paraphrasing) that it would be better for women to take nothing at all than to take these dangerous, harmful, and even fatal synthetic hormones. There you have it. These synthetic hormones are responsible for putting a woman's body into a state of *imbalance* rather than *balance*. Imbalance is where cancer has its opportunities. With this information, why would these hormones still be prescribed?

This knowledge made true hormonal replacement even more exciting to me. If menopausal women could rebalance our hormones, then we could essentially trick the brain into believing we are still reproductive. I was jazzed.

It was time to write a book on bioidentical hormones. It was called *The Sexy Years*. I termed the symptoms of menopause the Seven Dwarves of Menopause: Itchy, Bitchy, Sleepy, Sweaty, Bloated, Forgetful, and All-Dried Up. Writing the book was an education. In researching it, I had the privilege to interview the brilliant and courageous doctors who understood this phenomenon at that time. I learned that my "estrogen dominant" cancer meant that I was not making enough progesterone—clearly a huge factor in why I got cancer that I did not understand at the time.

The Sexy Years, published in 2004, was an instant number-one *New York Times* bestseller, which made me happy for every reason I can think of. Women were finally getting another option, a viable one, to get their life, mood, figure, and sex drive back. My interviews with cutting-edge, knowledgeable doctors allowed women to age in a new way, without drugs, while keeping their memories intact, their sex lives active, and their beauty restored. No wonder they loved me! (Ha ha.)

The book outraged many doctors, I believe, because it exposed their ignorance of how this natural passage, menopause, really works, and of the realities of real hormone replacement. The solution is not in a synthetic pill that matches nothing a woman makes in her own body—that only confuses the body, and it's not good for the human body to be confused. The drug companies took shots at me and ridiculed me.

But I felt like the Erin Brockovich of hormones. The book was a phenomenal success. I was becoming the messenger for

It's great to be alive while you're living,

a new kind of health, one that changed the way women age. I went on every talk show, and the response from the public was overwhelmingly positive. Lecture requests came pouring in, and they eventually led to "health tours" where seven thousand and sometimes nine thousand women came to get clarity for why they felt so crappy.

What I loved most was the win/win aspect. I had taken my *problem* and turned it into a great asset for myself and for others. All was good, for me and for women.

The book sold over one million copies!

Problem solved.

Alan also realized that his hormones weren't what they once were when I pointed out to him one day that he was sleeping all the time like our old cat! Hormone replacement is much easier for men.* Alan got his blood work done, and the doctor determined his deficiencies—testosterone and DHEA. Once he started rubbing on the cream, the two of us began dancing again. It's great to be alive while you're living, and this "balance" brought us back.

* For testing, call 1-800-327-9009.

. . .

When you leave yourself open to follow the flow of your life's journey, there are amazing twists and turns. Without looking for it, I found a new life mission, taking care of women in a way no one had. Up until then, women went through their passages with a pill for every ailment, and here I was saying there is another way. My life without drugs was inspiring to many women. The concept of putting back what you lost in the aging process with natural remedies appealed to so many.

Hormone replacement has to be individualized. There is no "one pill fits all." What I need is different from what the next woman needs. Without hormonal balance, lives were being ruined, and women were losing themselves. I called hormone balance the "juice of youth," the answer to good health.

Alan had been right again. Had I not been on the air talking to women all those years on the Home Shopping Network, I don't believe I would have had such a powerful connection with them. So this new work was a win/win: a win for me and a win for women.

> Never give up, and be confident in what you do. There
> may be tough times, but the difficulties which you face
> will make you more determined to achieve your
> objectives and to win against all the odds.
> —MARTA VIEIRA DA SILVA

My next book was *Ageless,* and once again it shot to number one on the *New York Times* list. Alan's marketing plan was inspired. He could garner free media by using my celebrity to get on all the national shows. Everyone does it now, but he was the first.

There was so much to learn about bioidentical hormone replacement (BHRT), and the knowledge was growing so fast, that in just a couple of short years, it required another book. More and more doctors were learning about BHRT. I made it my mission to gather my hero doctors, those who didn't mind that the messenger for BHRT was the woman who had once played Chrissy Snow on television. At first I had been able to find only a handful, but now for the second book, I found more than a hundred. I interviewed each of them for hours and then synthesized their information down to readable interpretations for laypeople like myself. I figured once I understood it, then we all could understand it.

A movement was starting to take place and it was growing fast. Women were demanding better treatment and relief from their doctors. They were calling their doctors in droves saying they had read Suzanne Somers's book and "wanted what she had."

It has been my experience that doctors are "down on what they are not up on," and BHRT was not and still is not taught at medical school. So frankly I felt, and feel, that in many cases I knew more than a lot of the doctors about this subject. I was a walking, talking example of BHRT's health-giving, life-enhancing power. People looked at me and Alan with our energy and vitality and our great health and wanted it too. I liked aging. What woman says that? Without all

When you leave yourself open to follow the flow of your life's journey, there are amazing twists and turns.

the crappy symptoms of menopause, what's not to like? You have your acquired wisdom and perspective in a way no young person can ever have. It's a gift, that *knowing-ness* from having lived awhile.

Besides, at this stage of your life, the weddings are paid for, the tuition is over, the angst is mostly gone, and now you're free to enjoy the rest of your lives together. What a tragedy that so many marriages break up over menopause, just when life gets really good.

Other doctors came to my lectures, and they saw and heard that my research was all science-based and backed up by doctors. They were aware that the information in my books was given to me by knowing doctors and scientists who gave generously of their time.

We're at the restaurant Nobu in Malibu, sitting with two world-famous people. I spot a couple approaching our table, and I alert all to expect iPhone follies. But instead the woman, tearing up, tells Suzanne, "Thank you for saving my life." The man also wells up and says, "Thank you for saving our marriage."

They never even noticed the world-famous people with us.

That's Suzanne the author.

Thousands of women who have read Suzanne's books turn up to experience Suzanne in person. These women are all with her. They vibrate with the truth of every word she speaks. They want what Suzanne has, and they now know it's possible.

That's Suzanne the lecturer.

I was learning so much and now had a much better and deeper grasp of BHRT and the implications of hormone imbalance. I was finding more doctors who had the courage to step out of their comfortable standard-of-care box, those who had gone back to school and got with the BHRT program.

"You're taking advice from *that actress?*" some conventional doctors would ask their patients. I think they felt stupid, and I was easy prey to pick on. Then came the big one: a group of doctors, many of whom I had not interviewed or featured, took me on big time. One doctor I had interviewed but eliminated was angry that I had decided she wasn't up to the same standards as the other doctors. After interviewing her, I discovered she wrote a column for a gossip magazine, and that had made me feel uneasy about her qualifications. I had removed her from the book because I was concerned she would invalidate the other great doctors. I also found her not as well versed as some of the others. That was my prerogative—it was my book.

These doctors banded together and wrote an op-ed for the *New York Times*. Its purpose was to discredit me and scare women away from my work. But they didn't know that I live my message and I don't go down easily.

This quote by Arthur Schopenhauer has been my go-to when the media and science community goes after me:

All truth passes through three stages. First, it is ridiculed. Second,
it is violently opposed. Third, it is accepted as being self-evident.
—ARTHUR SCHOPENHAUER, GERMAN PHILOSOPHER (1788–1860)

I had to hang on. I knew I was right. I knew my science was
sound. But BHRT was a new concept, and I was not the messenger
they thought should be turning science on its head.

These uninformed doctors had no idea with whom they were dealing. Su-
zanne is a major survivor—she is smart and knows her stuff. Her lectures
to thousands of women, and now men, were changing lives. When she did
an interview for Larry King, I sat in the green room and watched her on a
monitor. They thought they were dealing with that dumb blond character
on TV. But every word Suzanne writes is passed through all the doctors in
the book, as well as the medical staff at Life Extension.

The doctor who rounded up the other docs to write the New York
Times *op-ed was beating up on Suzanne because she wrote about a hor-*
mone replacement protocol called cycling. This doctor dismissed the pro-
tocol as having been created by someone who didn't live up to this doctor's
standards. Suzanne then pulled out an actual prescription from her purse
written by this very doctor using the exact same hormone protocol. It was
a delicious moment, and I cheered sitting all by myself in the green room.

That night a twit guest who was head of the North American Meno-
pause Society was also on Larry's show. He rambled on about bioidentical
hormones being the same as the fake ones that were made from the urine
of a pregnant mare. (Hello PETA?) It's a torturous process for the lady
horse, and horse hormones have nothing to do with human hormones.
Suzanne suggested he was there to defend the drug companies that manu-
facture the fake hormones. He emphatically denied it and emphatically
denied taking money from the drug companies. Suzanne then pulled from
her magic purse a document showing that the North American Meno-
pause Society was funded by the companies that made the fakes, and that
one of the companies had honored this twit for something that likely made
money for this organization.

Suzanne's performances on Three's Company *had been so powerful and believable that some people really thought she was a naïve lovable bumpkin. But Suzanne is autodidactic. She sucks up medical information like a sponge. She can learn anything she wants quickly, going back to the days when she was thrown into teenage mothering with no child support or alimony and no training of any kind and barely a year in college. She was forced to learn how to care for her baby by herself, and to think on her feet when the rent was late or a check bounced. She learned fast. She survived.*

Now she interviewed dozens of the greatest scientific minds in the world for hours at a time and then went back to them for clarification. So she had access to information most doctors never get, ever.

At one point she said she wanted to interview Ray Kurzweil, who Bill Gates said was the "smartest man in the world." (I concur.) So she called MIT, and Kurzweil's assistant asked if Suzanne had an appointment, and if not, what was the nature of the call? Suzanne said, "I just want to talk to him about being the most fascinating man on the planet." A moment later she heard, "Hi, Suzanne, this is Ray. How are you?" From that call has grown a wonderful friendship with this brilliant man whom we love.

D o you think my husband is protective?

In the end, it's my women who have won. These doctors tried to keep cutting-edge information away from women and had to discredit me because I was rocking the boat. As a child I had had the greatest training for survivorship, and as a result, I've been able to take each life punch and bounce back (the shmoo), turning negatives into positives. Through Alan, I have learned over the years that hanging on to the old crap, as he calls it, is a waste of time. I moved on, and we moved on.

> After a cruel childhood, one must reinvent
> oneself. Then reimagine the world.
>
> —MARY OLIVER

For my next book, *Breakthrough,* I would experience the same type of fight with establishment folks, but life has a way of providing balance. One day out of the blue, Michael Patrick King, producer of *Sex and the City 2,* called me and said, "I just read your book, and I wonder if you'd mind if I mentioned it in our upcoming movie?"

I was dumbfounded. "Of course," I stammered.

"That's great," he said. "And we'd love you to come to the premiere when it comes out."

Sometimes life hands you a gift, and this was one of them. To have a book or product mentioned in a movie is worth millions in free advertising. In fact, generally advertisers *pay* to be placed in a movie, like the bottle of Evian on a desk, or the Casamigos tequila George Clooney is drinking, or the Hermès purse an actress carries. Here was a producer asking if I would mind if he mentioned my book. Wow! All I could think: *We can help more women.*

We flew to New York City for the premiere, a major star-studded event with fans lining both sides of the Manhattan streets leading up to the theater. As I got out of the car, the fans began yelling "Suzanne, Suzanne." I waved back. It's fun to be recognized, and I was proud of my body of work leading to

Sometimes life hands you a gift.

that recognition. Alan always pulls back at these events: he's always watching, protecting, and keeping me safe. He worries that these events are so up close and personal, and you never know what can happen. He often wears dark glasses so he can watch without seeming to look disinterested. It's like having my own personal Secret Service agent, and I find it very sexy.

Once inside, we were seated in the VIP section. To my left, a row in front, was Howard Stern. Darren Star, the creator of the original TV series, was seated behind me. Everywhere I looked were other famous people.

As the movie unfolded, I was astounded that *my* book had become a subplot of the entire movie. I looked at Alan. Howard Stern looked back at me. Darren Star poked me in the back. *Wow.* Never in my wildest dreams could I have imagined such a break, as an author, as a messenger to women, and as a pop culture icon. What this would do for women and, no small thing, what it would do for sales globally.

I felt so satisfied with myself and my work. I had found my encompassing passion: quality of life. And I had finally found a productive use for my celebrity where I could help millions of people enjoy a healthy life.

WHAT I KNOW NOW

Hormone imbalance is a major reason for midlife unhappiness. So much of the contentment and happiness that both Alan and I experience daily is due to being hormonally balanced. He feels right, and I feel right. We aren't fighting deficiencies. It's a beautiful thing. The Seven Dwarves are gone, and it's just two people really having a good time. It's why I keep writing and lecturing, educating people to seek out a knowledgeable doctor. The payoff is great health, a great life, and a happy relationship.

CHAPTER 18

BROADWAY

God grant me the serenity to accept the things I
cannot change, the courage to change the things
I can, and the wisdom to know the difference.

—SERENITY PRAYER

I think every actor's dream is to star on Broadway. Besides the
Annie Get Your Gun offer, I had been offered several other Broadway shows, but the timing never worked out or the project wasn't
the right fit.

Now we had a meeting with Emmy Award–winning veteran
TV writers Ken and Mitzie Welch, best known for the hilarious
sketches on *The Carol Burnett Show,* including all those memorable
ones with Tim Conway and Harvey Korman. Years before, they had
written a piece of special material for my nightclub act. Alan and I
loved it, but it was too sophisticated for a Vegas stage. We sat on it
for ten years, and one day I said to Alan, "We should take another
look at that great material." That was the genesis for my one-woman
Broadway show at the Brooks Atkinson, *The Blonde in the Thunderbird.* We made a deal to open in the summer of 2005 at the greatest
location, 47th Street and Broadway, in the best of all the theaters in
my opinion.

We pulled together a stellar team: Roger Ball as production and lighting designer, Bob Ludwig as sound designer, and Doug Walter as musical director. I'd been fortunate enough to work with these extraordinarily talented men for over thirty years. They are very dear to me, and we all have had a lot of fun together.

I worked with Mitzie day after day. I studied with an opera singer/teacher to get the Vegas out of my sound, and I dug deep into my soul to ask why I wanted to return to this story of alcoholism. It was a story of optimism and passion. I felt it was worth telling in musical form.

Onstage was going to be me . . . solo for ninety minutes, with no intermission. I decided against costumes; I clad myself in all black so you could see body shape but no skin.

We tried out the musical out of town in San Diego, and the response was incredible. Alan had a camera crew stationed outside the theater, and when it was over, people just walked up to the camera to tell how moved they had been. That's what I wanted. Theater should make you think and feel; it's part of the live experience. I wanted to pull people into the story so they saw their own lives in it. I chose to be raw naked in my emotional exposure. I let people see the good the bad and the ugly. The ugly is not easy when you're telling the truth. I wasn't playing a character; I was being *me*!

We rehearsed and rehearsed. At one point in rehearsal, my assistant came over, interrupted me, and whispered in my ear, "You have a phone call."

I said, "Can you take a message and I'll call back?"

"It's President Bush Senior."

Gulp. "Hello, Mr. President, what a nice surprise!"

"Well, I was just sitting here, Suzanne," he said. "And I got your letter and decided I'd rather talk to you than to send a letter." I had met the president several times before, and for some reason we had an instant rapport. I had sent a letter asking him if I could use a piece of film footage of him on C-SPAN where he was speaking at a black-tie state dinner. He had said, "The reason Marlin Fitzwater isn't here tonight is because he busted his ThighMaster." It was hilarious, and frankly, I was flabbergasted that the president of the United States was unknowingly helping to sell it!

"Where are you?" I asked casually (as casually as one can while talking to a former president). "Last time I saw you, you were jumping out of an airplane!"

"Kennebunkport," he said. "In fact, I'm looking out the window at the boats going by."

"Well, how nice," I said, trying not to seem rushed (which I was). "So are you going to let me use the film clip in my Broadway show?"

He laughed, "Only if I'm invited to opening night."

"You got it," I said. "I'd love to talk to you all day"—I really would have, could have, he was that easy—"but I have a whole rehearsal room waiting. I'd love to sing 'Happy Birthday' to you on your birthday again."

"Well, I'd love that," he said, and we hung up. He is a sweetheart and remains a friend today.

After months of rehearsals and tryouts, we opened on Broadway in previews for one month. Wow, every night—standing ovations. They wouldn't let me off the stage. The crowds outside afterward were of people crying, laughing, and emotional.

Broadway was a glorious experience for both of us. Alan was the producer and was good at it. He was calm and collected, working with all the division heads, and everyone respected him. We were definitely outsiders and had a lot to learn, and we knew that the Broadway family does not take readily to outsiders. You had to pay your dues.

One day as a surprise for me, my hairdresser Mooney decided to decorate the greeting room at the Brooks Atkinson. He and his partner used inexpensive chocolate-brown pillows and soft blue accents, very simple and in very good taste. Broadway theaters are quite musty, so this made for a nice place to meet friends after the show.

None of us knew there was a protocol for such things. I came to the studio the following afternoon and the head stage manager, an IATSE member, met me at my dressing room door. Upset, he said, "You're takin' away someone else's job. You want your dressing room fixed up, you come to me." Yipes! He wasn't kidding around. What had been done as a nice gesture by Mooney turned into a huge problem.

When you are on Broadway, you don't want your stage crew upset with you. Curtains have to fly at the right times, sound has to be plugged in, electrical has to work, and lights have to come on at the appropriate times. If you have an angry and upset stage crew, it's possible none of those things will go smoothly onstage, and then you are left with egg on your face in front of the audience.

What could I do to make this right? I thought about it, and the next day when I arrived I decided to go down underneath the stage where all the crew "lived" during work hours; it's where they ate, hung out, and worked on things. I made my way down the back stairs and asked if I could speak to all of them. "I'm new here, and the unions in California are much different. In California TV studios, everybody is free to do the next guy's job if he's busy. There are very few rules. I didn't know how it works here, and I want you to forgive me for being so ignorant. I was not trying to take anyone's job away. It was done as a surprise for me. We'll take everything down, and I sincerely apologize for offending you. I'm really sorry."

The next day I arrived at the theater, and the head union dude asked if I would come on stage—he wanted to talk to me. *Oh God, I thought, now what?*

All the stagehands were on stage, and the head guy says, "Miss Somers, *you* didn't have to do that yesterday, and we just wanted you to know how much we appreciate being respected like that. We want to make you an honorary member of IATSE." Then they handed me a union T-shirt. I wore that shirt bare-legged and with pride around the theater before shows. These were good guys.

· · ·

We were finally ready for opening night and the press. We put together quite an event. After the opening, I was to leave the theater by the stage door and get into a waiting white '57 T-Bird. I would be dressed in a fabulous Richard Tyler ensemble of gold satin.

As I stood before the curtain that night, I could hear the excited crowd. I have stood behind curtains so many hundreds of times in my career that I can tell the mood of the audience from this sound. These were my friends, relatives, and family; Bruce and Caroline and the girls, Leslie and Daisy, Alan's sister and nephews. It meant so much to me that my sister, Maureen, and her husband, Bill, and my brother Danny, had come. This was their story, too.

Barry sent his regrets. I think he was just so nervous for me that he couldn't take the stress. We later laughed about that one. He hadn't wanted them to go after me. He kept saying, "You're Hollywood— they're going to kill you. They killed *me*." I didn't believe him. I'm harmless. I come from a good place in my heart. I'm telling the raw truth—I'm emotionally *naked* out there.

I took one last look at Alan standing in the wings. He gave me a thumbs-up and mouthed *I love you*. I loved him. He was always there, always had my back.

The show went perfectly, followed by the longest standing ovation. I had a hard time not crying from joy. I/we had done it. We had pulled it off.

My dressing room was filled with our nearest and dearest. Everyone was excited. Flowers filled my little space. I felt such love and joy and support. Everyone left so I could dress and proceed to the big after-party. I stepped out the stage door to such a huge crowd of people, it shocked me. Forty-seventh Street was so jammed, cars couldn't get by. It was a love fest. Everyone wanted autographs and photos. The T-Bird was waiting. I sat on top of the backseat of the convertible like a movie queen in a cloud of bliss hard to describe.

We rode the long way through Times Square to the restaurant a few blocks away, and when we arrived at the after-party, there was another throng of people, fans, paparazzi, so many I could hardly get into my own celebration.

The party was fabulous and more. Big, flashy, splashy, and wonderful, and by around three in the morning, it was all over. Alan and I returned to the Lowell Hotel, our home away from home. I barely had the energy to remove my makeup, but I did, then fell into bed wrapped in Alan's arms. Then we cried together. It had been such intense work, and it had gone so perfectly. Sleep came, deep, peaceful, satisfied sleep.

That was Sunday night. On Monday morning I was scheduled to appear on *The View*. We got up early, and I washed my hair and put on makeup and my good outfit. We jumped into the limousine to get to the ABC studio.

Something felt off on the show that morning, so I was glad when it was over.

"Oh my god!" I exclaimed to Alan excitedly as I got back into the car. "I forgot all about the reviews! Have you seen them?"

"Yes" was all he said. In my euphoria, I hadn't even noticed how quiet he had been all morning.

"What?" I asked, not wanting to hear his answer.

Softly he said, "They killed you. They hated it. They hated you, they hated your hair, they hated everything."

Always one to see the glass half full, I went back to work the next evening thinking, *Screw them*. But I didn't know the heft that a Broadway review carries; tickets had already been sold for the week, but from next Saturday on, it looked bad. Roger went to the box office each day to look at the rap (tickets sold) and came back to my dressing room shaking his head. If you were coming to New York for your summer vacation and you were going to see one Broadway show, would you choose the one that had the worst reviews and pay three or four times more to see it? The reviews were the kiss of death.

I knew what we had to do. On Saturday night, I called everyone involved into my dressing room to tell them the sad news. This would be our last show.

Broadway, it can break your heart. I now knew what this quote meant.

I just wanted to go home. But couldn't yet, as I had committed to appear on the Home Shopping Network in Tampa between nights off on the Broadway show. So at four-thirty on a Sunday morning, Alan and I dragged ourselves out of bed and started the terrible job of packing our things; it was a lot because we had been committed to stay for quite a while. Boxes and boxes, a large van was waiting outside. I was distraught and exhausted. In hindsight, we probably should have left New York and then flown back afterward and packed in a more relaxed fashion, but I just wanted to get out of town. We flew to Tampa in a jam-packed plane full of our things: clothes, computers, exercise equipment, and accumulated papers—I was in the process of writing another book, *Slim and Sexy Forever.* (Think I'm an overachiever?)

Once I was in Tampa and on the air, I thanked all my "ladies" for the tremendous turnout. They came filled with enthusiasm. Because of the interactiveness of electronic television, all the talks I had been having with them, all the intimacies I had revealed about me and Alan and our family, and all the photos in the books depicting our lifestyle had connected us. They knew I wasn't phony, and they knew on this day I needed them to take care of me.

On the second night of my HSN appearance, we flew home to Los Angeles. There was too much baggage on the plane; hardly any room to sit. It was Roger, me, and Alan. Roger has been with us through everything for the last thirty-five years. He is our show designer, our lighting designer, and our head of production; he is in our office every day when we are not on the road. Basically, Roger does everything for us that's production related. He is the best, a big part of our family, and an essential part of our business. We pulled out the tequila and decided to get a little drunk. If ever I needed or wanted to get a little high and escape, it was now.

Somewhere in the middle of Arizona, the plane started making funny noises. Thankfully we were two tequilas in, and I didn't feel panic or fear until the pilot walked back to us and said, "I don't feel comfortable flying this plane any longer. The fuel tanks aren't feeding from one wing to the other, and I'm afraid we will run out of fuel. I'm bringing her down while we can."

> *I found forgiveness and grew as a person. I could not change what had happened, but came out stronger for having lived it. I'm better because of it. This is "the perfection of life" I speak about. We all have our personal struggles to work through, and mine brought me to who I have become today. I found my life's meaning and hopefully through my searching I have given hope and strength to others.*

That sobers you up. Suddenly Broadway seemed insignificant; living not dying was all we were thinking about. We landed in the middle of the night somewhere in Arizona with no way to get home unless we hired a driver to take us to the nearest private airfield, which was about an hour and a half away. I was so tired and stressed, I felt like I was going to lose it. I rarely feel like that. It had been such a journey the last couple of days: the lack of sleep, the sadness, the monumental packing job, the eighteen hours in the air over two days of being "on," flying home, and now this frightening landing in the middle of the night on a dark tarmac. The pilot helped us find a driver who would take us and *all* our things, no easy matter. Finally a guy named Mohammed showed up. He had a heavy accent and said his friends call him Fred.

All the way in the dark of night, as we were driving to wherever, Fred was speaking Arabic quite loudly to someone on his cell phone. Please read nothing into this except that it added to an already stressful and unbelievable few days.

As we rocketed through the darkness, Mohammed was on his phone speaking in Arabic. I had no idea where this guy was taking us. We were in the middle of the desert; it was three a.m., and his speaking loudly on the phone was really bugging me. (Why do people speak so loudly on their cell phones?) Was this Islamophobia, or would I feel the same way about a guy named Ilyich speaking Russian? Absolutely. I guess we were nervous about the plane running out of fuel, the show closing, being exhausted, rocketing through the middle of the desert, going who knew where, a stranger driving too fast—it was all bad!

So far it had been a series of negatives. Surely, the sun would shine soon.

And shine it did. We boarded our new plane with a bubbly stewardess with sun-streaked surfer hair, a big smile, big boobs, and a great ass. She served our favorite drinks as we took off and headed for our precious home. Soon we would be safely in bed with our cats staring at us, and our normal life would return.

We got home to our love nest in Malibu. I turned out the lights, we held each other, and as I was at that place between awake and sleep, Suzanne said, "I'm bloated. I shouldn't have eaten that cake." Oh, Jesus—I knew what that meant. I moved as far away from her as I could without falling off the bed and covered my head with the pillow to snuff out what sounded like Miles Davis playing crazy shit all night.

Sleep was eluding me; I was tossing and turning, rolling over, twisting, covers off, covers on, bad dreams. I really shouldn't have had the cake. This went on for days. On one night I woke up from a bad dream with *Why, why, why* screaming in my head over and over. I turned on the TV to quiet my brain, and a guy being interviewed on a New York show said, "Let it be."

We get our messages in mysterious ways, even from late-night TV. It hit me like a brick. Paul McCartney's famous three words were what I needed to hear. In mounting the Broadway show, I had accomplished what I'd set out to do. The people who came had heard what they needed to hear. I was finished. The message had been delivered, and it was time to move on.

From then on I was all right again.

"Pick yourself up, dust yourself off, and start all over again."

I would. I did. I have!

WHAT I KNOW NOW

My one-woman show was the universal story of the alcoholic and those who live with them. Alcoholism is an addictive disease no different from abuse of any kind. It knows no boundaries, and too many people are touched by it. Lives get ruined as a result. Finding closure is not for sissies, but for those who have the courage to do so, it is life-changing—it frees you. For me, it took therapy, writing, and creating to find ultimate closure. It took a massive amount of personal work to get to the other side, to wellness, but then I was free and filled with gratitude. I found forgiveness and grew as a person. I could not change what had happened, but came out stronger for having lived it. I'm better because of it. This is "the perfection of life" I speak about. We all have our personal struggles to work through, and mine brought me to who I have become today. I found my life's meaning and hopefully through my searching I have given hope and strength to others.

CHAPTER 19

FIRE

A goal in life to strive for: To be untouched by
triumph and to be untroubled by failure.

—CAROL BURNETT

We were in the news again, but in a way I had never dreamed. The morning of the fire, I was on the balcony having a cup of coffee, and I said to Alan, "Hmmm—it's one of those fire days."

I was referring to a Santa Ana condition, where the winds blow toward the ocean from the desert. It's a very warm wind, and if conditions are right—if it's windy and dry enough—then someone stupidly tossing a match or a burning cigarette can be just enough to devastate lives. But nothing like that could ever be a threat to us. After all, we lived on the *water,* and the fire department was about five hundred feet down the road from us. We were safe. We were protected.

I did several things that morning that, in retrospect, strike me as strange. I looked at my Native American moccasins that I had been collecting for forty-five years and thought, *These are so wasted in this house. I should bring them to Palm Springs.* And then I talked myself out of it.

We had planned to go to Palm Springs the next day because I

was giving a dinner party for my desert and L.A. friends who were coming in for the event. Instead, I said to Alan, "We have a light day. Why don't we go today instead of tomorrow?" This decision most likely saved our lives. I went to my closet and pulled out my favorite black leather jacket, then decided the weather in Palm Springs didn't require it. (Damn, I wish I hadn't talked myself out of that one.) I took a couple of favorite pieces of jewelry but left the rest in our fireproof safe.

My housekeeper said to me out of the blue, "I don't feel right in my body today."

"What's wrong?"

"I have a *burning* in my stomach." I encouraged her to go home, but she said, "I'll wait until you leave, and then I'll go."

We left the house at approximately two o'clock. In the meantime, my housekeeper's daughter called and told her she didn't have a ride home from school, so she left an hour after we did. This move probably saved her life.

At a little after four, we arrived in Palm Springs. As we were putting things away in the kitchen, the phone rang. "Your house is on fire," my neighbor told me. "No," I said, "we just left—impossible."

"Turn on your television set," he urged.

And there was an announcer doing a play-by-play, saying, "I don't know whose house this is, but it's a goner." I thought, *I know whose house this is.* It was unmistakable. Alan and I stood a foot away from the TV set watching our house disappear, and then to add insult to injury, my Jaguar blew up. I looked at Alan. He was holding his hands over his mouth in shock, as was I. I said quietly, "Well . . . that's that." The house had blown up and was totally *gone* in what seemed like minutes.

It is thought that someone on the road above—Pacific Coast Highway—tossed a burning cigarette at the stoplight below Pepperdine University. The fire started so fast and was so hot that it raced down the bluff, set fire to the large tree in front of our home, then got so hot that a fireball jumped the house and hit the ocean. There the torque of the water blew the fireball under our house, where it ignited the gas line and blew up the house! Had we stayed, had our housekeeper stayed, none of us would have gotten out.

Yes, we had been protected, but it was a lot to wrap our arms around at that moment. Three hours before, we had had our home and all our belongings, and now it had all burned to the ground. Everything was gone. It would take a while for me to become philosophical. We were still in a state of shock having watched our life get blown up. Newsmen were everywhere on the Malibu road, and reporters were saying, "It seems this is Suzanne Somers and Alan Hamel's house."

The phone rang again—this time it was Steve Lawrence. I love Steve, he is very Vegas, and he said, "Suzanne baby, your house burned down." I don't know why, but it struck me as funny, and I started laughing. He said, "Oh baby, you always had the greatest sense of humor."

Losing everything is a profound experience. People tried to comfort us by saying things like "It's just stuff." That made me angry. I'd think, *Then, why don't you go burn all your stuff and see how you like it?* I can say it's just stuff, but others can't. Then again, I also think I was oversensitive.

We were luckier than most—we still had our home in Palm Springs. But it has always been a second home—all the good things, the stuff of memories, were in the Malibu house. We had had a storage room under the house and a large wardrobe where many of my costumes and good clothing, star clothes, including the outfit I wore getting my star on the Hollywood Walk of Fame, things that had meaning, were all stored. Our photographs were in this house, the computers, things I treasured, like the china set my mother had bought me piece by piece.

I must tell you, one of the shallow things you think of when everything burns is, *With all the clothes I had, why did I wear this?* I had been wearing comfortable black sweats, a black T-shirt, and my favorite run-down, whacked-out boots. I kept very little clothing in Palm Springs, so essentially this was it!

The next day we got up early to go back to Malibu to see if there was anything left to salvage. When we arrived, it was quite a scene, with at least twenty news trucks from Fox to CNN, from network crews to local. Reporters everywhere, and camera people. When they saw us pull up, they swarmed our car. We were both emotionally fragile and hadn't intended on this being so very public.

"Miss Somers, how do you feel? How do you feel?" The reporters were relentless. It reminded me of a scene in the old Mary Tyler Moore show where she and Ed Asner and the others in the newsroom emotionally moved together in a pack. I walked, and the reporters smashed in around both of us. I couldn't even see my house.

We were alive. We had each other. Our kids were healthy and safe.

Finally I said, "I don't know how I feel. I need a moment to see what's left and feel my feelings." At that they backed off and gave Alan and me our space.

And there it was: ashes and timbers. Humorously, a pair of Alan's purple underpants were hanging on an ember, flying proudly. That made me laugh. But it was somber. Sobering. It was all a charred mess. Nothing to salvage. At least we had the fireproof safe, I thought. In it were my most prized treasures: my jewelry, and my first seven books in longhand. It would have been the biggest hurt if they were gone.

I was not crushed about losing our home, since I always believed that wherever Suzanne was was home. I thought about the personal things that burned and missed nothing aside from the Tom Ford leather jackets designed at Gucci. Well, we both certainly missed Suzanne's Indian collection, but for Suzanne it was more emotional. For me, believing in the Indian afterlife, all those beautiful artifacts had gone to happy hunting grounds.

As I write this, it's been some years since the fire, and we have lived in four rentals, which is a huge pain in the ass. Rentals are not lovingly looked after, and I've spent a good deal of my time bitching to the owners about fixing this or that and having to deal with workmen coming and going.

Years ago we rented a beach house that we owned to Michael Landon, who was between marriages. One day he called me to say his washer wasn't working. I promised to send the repairman over before day's end, but thought, This is Michael Landon! *I sent him a new washer instead and had it installed that day before he returned from the studio. He sent me flowers.*

As I told *Extra,* "I don't have a son or daughter in Iraq. I haven't lost a loved one. We will rebuild. I truly believe we will learn something great from this experience." I believed what I said. We were lucky to be alive. We were lucky we hadn't lost a child, and we would rebuild!

Suzanne, the worst is over. I lived by those infamous words of Mrs. Kilgore from so long ago. I had been through worse. We were alive. We had each other. Our kids were healthy and safe. All was good.

I learned about sifters, companies you call when your house on the beach burns and they come and sift through the sand with you all day, looking for anything of any value. Remarkably, the day before, I had taken off my wedding rings to wash my hands and popped them in a little dish, then forgot them. I remember being in the car feeling my finger, as you do when something has been such a part of you for so long, and feeling that little bit of panic that I had left them.

Sifting, sifting, sifting . . . the guy would look through his sifter and toss. At one point, he was about to toss, and I said, "Stop!" It was my wedding ring, the ring Alan's father had found in a potato bin so many years ago, the ring that fit me perfectly, the simple gold band with an initial *S* engraved inside. Unbelievably, there it was, blackened but not melted. I felt so happy. I put it on my finger, never to be removed again ever.

I showed the sifters the approximate area where the safe would have been so they started going through the sand there, sifting tray by sifting tray. The safe was large and heavy, so it would have fallen through the collapsed floor, and sure enough there it was, stuck deep in the sand looking worse for wear but intact. *Thank goodness.*

We had to hire a safecracker. A crowbar and a little push, and then, bang—the door opened. It had taken him less than a minute. Wow! So much for the security of safes. And inside it . . . all was ashes. Everything: the money was dust, the jewelry was melted and a mess. And worst of all, the manuscripts of my books, my bestsellers, were all burned. Especially sad was *Keeping Secrets*, its thousand handwritten pages now a charred mess. I had always planned to give it to Bruce. It had value, sentimental and otherwise; the book had been a major bestseller, the story of his mother's life written in longhand. He could have kept it for his children or donated it to a university.

> All negative experiences are a waste of time if nothing is learned from them.

"How could this happen?" I asked no one, but the safecracker said it was "probably 'cause you kept bullets in there. If the fire gets too hot, the bullets explode."

I looked at Alan, who sheepishly said, "Where else was I going to keep them?" I find it funny now, but at that moment I felt steam coming from my head. Slowly I said, "You kept your ammunition in the safe?!"

All negative experiences are a waste of time if nothing is learned from them. Here's what I learned. I learned about letting go of attachment to things. It *was* just stuff. It could all mostly be replaced. Do I miss things? Yes, I still miss that jacket. Alan misses his father's gold cuff links and his favorite jacket. I wish my Native American collection wasn't lost. I wish I'd given it to a museum. And I miss my handwritten manuscripts—those were irreplaceable.

But I learned something else, too: the kindness of people. Malibu is a small village, with only thirteen thousand people. Everybody knows everybody. That's what always attracted me; it was a small yet sophisticated town. I'm from a small town, and I do better in an environment like that. The people of Malibu know that when there's a fire, it could just as likely have been them.

During the days I was in the sand digging through things, people came by and brought us soup and food. Jane Seymour brought us two boxed salads. It meant so much. We were dirty messes, and we were both starving, and here was this nice woman bringing us salads.

James Perse, the famous high-end soft cotton T-shirt maker, sent us each a bag of new sweat pants, cozy T-shirts, and sweaters, things you really want when you have no clothes. Each gift brought me to tears. When we went into the village at night to eat, no restaurant would let us pay. Even the paparazzi were kind and respectful, taking photos only from a distance, not invading our space up close

These acts of kindness helped us heal.

and personal. Then the most incredible of all, our neighbors down the street came to us and said, "We're leaving for three months. You will use our home." We knew this man and his wife, David and Linda Shaheen, only casually—we had been invited to one of their garden parties once. I just stared at them and quietly and humbly said, "Thank you."

These acts of kindness helped us heal. We moved into their home with our new T-shirts and started the process of rebuilding our lives. Their home was gorgeous. The first night I soaked in their amazing master bathtub, looking out at the sea, and I knew we were going to be okay. I promised myself if I ever had the opportunity to help someone in need, I would be there. I would do the same for them.

One day I turned on the news, and a nuclear power plant in Japan had been decimated by a tsunami. It was chaos there, which is very uncharacteristic for the Japanese. Dr. Kotaro Yoshimura, the doctor who pioneered regrowing women's breasts after cancer, and who made Suzanne's remarkable stem cell breast regrowth possible, lived in Tokyo with his family. I heard Suzanne on the phone inviting someone to come live with us. When she hung up, I asked her, "Who's moving in?" She said she had invited Dr. Yoshimura and his wife and kids to stay with us till things cooled down in Japan.

"Suzanne—you invited a family of four, three of whom speak no English, to move in with us for an indefinite time?" My first reaction was Are you high? *Then I remembered Linda and David Shaheen, barely acquaintances then, now dear friends, who had given us their spectacular home for three months after the fire: angels. Suzanne has a huge heart, and that's one of the reasons we're together and always will be.*

CHAPTER 20

KNOCKOUT

Don't cry because it's over, smile because it happened.

—DR. SEUSS

I am proud to be a shmoo! You get hit, you bounce back, you get hit again, you bounce back again. But I didn't know that the shmoo was about to give me the ultimate test.

For three days, we had been on the air at the Home Shopping Network, doing three three-hour shows daily; it was very intense and taxing. It's an ad-libbed form, that's the fun of it, no script, but at the end of the day, my brain feels like it's been fried.

Alan and I always stayed at the same hotel every month and had been doing so for several years. I noticed with amusement that this time a large group of drug salesmen for a pharmaceutical sales conference were also staying at the hotel. Every day as I was coming and going, large groups of salesmen (mostly men) in suits were gathered in the lobby waiting for the next meeting to begin.

I said to Alan, "Ironic, isn't it? I'm their worst nightmare, and here we are all staying together." Ha ha!

My books had made a significant dent in the synthetic hormone business, a fact I'm sure the drug companies were not enjoying. Since the introduction of bioidentical hormones, the synthetic hormone business had dropped by a whopping 72 percent. If I were them, I'd probably want to shut me up.

Sunday night after our last show, we invited our entire HSN team to the hotel bar for a glass of wine and something to eat. We had all worked hard, and sometimes a glass of wine at the end of the day soothes, relaxes, and takes the kinks out. Today I've replaced wine with clear tequila, but back then it was wine. I also ordered a salad. I placed my drink and salad on the little cocktail table to my left and slightly behind me. The place was swarming with drug salesmen, but our little group was sitting in a semicircle in front of the fireplace.

Suddenly, after finishing half of my drink, I didn't feel good. I got sweaty and clammy, and the room started spinning. I told Alan I wanted to get out of there. By the time we reached the restaurant entrance, I felt I was in trouble. We got up to our hotel room, and I became freezing cold. Colder than I'd ever felt; I was shivering, cold to my bones. I asked Alan to lie on top of me. My whole body was shaking. And then I felt hot. I looked down at my arms, and my whole body was covered in a hot, itchy rash. My hands were swelling, as were my feet. Then I started having trouble breathing.

We had flown private, so Alan called the pilot and said we needed to go home—now. On the plane, I couldn't get warm. I was back to freezing. By the time we reached Palm Springs, I was fighting for every breath. I called a local doctor, Steve Nelson, a man I respected, someone I had interviewed for one of my books, and he said, "You are in danger. Go to the emergency room immediately." I knew he was right. Alan, who never loses anything, couldn't find his keys, so we asked our gardener to drive us to the hospital. I lay in the back of his gardening truck in a fetal position gasping for breath. Alan had called the ER in advance, and they were waiting in front with a wheelchair.

"Why can't you breathe? Why can't you breathe?" the ER doc was literally yelling at me.

Suddenly the professionals snapped to it. ER docs are incredible: they know what they must do—they are there to save your life. This one was saving mine. I had no breath left in me. It's an awful feeling to try and breathe and it's not there. You feel panic. *Where's the air? Where's my air?* An oxygen mask was placed over my face. Decadron, a powerful steroid, was shoved into my veins, and Benadryl as well, to stop the tremendous rash, welts, and swelling. Then albuterol was administered with the oxygen to get me breathing. I kept gasping for breath, and my lungs felt like they were twisting inside out. But with these interventions, I felt the breath coming back, still labored, but there.

I was so scared. *What is happening?* I had been in perfect health a few hours earlier. Thus began an odyssey so frightening, so life-altering, that even today I'm not the same.

I was given a CAT scan. I didn't want to do it. I knew through research that a CAT scan has a thousand times *more* radiation than they thought! I didn't want it, but something was terribly wrong with me, and we had to find out what it was.

It was just me alone in the CAT scan room. The operator sat in another room, glassed off. It was like being in a science fiction movie . . . *click, click, click* were its sounds.

I was wheeled back to the ER; I still couldn't breathe properly, so I was reconnected to oxygen. Then the ER doc came in with a nurse and closed the door behind him. Something was ominous. His tone was serious. "I brought the nurse with me because I hate what I have to say. You have a mass on your lung so large, it's covering your bladder. You have so many tumors in your chest, we can't count them. They all have masses in them. You have a blood clot in your lung, and you have pneumonia, so I'm going to check you into the hospital because the blood clot will kill you *first*."

I was checked into the hospital, and then the assigned oncologist told me the news that I had "cancer everywhere." He said, "What we can do is start you on chemotherapy today." In my frightened, exhausted, confused state, I said, "I'd rather die than take chemo." At that he said, sounding somewhat perturbed, "Then if I were you, I would think about getting your things in order." And he exited the room.

Asshole.

Silence. The air had been sucked out. How did you process something like this? I looked at Alan, and his face was contorted. Our eyes locked. Everything about my

Family is everything. life, our life, was suddenly out of control.

I couldn't move because of all the wires hooked into me. Yesterday I had been fine, on the air, laughing. What happened since then?

"Call Bruce. Call Stephen and Leslie," I told Alan. They needed to know.

If I had cancer *everywhere,* how long did I have to live? The thought was devastatingly painful. My heart was pounding, pounding. I told the nurse, "I think I need something to calm me down. I feel like I'm going to have a heart attack." My blood pressure, usually low at 110/80, was now at 191. More drugs were pumped into me. This time it was Ativan, a tranquilizing drug. Then they added heparin.

Meekly I said, "What's that?"

"This is to prevent blood clotting," the nurse answered.

Me. The woman who took no drugs was loaded up and asking for more of them. Calm came over me . . . I guess the Ativan was taking effect. I could see why people got hooked. This one felt dreamy. I fell asleep.

I woke up a few hours later, and another doctor was there, a lung cancer doctor. He was nicer than the first one but essentially confirmed the bad news. "Looks like lung cancer." I had never smoked a cigarette in my life. Lung cancer?

It was like living in a bad movie that kept getting worse but you couldn't stop watching. Alan hadn't said a word. Night came, I think, and he crawled into my little bed with me and held me. Our kids came the next day and fought for me. Leslie was a little warrior. "She can't have cancer," she told the doctor. "She had her stem cells banked last year, and you can't have cancer to do that. She checked out perfectly." Bruce was fighting tears. Caroline was doing research. I felt so grateful. Family is everything.

For six days and six nights, six doctors all confirmed the same thing: my body was riddled with cancer. It didn't make sense. I lived and ate like an athlete. I had love in my life. I thought good thoughts. Was this a result of the original breast cancer? How could it have come back? I had felt I was well and on the other side. I had done it right, my way. I had been so sure. And then I thought of all the women who followed me, who believed in me. Would this make them doubt all they had learned? I was overwhelmed with fear and sadness. I had no anger—it just didn't feel right to me.

By this time, I believe my cells had accepted the information and were shutting down. It might sound kooky, but really think about it for a moment; we are, as human beings, approximately ninety trillion cells, and they all communicate with one another. All these professionals had been telling me the same thing: "You have cancer everywhere." What I heard was *You are going to die. You are going to die.* My cells heard the message and accepted it: *We're dying? Okay. Let's start the process.*

It's not who you are. It's not what you do. It's not what you have. It's only, only, about who you love and who loves you.

On the sixth day, the doctors agreed to biopsy me "to be sure." The surgery would involve opening my throat to extract a piece of my lung and a piece of one of the "so many tumors, we can't count them." The surgeon said, "I have to cut right around your vocal cords. I'll try my best not to damage them."

I was devastated. Not to sing anymore? But then, who cares if you can sing if you're dead?

In retrospect, this is not how I think. I'm always the one to see the glass half full. But shock and awe are tremendously powerful. I was so drugged up, so confused, so *sad.* So *sad!* I loved my life, everything about it. I loved my family. I wanted more with all of them. I wanted so much more with Alan. I wanted more of us.

The night before the scheduled surgery, I woke up from a sound sleep and heard what I thought was a loudspeaker, scratchy background noise and all. I believe now that I was having a dream. I looked at Alan, asleep in my arms in my little hospital bed. I looked at my children, sleeping on uncomfortable furniture, and wondered, *Why haven't they awakened?*

Then I heard a voice, a voice I shall never forget. As clear as day it said, *It's not who you are. It's not what you do. It's not what you have. It's only, only, about who you love and who loves you.*

My husband was still wrapped in my arms; my children were still asleep. And I realized I loved them all so fiercely and had so much love in my life. I felt at peace. If this was the message of my life, then I was ready.

The morning of surgery, the energy in the room changed. Everyone had a job to do to prepare me. Finally I was put on a gurney and had one more moment to lock eyes with Alan. In that moment, our eyes said everything. It was the deepest connection and communication; we both welled up. What could we say? Alan managed to get out, "You're going to be okay." Then I was wheeled off.

I remember the ceiling and the clickety-clack of the gurney on the hospital floor. We went down (it seemed) an elevator, then through what I think were double doors into *very* bright light. The surgeon was standing over me with a mask, surgical gown, and gloves. I could see his kind eyes. "Try," I said, pleading, "please try to be careful. I'm a songbird. I can't imagine not singing ever again." Then I was in that place where you go, somewhere in space, somewhere out of the world that I knew.

"Suzanne, Suzanne," I heard.

I tried to open my eyes. It was Alan. *What was he saying?*

"Suzanne, you don't have cancer anywhere." They had all been wrong.

What if I had taken the chemotherapy? What if I had lost my ability to sing or talk—for nothing?

Back in my hospital room, I tried to find my joy. After all, I didn't have cancer . . . but I had no will. The intensity of the week had beaten me down.

Then it got worse. A new doctor walked into my room, all smiles: "I bet you're happy with the good news that you don't have cancer. Now, unfortunately, we feel that you are in grave danger, and so is the community."

"What are you talking about?" I asked.

"I am head of infectious disease for the hospital, and we have every reason to believe you have a serious, contagious disease."

"Like what?" I stammered

"Well, we think it could be tuberculosis, leprosy, or coccidioidomycosis."

It was as if an atom bomb had been dropped on our room and the mushroom cloud hadn't yet cleared. Leprosy? Tuberculosis?

Dr. Infectious says, "So now we have to move you to an isolation room to protect the community." At that, a team showed up to move my things. My children were ushered out "for their own good." Caroline's voice was stressed like a rubber band pulled too tight, saying meekly, "I thought it sounded like you had coccidioidomycosis."

My lion, my protector, came roaring back. Alan demanded, "I'm going with her."

"You can't," said Dr. Infectious.

"I'm going with her!"

She could tell he was not going to be messed with. We were already spent from the ordeal; we didn't know what all this meant. But I could feel Alan was taking back our control.

We got upstairs, and I was in a room with hoses and exhausts to filter my germs to outer space. Everyone coming and going was wearing what looked like bee suits, except for me and Alan.

Dr. Infectious came in, and I said, "I want to go home."

She said, "Oh, that's not possible. We have to wait until your cultures come back from the CDC."

"How long will that take?" I asked incredulously.

"Anywhere from three to six weeks," she said matter-of-factly, and left the room.

I e-mailed Dr. Jonathan Wright.

"Get out of there," he wrote back. "You are getting very bad medicine. None of these diseases present like that. Get home, and I'll take over."

When Dr. Infectious came back to my room, I felt crazy. "I want to go home," I said sternly. "I want to go home," I said louder. And then I screamed, à la Shirley MacLaine in *Terms of Endearment*, when the nurse would not give her daughter, Debra Winger, the drugs to take the pain away, *"I want to go home!!!"*

I wanted out of this loony bin, this house of horrors of bad medicine, all these arrogant doctors, smug in their righteousness. One great internist backed me up, but the rest seemed to enjoy having me under their control. I felt that my being a messenger for alternative health was a factor. I started pulling out my IVs. Alan collected my things. Dr. Infectious knew if she stopped me, I would use all the force of my status to overrule her authority. I was not going to stay.

Finally she said, "Okay, we're going to let you go home. But we're quarantining you to your property for the next six weeks or until we get your cultures back. And you must take the medicine I'm sending home with you to address all the possibilities of these diseases."

"Fine," I said.

A wheelchair arrived. I took my bag with five thousand dollars' worth of medicine that I intended to throw out. I considered it my getaway bag and worth it so I could be freed from this place. We were wheeled out the back door to our car. As I sat in the front seat, I felt defeated. Spent. It had all been too much.

Once I was home, I called Dr. Wright and gave him the names of the medicines. He called back shortly and said, "Any one of those medicines could kill you, and taking them all together is suicide."

"That's all I need to hear," I told him, and got rid of them all.

I sat on my porch in my robe—and cried and cried.

Two weeks later the phone rang, and it was the one doctor I trusted at the hospital. He said, "Your cultures came back, and you have coccidioidomycosis, otherwise known as Valley Fever. It's serious. It's a fungus found in the top two layers of soil in the south-western desert. Do you garden a lot?"

"I do. I work in my vegetable garden, and I dig up artifacts with my friend in Santa Fe on his pueblo."

"Well, that's probably where you got it."

Cocci, as it's known, has cancer-like effects. It can kill you by eating away at you as cancer cells do. (Think mold on your bath-room tile.) It gets in your body and finds a happy place and then starts taking over. The remedy is antifungals. *Shit.* I didn't want to spend my life on the Diflucan I had been sent with this latest diag-nosis. It was already blowing out my kidneys. Yet I couldn't connect the dots between the violence that had brought me into the hospi-tal and this diagnosis: the anaphylactic shock from which I almost died, the rash, welts, blood clots, and pneumonia. None of these things added up to cocci.

What had happened to me? Had someone put something in my drink at that bar that night? Could it be that sinister? If Suzanne Somers had cancer, the bioidentical movement would be over. Ev-eryone would say, *Look, she took those hormones, and now she's dying of cancer.*

There was something more to this.

I was in L.A. at the office of my internist and anti-aging doctor, Michael Galitzer, and he said, "I don't get it. I was an ER doc, and when someone in anaphylactic shock came in, the first thing we did was check their eosinophils."

"What's an eosinophil?" I asked.

"It tells if there has been an allergic attack or a poisoning."

When I got home, I looked at my lab work from the hospital, and there it was. Normal eosinophil levels are from 2 to 5, but mine had been at 16—off the charts. That night I had been having an allergic attack, one severe enough to bring me to the hospital. But what was I allergic to?

A few months later Dr. Nick Gonzalez, a great man and a great cancer doctor who believed in a nondrug approach to treatment, was speaking at a conference in Salt Lake City. I was speaking at the same conference. He said to me, "I do radionics. It's very sophisticated hair testing. Give me a piece of your hair. I'd like to run some tests."

"I've been coloring my hair for years."

"Doesn't matter. Our equipment is so sophisticated, we can take a strand of hair from a thousand-year-old cadaver and tell what it had for dinner."

Two weeks later the results came back: "You were poisoned by succinylcholine."

Succinylcholine is a drug used in surgery. If you're overdosed, you go into anaphylactic shock and get rashes and welts all over your body, and your extremities swell. It reads like cancer on a CAT scan. It can kill you. ABC News did a piece on it that I'll quote:

> Succinylcholine is such a perfect murder weapon. The best poisons usually have three things in common: small effective dose, also called Median Lethal Dose (or LD50), ease of administration, and rapid and definitive action. The fourth characteristic, the difficulty in detection by a forensics team, is a big premium most poisons don't possess.

I was dumbfounded. "But what about the cocci?" I asked.

"Probably this drug degraded your immune system so quickly that it dislodged a dormant fungus in your lung. That's the mass they saw in your lung. Many people walk around their whole lives with fungus and aren't bothered by it if they have a strong immune system."

This was hardball! I could never prove it. Nor could I talk about it, lest I come off as a nutcase.

I've always believed in the goodness of humanity. I'm a trusting person. The feeling of violation and horror I experienced in suspecting someone tried to take my life stays with me today. There is evil in the world. I could have allowed myself to become bitter and fearful, but this is where having Alan comes into play. He is my protector, but even he couldn't protect me from this sinister act. I realized that when someone wants to harm you, they will figure a way. My soul had been damaged. My heart had been broken. The person or persons who did this to me tried to steal my life. They left me with an empty soul, and that was killing me.

For the first time ever, the shmoo was nowhere to be found.

If there is one word never attributed to me, it is *sadness*. Even as a child, when all seemed hopeless, I had never become depressed. I had been frightened, I had had a deep-seated fear of the unknown, but I had always been able to see the light, to see what was good about the new day. But this was different. For weeks, months, a year after this terrible episode, I became a different person. I couldn't find my joy. I was going about my life, but every day I felt like I was paralyzed. As a child of an alcoholic, I was an expert at pretending all was well when it wasn't, so my joylessness was my own burden.

By now, Alan and I had moved into a beautiful leased house on the hill in Malibu, while we waited to get permits to rebuild our burned-down home on the beach. I busied myself with redecorating the new house. I entertained quite often, had friends over, did anything to fill my days, anything to escape from the terrible depression I was feeling.

For the first time in my life, too, I couldn't find my joy with Alan. I felt all alone. I cried for no reason. Alan, too, was having a difficult time. One night I woke up in the middle of the night, and he was vomiting.

"What's wrong?" I asked.

"I don't know," he said flatly.

What was happening to me? To us?

My sadness and depression begat more of the same. My thoughts were dark; I couldn't find my way out. I was disappointed in myself, which only added fuel to my journey toward darkness. Depression is a terrible thing. I didn't understand it at all, but it felt so real, so concrete, so leaden. I had thought it could be handled like what

Cher said in *Moonstruck*: "Snap out of it." But I couldn't snap out
of it. I didn't understand the delicate alchemy that comprises who
we are as individuals. Stress blunts important hormones, as well as
minerals and nutrients in our brains. I didn't want to feel this way.
Depression physically hurts. I tried to shake it. I wanted to be happy
again, but it just got worse and worse. I couldn't find my way out,
and I was very afraid of the darkness that had become my mind.

It didn't enter my thinking that what I needed was to go to a
holistic psychiatrist, someone who could connect the dots of what
extreme stress and trauma had done to
me and unleashed in my body. As I would
later learn, the barrier wall of my gut lining had been shredded like a tire on a freeway, and all the toxins from all the drugs
I had been given were leaking out into my
bloodstream and making their way up to
my brain. When the brain becomes toxic,
it shrinks to make way for the toxicity, so
my brain wasn't working right. This was
all information I would later write about.

*It requires great
humility to get
emotionally well. You
have to see the part
you've played in the
dramas of your life,
and you have to face
yourself in the most
raw and naked ways.*

I thought it was me, Alan, us. We weren't "right" anymore.

Was our love affair over—had it fizzled out? Something had
changed. Something was missing. I would sit on my balcony looking at the ocean and feel . . . nothing.

Alan cried one night. I had never seen him cry except when his
father and mother died. I knew I was breaking his heart, and I felt
powerless to stop the pain.

*It was just awful. The worst part was that I couldn't fix it or even know
what was wrong. We weren't the Suzanne and Alan I knew. I could tell
we still wanted to be together, but some dark force had entered our lives.
Not knowing what it was, we couldn't get rid of it. I knew that I would not
accept a life without Suzanne. A life without her would be a return to the
only two weeks of my life when I lived alone. A time when I felt so lonely*

and empty that I would get creative in the dopamine elements I ingested to remove the pain. Whatever this was we were experiencing, we had to figure it out and rid ourselves of this ghastly feeling that the woman I loved was bordering on being a stranger.

In our early years, when we argued (which we did with regularity), Suzanne would throw things at me that never hit their mark (not good for the daughter of a baseball player). We'd exchange expletives, then laugh and make love. One night I remember I picked up an eleventh-century Chinese vase we'd received as a gift and threw it across the room and watched it shatter against the wall. Suzanne freaked out. How could you do that to my favorite vase?! she screamed. She never threw another thing at me.

You are in control both of the life you want and of the person you want to be.

But this was different, and it was a hell that just got worse every day. One night I awakened and sobbed and then threw up. That wasn't like me either. I had only cried when I lost my dear parents, and I'd thrown up only when, as a twenty-something, I drank too much cognac. Sick was not in the cards for me. I'd never had the flu or a cold and never been to a hospital. This thing was tearing us apart. I was determined to uncover the source, destroy it, and get back to our normal. I wanted us to return to being one again.

I needed a distraction and decided to write another book. This time I wanted to tackle cancer and feature doctors who were treating cancer without drugs. During my brief hospital stay, when I was *misdiagnosed* with cancer, the only thing the doctors had in their arsenal was chemical poison, and I had preferred to possibly die rather than fill my body with their worthless drugs. That experience fired me up: if I could be beaten down in such a short period of time, then it must be happening to many others.

And others needed to know there are other options. They needed to know that the present protocol of cancer treatment was in almost all cases an abject failure. I was going to find out about other options. Maybe that would help lift this dark cloud.

I started interviewing and gathering the most cutting-edge, new-thinking cancer doctors in America. The project gripped my mind, but at the end of every day, my dark emotions came flooding back. I had to find a way to win. I had to find a way to turn this around. I had the best ammunition: I am a writer.

The book would be called *Knockout*. When published, it would become a phenomenal success, another number one *Times* bestseller; it is still selling globally. Today, regularly, people tell me, "Your book *Knockout* saved *my* life." There it was again, my lifelong saving grace, turning a negative into a positive. I had done something to *right* the *wrong*. But I'm getting ahead of myself.

I cried with Alan often. For the first time in our beautiful lives together, he couldn't reach me. I didn't want to live without him, and I didn't know if I could live *with* him. I didn't know what I wanted. I felt like such a mess. Finally a dear friend suggested his therapist. Years earlier I had been so helped by therapy with Mrs. Kilgore, it had changed my life. So now it was worth a try. Rather than doing something rash, like bolting or walking away (the thought today gives me horrors), I began therapy with another great woman.

We are about balance.

For the first two weeks with her, I cried and cried. I felt hopeless.

She said, "You are experiencing PTSD. This episode has triggered every loss you've ever had. The trauma of everything that has happened to you is all front and center. The feelings are real. But we can turn this around."

I believed her. I wanted to believe her. For the first time in too long, I felt the skies could open up. And so we began: two and three times a week for an hour at a time. It was unraveling, slowly, slowly, talking, talking. It requires great humility to get emotionally well. You have to see the part you've played in the dramas of your life, and you have to face yourself in the most raw and naked ways. I thought I'd done all that, that the worst was over, but it wasn't. Being told that I was dying, buying into it and believing I had reached the end of my life, had left me so deeply, traumatically sad that my emotions and my heart had shut down. In doing so I was re-creating a crisis, but this time I was sabotaging our relationship. I was resorting to my old ways of coping; if I could run, I could outchase the pain.

This woman gradually helped me to repair, rebuild, and reprogram the information I had given to my cells. I was not going to die; that thinking had to be reversed. I never realized how much our thoughts control who we are. Cells have no emotions; they are little workers. You give them a message, and they carry out their mission. *I'm happy* is a message. *Life sucks* is another. *I'm depressed* is a message. *I'm worried. I'm insecure.* All are messages. But so are *I feel confident* and *I feel strong.* You are in control both of the life you want and of the person you want to be. It requires a shift in your thinking, a change in your attitude.

> *Traumatic events have a purpose, if a lesson or lessons are learned.*

I deserved my beautiful life. I had all I wanted. I was a good person. This therapist was helping me to believe that again. A terrible thing had happened to me that was not my fault. They got me when I was down and powerless and in shock and told me I was going to die. And I had believed it. In all the life experiences I'd had, I'd never been done in. I'd never given up, not until this one.

It took a year, but as with all therapy, I started feeling better along the way.

I started living again. I took joy in the meals I made for us and in the garden where I grow our beautiful food. I felt privileged to be back in my husband's arms, so we could make love and be together as we always had been. It took me a year to heal, but I did. And he did. Alan never gave up on me or on us. He also forgave me for giving up on us, and our beautiful life returned.

WHAT I KNOW NOW

Not a day goes by today when I don't say a prayer of gratitude for the gift I feel at coming through this ordeal and still having each other. How many rash and stupid decisions are made that change lives, ruin lives, when a person is chemically imbalanced? More than ever, I now realize and deeply know, we are about balance. The body, the mind, the spirit, and the gut, all require balance to operate properly. My balance had been destroyed, and the work I needed to do, no matter how hard, no matter how long it took, was to restore myself—or lose my life as I had known it.

Today I look at Alan throughout each day and thank God that he hung in and that we made it through (the rain, as Barry says).

Traumatic events have a purpose, if a lesson or lessons are learned. I have been referred to as autodidactic. I had to look it up when I first read that about myself: I am autodidactic. I taught myself. I figured it out. And what I figured out is that we are sent what we need in life if we are open to hearing, seeing, and feeling.

We humans are fragile. I am not perfect—none of us are. I learned from this experience never to get cocky; life events can change the chemical terrain in the body and brain, and you can become someone or something else. I learned the hard way about this delicate balance. I learned more than ever to appreciate what Alan and I have as a couple. My love for him has always been deep and passionate, but I now add another word,

We are sent what we need in life if we are open to hearing, seeing, and feeling.

and it is *fierce*. I would do anything for him. I would give my life for his. I will never knowingly hurt him ever again. Because this awfulness came so unexpectedly, it was beyond what we both understood, but coming out on the other side has made me love him even more deeply.

My life with Alan is our life. I love every day with him. We are and were a perfect team. I know, there is no perfect, but I'm telling you this relationship is nearly perfect. After all these years, who wants to play games? He's my life. My life is *our* life. We're now old enough, or more likely wise enough, to hear each other. We get into each other's heads. We see things

We humans are fragile.

from each other's point of view. We laugh a lot. We date a lot. We enjoy each other. We are two halves that make a whole.

TODAY

The older you get, the better you get, unless you're a banana.
—BETTY WHITE

My dear friend Les Moonves, who runs all the Sumner Redstone companies including CBS, told me at dinner recently, "Suzanne, you're still standing."

Alan and I made a conscious choice, after I was fired from *Three's Company,* to do it our way. When the CEO of CBS says this to you decades later, in a business that forgets about you in a heartbeat, then I think we did it right. My career's longevity is not about my age—it's always been about my journey. The journey is more important than the destination. Along the way, you succeed, you fail, you get knocked down, and you pick yourself up. It's all learning. We are put here to learn and grow and develop our wisdom. We are here to learn from our imperfections, accept them, embrace them, and then do the work to make ourselves the best persons we can be knowing there is no "perfect." To go for perfect will bring disappointment. Understanding this relieves stress, allowing you to be present in every moment. That is the goal: to be present. To be present is to achieve peace, and peace is attainable.

I am at peace.

. . .

It's around midnight, and we're walking down the back hallway of Casino Rama outside Toronto. It has been an amazing night. Five thousand wild fans. What a trip! The audience showed their appreciation with a long, thunderous standing ovation.

I was smiling to myself as we walked hand in hand. Lost in thought, I knew why that audience leaped to their feet at the end; I told them the truth. The truth is mesmerizing. I loved doing this show for them tonight. I love making people feel good. For the last year, I've been back performing nightly off and on in Vegas as well as on occasional random stages around the country. I'm grateful every minute for having achieved superb health. It allows me the energy, strength, strong bones, and fast-working brain needed to be out there night after night at seventy.

We are here to learn from our imperfections, accept them, embrace them, and then do the work to make ourselves the best persons we can be knowing there is no "perfect."

I thought seventy was supposed to be old, but for me it's not. The body is a magnificent machine. What craziness to abuse something so valuable. That has become my life's work: getting people to value their bodies. I want to change the thinking. Age is a number only; living at any age is about vitality and energy. Satchel Paige, the first black baseball Hall of Famer, once said, "How old would you be if you didn't know how old you were?" I love that quote, and that's how I live my life. I'm as young as my energy.

I have my priorities straight. I don't want to travel like I once used to, but this night was special. We were back in Canada, the land of my husband, and we knew so many in the audience. It was warm and thrilling. For 106 minutes I sang, danced my dumb dances (the kind you do in your bedroom when no one is looking), talked, and made them laugh.

I talk a lot in my show. I tell my story, of a life I never dreamed could happen, and each piece links together perfectly. My rough childhood was in retrospect a gift to grow and learn and toughen up. My teenage marriage brought me my beautiful son, who taught me to love and that we could survive against all odds. A chance meeting in a TV studio in San Francisco, where I was hired and fired the same day, brought me to Alan, the man who would become my husband and life partner in everything. Seemingly insignificant, un-

To be present is to achieve peace, and peace is attainable.

likely life events are all tied to one another: using a tube of lipstick for collateral got me my audition with George Lucas for *American Graffiti;* a chance encounter with Johnny Carson in the NBC commissary ultimately led to *Three's Company;* and my firing became rocket fuel for the life and business Alan and I made together.

I walk into the elevator, with two security guards and the hotel management team, and stand at the back with Alan, who is always by my side. I may be the one who goes on stage, but we do this together. Whenever I'm out there, I'm aware that he is there somewhere, always within reach, always looking out, protecting, analyzing.

Once we get to our hotel room door and thank the guards and hotel management, we begin the ritual. I fill the tub with warm water and throw in a small bag of Epsom salts. We already had two stiff tequilas at the after-party, and my head is buzzing a bit in that nice way, so delicious after a big energy-fueled show. The after-party is almost as fun as the show, when my endorphins are exploding and my adrenaline is pumping; the hugging and laughing and warmth of being with friends and family are so delicious and such a part of these evenings.

We will sleep deep and well, wrapped in each other's arms as always. We fall asleep knowing we are two of the luckiest people on the planet. Every night, as his hands cup my breasts and I spoon to fit perfectly to his contours, he whispers the same thing into my ear: "I love you so much." He says it as if it's the first time he's ever thought of it. I feel safe, warm, sexy, protected, and exquisite. Soon we're making love. It happens like this all the time, thinking we're going to sleep, and then we're entwined with each other. I kiss him tenderly, then fiercely. He's mine. I love him, he loves me. Thank you, God!

How privileged I feel in all aspects of my life and love. How privileged I am to do what I love with the person I love. I am a big walking ball of thanks. Maybe that's what people have responded to in my books. I'm them. I had to figure it out on my own. I didn't have opportunities, so I made opportunities for myself. That I found the perfect partner with whom to accomplish this happy and fulfilling life is the greatest gift. I constantly receive lovely notes and letters from my readers that hearing about my journey gave them the confidence to go for their own dream. If that is so, then God bless all that happened, good and bad. That is why forgiveness is so vitally important. Anger keeps you imprisoned. I broke through the shackles and found grace.

> *Age is a number only; living at any age is about vitality and energy.*

So here we are, thirty-seven years after the firing and that infamous clusterfuck of a meeting with ABC. Suzanne went on to do Step by Step *for seven years,* She's the Sheriff, Candid Camera, *music specials, movies, Vegas, Broadway, and HSN, and she became one of America's most influential advocates for women's health.*

Suzanne ends her Vegas show with a quote that grabs me and the audience night after night. It's by Lao Tzu: "If you're depressed, you are living in the past. If you're anxious, you are living in the future. If you're at peace, you are living in the present." I live in the present. We live in the present. I live each day for her, for us, for our family. The past is what made us, built us. The present gives us everything.

My uncle Benny and auntie Bella owned the Daily Bargain Store on Dundas Street in Toronto, a tiny working-class enterprise. They lived in the back of the store and hadn't been apart for sixty years. Suzanne and I are Benny and Bella. We're together 24/7 and haven't spent even one night apart in over thirty-five years. We are one. We are interdependent. We can speak in shorthand.

I handle the day to day of our business. Big decisions are made by both of us. Sometimes in bed, with lights out, with one last scrumptious lingering hug, we will do a quick chat about business, maybe go for it, then laugh ourselves to sleep. I love always being with her; I never need "my space." I've never had a night out with the boys, and Suzanne never needed one with the girls. We never even thought of separate vacations. And we've never stopped laughing, at least not for long. We've driven thousands and thousands of miles together with hours of beautiful silence, through magnificent national parks and through the Southwest. We've seeded our organic garden and harvested its bounty. We've hiked in the mountains near our home, a godly experience being at the top of Mount Jacinto while holding and kissing each other.

I don't know what else may be out there, but I do not believe that a relationship gets any better than ours. How did this happen? How did a big-city guy from Toronto meet a small-town girl from San Bruno, fall in instant love, and evolve together beautifully for fifty years? How do we keep this incredible gift going indefinitely?

Ray Kurzweil, when asked how long he will live, says, "Indefinitely." I have adopted his answer, since naming a number like "I'm going to live to be a hundred and ten" means, as Suzanne says, programming my cells to buy into that, and they will likely respond accordingly. I am very fortunate that Suzanne's work in cutting-edge medicine has given me the benefit of the halo effect. I do whatever "Dr. Somers" (she has an honorary doctorate from National University) tells me to do, and it's working out beautifully.

> Anger keeps you imprisoned. I broke through the shackles and found grace.

We are also blessed with a great bunch of children and grandchildren. Our children are all in their fifties now and parents themselves; they followed their passions, while living on very little, until they all succeeded big time. Stephen creates and produces big movies, and Leslie runs her fashion business. And Bruce, Suzanne's son, has his own successful production company. He and I love *each other. I consider him my son—period. When we're all together today, I am proud to be their father and happily stand in their shadows.*

My mother's passing taught Suzanne and me a great lesson. The combination of peak health, fun work, a great family, giving back, and lots of love to go around is our personal formula for success. And health is at the top of the list, because without health, the rest is substantially degraded. After health, it's all bookkeeping.

Suzanne and I laugh a whole lot. Our senses of humor are very resonant. We can lock eyes from across a room and laugh at the same time about the same thing without a word shared. When we are naked, we laugh at the little aging surprises that occur in our bodies. "Where did that come from?!" is always followed by peals of laughter. We often laugh during lovemaking. Suzanne has a rule that I always enjoy breaking. If I'm feeling amorous at four o'clock in the morning, that's okay by her, but just make it fast.

Anytime after seven in the morning, we can go Tantric. Suzanne's gynecologist Prudence, who in the fifties would've been called a great broad, gave me a book about Tantric sex. Whenever the three of us are together in her office, we often giggle and make jokes when we talk about sex. I think Tantric sex is the greatest. Suzanne, on the other hand, often accuses me of loitering with Tantric, which triggers big laughs from both of us.

One night we were sitting at Big Al's Bar (in our home), and I said, "I love being at home with you." And Alan said, "Home is with you. I don't care where we are—you are *home*." I was stopped by that and so moved. I realized I'm not as evolved. I'm always looking for nirvana, perfection. And yet for sure, it doesn't matter if I'm in some crappy chain hotel with him or wherever—when I'm with *him,* I am home. He *is* home.

This morning, while lying in bed together, drinking Alan's great organic coffee, and watching our favorite TV program, *CBS Sunday Morning,* we were holding hands as we so often do. We hold hands on our walks; we hold hands always. We've never talked about it, it's just automatic. It caused me to think about aging and what *old* means: it's about wanting more time, it's about never wanting this beautiful life to end.

Even today, almost fifty years later, I don't quite understand what we have. I don't try to analyze why. Fifty years, and we're still joined at the hip, still kissing and still hugging and telling each other how much we love each other at every opportunity. Our friends tell us we shouldn't be so close, because when one of us goes, the other will suffer big time. Should we push back from our feelings? Do we discontinue our great love? Do we stop sleeping and holding each other? That just doesn't make any sense to me. Of course, I want this to continue forever and ever.

How is it fifty years later? Well, we don't pull off the freeway to make love anymore. And we don't pull into the Papaya Restaurant parking lot to make love on our way to the airport anymore. And we don't make love in the water at Waikiki Beach surrounded by hundreds of people anymore. Or on the beach in Eleuthera anymore, noticing afterward that a group of uniform-clad school kids were watching from above. And we don't make love in the car anymore, now that cars have gone from bench seats to bucket seats.

We still make love a lot, and it's light-years beyond frantic groping. It's love making. I still can't get over that Suzanne lets me do anything I want with her. She is easily the most felt-up woman in America. As I say this, I envision my grandkids with fingers in their ears, eyes shut, making trilling sounds at the thought that their granny and granddad still do it. I love to kiss her and hold her tight. I love to awaken and look over at this incredibly beautiful woman I am privileged to share everything with. Suzanne with no makeup looks like a teenager. I joke that the first thing I say to her when she opens her eyes is "I'm sorry." (Big laugh.) That kind of covers it for at least half the day. Guys understand.

Fifty years together needs careful tending like a beautiful garden. You can't get lazy. You can't take it for granted. As time goes by, it's even more important to give each other a lot of attention.

We respect each other. We make it a point to meet at Big Al's Bar a couple of times a week for a "date." We laugh. We talk. We dance in the kitchen. We are great friends. We don't bicker. I don't remember the last time we had an argument or had cross words. Why don't we argue or fight anymore? What's the point of wasting time being angry with each other? We're great lovers and great friends. We appreciate each other and take care of each other. We've found peace together, and for that we are both extremely grateful.

Gratitude is a state of being that leaves little room for anything else. If you choose happiness on a daily basis, life works out. I do a little exercise every morning when I wake up. As I'd said earlier, the human body is composed of approximately ninety trillion cells—I wonder who counted?—and they all communicate with one another. My morning meditation is this: I visualize and isolate just one cell, and I tell it how grateful I am for my life; that my problems have become my opportunities; that I love my husband with all my heart; that I love my children and grandchildren, my work, and the food I get to eat. You get the picture. I then release that cell, and in my mind's eye, I visualize it telling all the other ninety trillion cells that I am grateful and happy for all the love in my life; these things that will allow us to live a long, happy, healthy life together.

> Gratitude is a state of being that leaves little room for anything else. If you choose happiness on a daily basis, life works out.

When I finish this meditation, I am bursting with happiness. Imagine if I woke up in the morning and instead programmed a thought of anger or hate or resentment. That little cell would have to go off and deliver the bad news to the rest of the group. How would that manifest in the body, emotions, and mind? You see how it works. By this simple exercise, I am programming and choosing happiness!

Today I feel that Alan and I are only partway through the journey. I'm curious as to how long we will both live. We consciously take care of our bodies. We watch what we feed ourselves; we know thoughts create, so we consciously practice taking the high road and thinking good thoughts. We laugh together a lot. We take our hormones and our supplements. We rest our bodies seven to eight hours nightly. We live a calm yet exciting life. We can dip in and out of our business and glamorous events as often as we desire, and we do. As I write this page, I'm thinking about tonight, when we'll attend a very glamorous star-studded Hollywood party. I'm going to wear my beautiful tiger-striped sequined Balmain minidress, gold high heels, and red lipstick. It's all great. We take care and cherish what we have because it's worth it. Neither of us wants it ever to end.

I have told myself the truth. I believe if you don't phony it up, if you have the courage to be humble, people take to it. We all respond to truth and authenticity.

I often think about why things turned out the way they did. Why, having come from all the fear and pain of being a child of an alcoholic, did it work out for me? Through no smarts of my own but rather a terrible accident my son had to endure, I was forced to do the work of healing. The serendipity of life placed me in the right place at the right moment to meet the man of my dreams and to go on to live a life of such joy.

Today I have my answer; I have told myself the truth. I believe if you don't phony it up, if you have the courage to be humble, people take to it. We all respond to truth and authenticity. For me, I had no choice; my lack of training, education, and skills forced me to educate myself, and over time I came to appreciate that I had a voice within *me* that believed in me, that we all do. I learned that deep down I could figure things out, and I did.

I wrote this book to give hope to all who might have given up on their dreams. I hope it helps to know that there are two people who against all odds made it. That the two of us came from opposite sides of the continent and a different country yet seemed destined to find each other. The unlikeliness of us finding each other shows that sometimes the universe has a plan for you if you are open to it. I wrote this book to express gratitude for having learned (and in many cases the hard way) what is important.

Love is the answer. The journey in life is to teach ourselves what we want. Those two great questions in life: *Who am I?* and *What do I want?* Most people are never able to answer either question. Now I know. I have my answers. I hope you find the same peace. Every day I am cognizant of the profound and prophetic words that came to me while delirious in the hospital: *It's not who you are, it's not what you do, it's not what you have; it's ONLY . . . only about who you love and who loves you.*

I live by those words. I am loved and I love fiercely. I wish the same for you.

L ife is not how you start but how you finish. I want our children and grandchildren to *want* what we have and to find what Neale Donald Walsch calls, in his incredible book *Conversations with God,* "the grandest version of the greatest vision you ever had about who you are." What is imaginable for their lives? I want them to know it's not about luck. It's about your personal vision: seeing what you want, then doing the work to get it. To manifest it. To know it. And never to stop dreaming.

> *Love is the answer.*
> *The journey in life*
> *is to teach ourselves*
> *what we want.*

Our story is certainly not over, but in looking back, the big picture becomes clear—it was all perfect. All the good, all the bad, all the happy, all the sad—it's all been for a reason.

You can't give up. Ever! Happiness takes work. A great relationship takes work. Every choice matters; every thought creates. We are all in control of our joy. Inevitably, it's the dark times and the negatives that are our best teachers.

Life is the process of learning from all of it.

The lucky ones do.

PHOTOGRAPHY CREDITS

All photographs unless otherwise noted are courtesy of the author.

INSERT 1

Page 1: Hank Saroyan

Page 4, top: 1973 Universal Pictures

Page 4, middle left: Hank Saroyan

Page 4, bottom: Carson Entertainment Group

Page 5, top: Harry Langdon Photography

Page 5, bottom left: © Ron Galella/Ron Galella, Ltd.

Page 5, bottom right: Getty Images

Page 6, top left: © Ron Galella/Ron Galella, Ltd.

Page 6, top right: Getty Images

Page 6, middle: © Ron Galella/Ron Galella, Ltd.

Page 6, bottom: © Ron Galella/Ron Galella, Ltd.

Page 7, top: AP Images

Page 7, middle right: © Ron Galella/Ron Galella, Ltd.

Page 7, bottom left: © Ron Galella/Ron Galella, Ltd.

Page 8, all photographs: © Ron Galella/Ron Galella, Ltd.

INSERT 2

Page 1, top: Harry Langdon Photography

Page 1, bottom left: Harry Langdon Photography

Page 2, top right: © Ron Galella/Ron Galella, Ltd.

Page 2, bottom left: Jeff Katz

Page 3, top right: Harry Langdon Photography

Page 4, second row, left: © Ron Galella/Ron Galella, Ltd.

Page 4, second row, right: AP Images

Page 4, third row, left: Disney/ABC Television

Page 4, bottom left: Cindy Gold

Page 4, bottom right: © Ron Galella/Ron Galella, Ltd.

Page 5, top right: AP Images

Page 5, middle left: Courtesy of *The Dr. Oz Show*

Page 5, middle right: Getty Images

Page 5, bottom left: Getty Images

Page 5, bottom right: Disney/ABC Television

Page 6, top right: Jeff Katz

ABOUT THE AUTHOR

SUZANNE SOMERS is the author of twenty-six books, fifteen of which are *New York Times* bestsellers, including the #1 *New York Times* bestsellers *Sexy Forever, Knockout,* and *Ageless; Tox-Sick; I'm Too Young for This!; Bombshell; Breakthrough; Keeping Secrets; Suzanne Somers' Eat Great, Lose Weight; Get Skinny on Fabulous Food; Eat, Cheat, and Melt the Fat Away; Suzanne Somers' Fast & Easy;* and *The Sexy Years.* Suzannne is a dedicated women's health advocate and an award-winning comedienne, lecturer, entertainer, and entrepreneur. For more information about Suzanne, visit SuzanneSomers.com.